Thoroughbred Studs
of
Great Britain

Thoroughbred Studs
of
Great Britain

ALAN YUILL WALKER

Weidenfeld and Nicolson
London

ISBN 0 297 81206 8
Typeset by BP Integraphics, Bath, Avon
Printed in Great Britain by Bath Press Ltd, Avon.

CONTENTS

CONTENTS

vi

CONTENTS

AUTHOR'S ACKNOWLEDGEMENTS

There are many people to whom I am very grateful for the publication of *Thoroughbred Studs of Great Britain*, but none more so than the following: my editor, Jane Blackett, for whom nothing was too much trouble, together with John Boyce, editor of *The Thoroughbred Breeder*, and Sue Cameron of Sagittarius Bloodstock, whose expertise at proofreading obviated too many errors. So far as the photographs are concerned, I am equally indebted to Anny Hedges of Triple Crown Advertising and Michael Harris, editor of *The Racing Post*. My sincere thanks are due to them all.

FOREWORD

My late stepfather, Sir Cecil Boyd-Rochfort, never failed to impress upon me the benefit of training successive generations of the same breed so that one became familiar with the various idiosyncrasies of the families. At Freemason Lodge, he was in the fortunate position of training for a number of leading owner-breeders which gave him the opportunity of doing this. The same applied to Sir Noel Murless, my predecessor at Warren Place, who held exactly the same opinion.

It is this question of continuity which makes Alan Yuill Walker's *Thoroughbred Studs of Great Britain* such an invaluable book of reference. Here in one book for the very first time are all the essential facts as to how these famous and not so famous studs started and have continued down to the present day.

I have known Alan for nearly thirty years since we were at the Royal Agricultural College, Cirencester, together. We used to go rushing around saying 'the answer must lie in the soil', but he was always much more concerned than I was with what was happening on the Turf!

In those days Alan was quite a serious punter, but since that time he has become fascinated not by the starting price of the last winner but by the breeding and the breeder.

I thoroughly recommend this book to anyone interested in racing and breeding.

Henry Cecil
Warren Place, Newmarket

INTRODUCTION

Thanks to modern technology, the general public are better informed than ever before, with television bringing graphic pictures and commentary instantly into millions of homes. As with all spectator sports, racing has participated in this great bonanza. Nowadays virtually all the big races in Great Britain and Ireland are shown live on television as are many important races from other major racing countries.

Interest in racing worldwide has been stimulated by comprehensive television coverage of such gala occasions as the Ciga Prix de l'Arc de Triomphe weekend in Paris and the Breeders' Cup series in the USA. Additional events like the Japan Cup have all helped to promote the international aspect of flat racing. There is also extensive press coverage, both in the daily newspapers and the specialized racing publications, daily, weekly and monthly. Racing World Video Productions enable the enthusiast to enjoy a monthly visual review of just about every contemporary aspect of racing and breeding worldwide.

Today winning a big race that is televised involves almost everyone, from the trainer to the stable lad, being subjected to a barrage of questions. Indeed the horse has only just passed the winning post and a microphone is pressed into the unfortunate jockey's face to glean the inside story. Yet amidst all the euphoria, the breeder, who as the prime producer is the most important person of all, is invariably overlooked. This omission was never more vividly illustrated than after Saumarez had triumphed in the 1990 Ciga Prix de l'Arc de Triomphe. In this instance the name of the breeder, Mrs Peter Longton of Heatherwold Stud in Berkshire, was even missing from its customary slot with the horse's tabulated pedigree. In fact Saumarez, whose breeder is Norwegian, is the first winner of the Prix de l'Arc de Triomphe to have been produced by an English stud since Prince Royal triumphed in 1964. Prince Royal was bred at Moyns Park Stud in Essex by an American, Charles Wacker III. The last Englishman to breed an 'Arc' winner (Vaguely Noble in 1963), was the late Major Lionel Holliday, who lived in his native Yorkshire, but whose extensive breeding operation was centred on his famous Cleaboy Stud in Ireland.

A further injustice suffered by the breeding fraternity is the media custom of taking a horse's nationality from the country in which he or she is trained.

Hence Saumarez was regarded as English when trained by Henry Cecil, but French upon winning the 'Arc' for Nicolas Clement. It might be supposed that a horse's true nationality could be ascertained from the official suffixes (GB, USA, FR, IRE, etc) which are allocated upon registration with the Stud Book of the country in question. However these merely denote the country in which the animal was foaled. Hence the progeny of a mare belonging to a French stud which is foaled when the dam is visiting a stallion in Newmarket will have a GB rather than an FR suffix.

Just as the last decade has seen racehorse ownership in the United Kingdom completely dominated by the Arabs, so far as top flat horses are concerned, so the 1990s will assuredly witness a comparable Arab supremacy from a breeding point of view, albeit the volatile situation in the Middle East could have enormous long-term repercussions. The two principal families involved are the Maktoum brothers from Dubai (Sheikh Mohammed is the Minister of Defence for Dubai), and Prince Khalid Abdullah of Saudi Arabia. Between them they own twenty-five studs in England and Ireland with additional thoroughbred farms in Kentucky.

Such unprecedented involvement means that many of England's greatest studs have lost their original identity. Consequently there is a grave danger of their historical significance being lost with the passing of the years. For example, Beech House Stud is now just an appendage to Sheikh Hamdan Al Maktoum's vast Shadwell Estate. However it was here that Nearco spent the duration of his stud life and is buried. In the context of the modern thoroughbred, one cannot overestimate the role of Beech House where Nearco was mated with the homebred mare, Lady Angela, to produce Nearctic, the sire of Northern Dancer.

Thoroughbred Studs of Great Britain is an attempt to chronicle the history of some of our premier studs down to the present time. The yardstick for inclusion is that they are still operational although a few are undoubtedly borderline cases. They have been included for past glories rather than any great expectations for the future. One such instance is provided by Buttermilk Stud. This small private stud was owned previously by the late Mrs Leonard Scott, whose knowledge, experience and judgement were second to none. Joan Scott once admitted that the only advice to which she ever adhered came from one or two stud grooms of long standing. Writing in *The Field* in December 1990, John Hislop said of Park Top's breeder, 'Mrs Scott has sound claims to being the most successful breeder of the post-war era, considering her limited financial resources, small number of mares, their low cost, the price of nominations used and the quality of horses bred.' Yet how many members of the racing public have ever heard of Mrs Scott?

It should be emphasized that many additional studs have sound claims for inclusion here. This is particularly true so far as public (stallion) studs are concerned and those operating with a significant boarding element. Unfortunately with so many studs from which to choose (see Appendix II), the list of those that feature is an arbitrary one, the emphasis being on studs which have themselves bred winners of outstanding merit.

One of the perennial fascinations of bloodstock breeding is the sense of continuity which exists from one generation to another. Many studs that have survived down to the present time owe their success to one particular foundation mare acquired long ago. Although the whole concept of female families is a contentious one, there is no denying the contribution that certain mares have made to certain studs, witness Feola with the Royal Studs, Horama with White Lodge, Felsetta with Arches Hall, Pelting with West Blagdon, and many others. It is a fact that both of Sheikh Hamdan Al Maktoum's two champions, Nashwan and Salsabil, trace back in the female line to Aloe (Son-in-Law − Alope), a mare bred by Sir Abe Bailey in 1926.

The Maktoums and Prince Khalid Abdullah have established enormous broodmare bands by buying into the best bloodlines on a worldwide basis. Being ready, willing and able to pay handsomely for the privilege, they have managed to assemble a nucleus of mares within a decade that is matched only for strength and depth in Europe by the Aga Khan. His decision not to have any horses trained in England from 1991, following the Aliysa affair, is a body blow to British racing which removes the only real individual competitor to the Arab legions at a single stroke.

It has to be said that the future for many British owned studs looks decidedly depressing as the bloodstock business faces not only the general economic recession but also an internal financial crisis brought about by a totally inadequate prize money structure. During the second half of Mrs Thatcher's premiership, many commercial studs were operating at a loss following the boom years during the first half of the 1980s. By the time John Major was installed in 10 Downing Street, the picture had become even bleaker. As David Gibson, the current president of the Thoroughbred Breeders' Association, commented on seeing a draft copy of the chapter on his Barleythorpe Stud, 'Unless the markets cheer up soon, it will be only a history book!'

For a number of years prior to 1 January 1993, the disparity that exists between Great Britain and other members of the EEC (notably Ireland

and France) with regard to VAT has been another major cause for concern, notwithstanding persistent representations to Parliament by the Thoroughbred Breeders' Association and other interested parties. If this long-running saga is not resolved satisfactorily post haste, Messrs Tattersalls have announced their intention of vacating the resplendent Newmarket headquarters for Ireland. Such a momentous move would be yet another nail in the coffin of British bloodstock.

Since the end of the eighteenth century, Tattersalls' Park Paddocks, which has been developed into Europe's finest thoroughbred sales complex, has provided a shop window for what has become an international commodity. Traditionally the Newmarket December Sales have been the venue for breeders worldwide to acquire their breeding stock, both mares and fillies. Here the great majority of studs featured in this publication bought their foundation mares. They include studs like Overbury which procured Lundy Parrot, the third dam of Grundy, for just thirty-five guineas in the dark years of 1941. In 1978 the Holland-Martins sold a colt by Grundy for 264,000 guineas, a new European record for a thoroughbred at public auction.

The story of Overbury Stud, which progressed from breeding hunters to champion racehorses, provides one of the chapters here. This is a tribute to the many breeders and their staff who have managed to sustain Britain's great historical links with the thoroughbred, one of the most beautiful and graceful of animals, during the post-war era.

Alan Yuill Walker
Lambourn

Adstock Manor Stud

ADSTOCK · BUCKINGHAMSHIRE

From a breeding point of view, the opening of the York festival meeting in August 1980 provided one of the most remarkable days' racing on record. Four consecutive winners that afternoon were sired by High Line, highlighted by the Group 1 scorers, Master Willie (Benson and Hedges Gold Cup), and Shoot a Line (Yorkshire Oaks).

Three members of the quartet, including Master Willie, were bred by Messrs W. and R. Barnett Limited, grain importers from Belfast. They keep all their breeding stock at James Delahooke's Adstock Manor Stud, near Buckingham, where homebred High Line was foaled, reared and has spent his entire stud life.

The enormous success which the Barnett bloodstock has enjoyed over the last two decades would have brought tremendous pleasure to the late Matthew Prior, founder of Adstock Manor Stud in 1903. A renowned turf historian, he worked in close conjunction with his daughter Florence Prior – she died aged ninety-one in 1982.

Stallions to have stood at Adstock Manor in the early days were unraced Missel Thrush, who was sold to the Argentine for £10,000, 2000 Guineas winner Neil Gow, who was bred locally by Lord Rosebery at Mentmore Stud, and Kroonstad, winner of twenty-two races.

A couple of mares sold by Matthew Prior from Adstock Manor were to produce classic winners in France – Dora Agnes, dam of Dorina (Prix de Diane), and May Queen, dam of Strip the Willow (Prix du Jockey Club). To Neil Gow, Matthew Prior also bred Perce-Neige, dam of Oaks heroine, Rose of England, the foundation mare of Mrs Florence Nagle's Westerlands Stud.

Following her father's death in 1940, Florence Prior, founder of the *Register of Thoroughbred Stallions* and compiler of the *Half-Bred Stud Book*, maintained the stud on a reduced scale. From her homebred foundation mare, Dutch Clover, she bred that good sprinter, Runnymede. This grey spent his stud life at Benham Stud, near Newbury, where he was foaled.

In the autumn of 1951 Adstock Manor Stud was bought by Garry and Priscilla Delahooke, James's parents. Both keen followers of the Grafton and Whaddon Chase Hunts, they farmed close by at Newton Longville where they had kept the occasional mare for breeding. Their first homebred yearling was dispatched to the 1956 Newmarket December Sales. Accompanying her was a three-year-old filly belonging to Miss Prior, who continued to have a few boarders at Adstock. Named Greensward, she was destined to breed the Prix de l'Arc de Triomphe hero, Exbury.

Sadly Garry Delahooke died in October 1960 on the very day that the Adstock yearlings came up for sale at Newmarket. Excluded from the draft was the Relic colt, Old Tom, winner of the 1965 Lincoln Handicap. His dam was the Delahookes' original foundation mare, Sweetcake. At one time another of her sons, Deep Gulf, trained by Vincent O'Brien, was ante-post favourite for the Derby. Their half-sister, Hannah Darling, was runner-up in the Irish 1000 Guineas.

When Priscilla Delahooke died in 1969 (like her late husband, she was only in her early fifties), James, the second of their four sons, at a very early age found himself in the deep end so far as the stud was concerned. Just beginning to make a name for himself as an amateur rider, he had to surmount considerable financial difficulties to get the stud back on an even keel.

However there was a saviour at hand from a most unexpected quarter. In three successive years (1969/70/71), High Line triumphed in the Jockey Club Cup. Although stayers are not popular with commercial breeders, the late William Barnett was determined to stand the horse at stud himself. Consequently High Line (High Hat – Time Call), retired to cover his first mares at Adstock in 1972 at a fee of £600 (1 October). The first stallion based at Adstock since the days of Matthew Prior, he was described by Barnett's racing manager, Clarence Hailey, as a bigger edition of his illustrious grandsire, Hyperion.

Putting all one's eggs in the same basket is invariably a recipe for disaster, but such was not the case for William Barnett. He mated his mares almost exclusively with High Line, although the horse was shunned by others, and in the process elevated a modest broodmare band to the top of the pack.

The ace performer proved to be the Derby runner-up, Master Willie. Winner of the Coral-Eclipse Stakes, Coronation Cup and Benson and Hedges Gold Cup, he was repatriated to stand at Adstock alongside his own sire after completing six seasons with Northern Dancer at Windfields Farm, Maryland. During that period he sired the Barnett-bred Deputy Governor. Consigned from Adstock Manor at the 1985 Highflyer Sales, he returned to the USA to win two Grade 1 events on the turf in California. Incidentally Master Willie's dam, Fair Winter, won the Nassau Stakes to become the Barnett's first notable Adstock-bred winner – their most recent is the High Line filly, Jaffa Line.

High Line is by one of Sir Winston Churchill's celebrities in High Hat, while Centro is by another in Vienna, sire of Vaguely Noble. Mated with High Line, Centro produced three winners of the Jockey Club Cup in Nicholas Bill, Centroline, and Tale Quale. From 1982 to 1990, Robert Barnett (William's son) stood Nicholas Bill at Hunsley House Stud in North Humberside.

Their own-sister, Centrocon, is dam of Robert Barnett's champion mare, Time Charter. The only good performer sired by Saritamer, she gained Group 1 victories in the Oaks, King George VI and Queen Elizabeth Diamond Stakes, Dubai Champion Stakes, and Coronation Cup. Her yearling colt by Shirley Heights realized 300,000 guineas at the 1990 Highflyer Sales.

Recognized as one of the world's top yearling judges (a reputation earned in conjunction with his great friend Guy Harwood), James Delahooke spent six years from August 1979 to August 1985 masterminding Prince Khalid Abdullah's racing and breeding empire based at Juddmonte Farms, Wargrave-on-Thames.

At that time Adstock Manor Stud was managed by Sally Judd. Since the arrival of her successor, Ted Voute, the stud has specialized in sales preparation based on the American agent system with Kentucky breeder Robin Scully of Clovelly Farms being a major client. Meanwhile James Delahooke pursues his role as an independent bloodstock agent.

Angmering Park Stud

LITTLEHAMPTON · SUSSEX

No one has been more closely involved with owning, training and breeding over the last half a century than Lavinia, Duchess of Norfolk. At one time she and her husband had as many as forty horses in training at Castle stables, Arundel, with nearly thirty mares at their Angmering Park Stud.

In modern times the broodmare band at Angmering Park, just three or four miles down the road from Arundel on the edge of the Sussex Downs towards Littlehampton, has dwindled to about half a dozen (excluding pensioners and boarders). However, thanks to one mare, Castle Moon, the Duchess's fortunes were never better.

Castle Moon was foaled in May 1975, just four months after the Duke died. Only the previous year her half-brother, Ragstone, had provided his owner-breeder with a victory in the race he coveted above all others, the Ascot Gold Cup. It was a poignant occasion as Bernard Norfolk had been Her Majesty's Representative at Royal Ascot for an unprecedented twenty-seven years from 1945 to 1972.

The Norfolks founded Angmering Park Stud in a small way just before the Second World War. They were married in 1937 and one of the foundation mares was already named Lavinia when she was given to them as a wedding present by her stepfather, Lord Rosebery, owner of the famous Mentmore Stud in Buckinghamshire.

Two fine colts bred in the early days were Garrick (Queen Anne Stakes), and Caerlaverock, who was by Hyperion from a Blue Peter mare, a couple of key stallions in the stud's formative years. Amongst the Duchess's favourites were St Peter and St Paul, own-brothers by Blue Peter who won twenty-one races between them. Another, Burpham (by Hyperion), made a sensational Ascot debut by upsetting odds of 1–25 laid on Royal Forest.

During the late fifties and sixties the Arundel stable, presided over by Willie Smyth and his son Gordon, relied increasingly on precocious two-year-olds purchased as yearlings, the sky blue and scarlet colours being carried by such notable sprinters as Conspirator, Sound Track, Sovereign Lord and Skymaster. The decision was then made to procure some fast blood for the stud. At the 1962 Newmarket December Sales the mare La Fresnes was purchased from her breeder, Lord Derby, for 17,000 guineas.

As La Fresnes had previously produced very small foals, Roderic More O'Ferrall of Kildangan Stud suggested that she should be mated with Right Royal V, a commanding individual. The result was a singularly unattractive filly. Named Fotheringay, she won a small race locally at Goodwood as a three-year-old.

Fotheringay was to become an outstanding foundation mare. Her produce includes not only Ragstone but also Castle Keep (by Kalamoun) and his own-sister, Castle Moon. Ragstone completed four covering seasons at Lavington Stud until meeting with a fatal accident. It was here that Castle Keep (Grand Prix Prince Rose) also retired to stud, later moving to Ireland via Yorkshire.

The dip-backed Castle Moon, who scored three wins as a three-year-old, has excelled as a broodmare for the Duchess of Norfolk with three Group winning sons in Moon Madness (by Vitiges), Sheriff's Star (by Posse), and Lucky Moon (by Touching Wood). Incidentally all three are by sires who were quickly banished overseas due to lack of success at home.

Both Moon Madness and Sheriff's Star, a grey, were amongst the leading middle-distance performers of their generation. Between them they won sixteen races, nine of them Group events. Each gained two Group I victories, Moon Madness in the Holsten Pils St Leger (the Norfolks' only classic success) and Grand Prix de Saint-Cloud, and Sheriff's Star in the Hanson Coronation Cup and Grand Prix de Saint-Cloud.

Like the majority of Norfolk runners, Moon Madness was trained in the grounds of Arundel Castle by John Dunlop, whereas Sheriff's Star was trained by her eldest daughter, Lady Herries, whose yard is adjacent to the stud. Both horses followed their respective sires for a stud career in Japan. Meanwhile their half-brother, Lucky Moon, triumphed in the 1990 Goodwood Cup as a three-year-old.

During the 1980s Angmering Park achieved a couple of Grade I successes in the USA with Mountain Bear (Santa Barbara Handicap) and Mister Wonderful (American Handicap). Mountain Bear was bred by Lady Sarah Fitzalan Howard as was her half-brother Efisio. A Group I scorer in Italy, he retired to stand at Hever Castle Stud Farm in Kent.

Additional homebred winners of earlier vintage include Laser Light, Predicament and Trusted. The sprinter, Laser Light, who went to Ballykisteen

Stud, Co. Tipperary, came about through Sandy Scratchley upon whose recommendation the dam, Ruby Laser, was acquired as a two-year-old in Ireland.

For a number of years Sandy Scratchley, who raised Sing Sing and Burglar as his Yarbrook Stud, near Chichester, for Colonel Bill Stirling, was manager at Angmering Park, having succeeded the original manager, Colonel Frank Holland. The present manager is John Dunlop with Peter Willett acting in an advisory capacity.

Since its formation, Angmering Park Stud has only had two stud grooms, Harry Espin, a forthright Yorkshireman, and Alfred Goulder. With experience on the Continent at such famous establishments as the Razza Dormello Olgiata and the Haras de la Verrerie, Goulder has been stud groom since arriving at Angmering Park in 1959 so he knows more about the place than anyone.

Alfred Goulder rates Moon Madness and Mister Wonderful as the two best looking foals he can remember (both were born in 1983), neither Ragstone nor Sheriff's Star being anything special at that stage. Another Royal Ascot winner to bring reflected glory to the stud is Chilibang (King's Stand Stakes) – his dam Chili Girl is the only mare boarded there for Mrs H.J. Heinz.

Arches Hall Stud

STANDON · HERTFORDSHIRE

In 1980 Bireme won the Oaks and Shoot a Line won the Irish Guinness
Oaks and Yorkshire Oaks. Not only did the former provide a first classic
success for her owner-breeder, Richard Dunbavin Hollingsworth, but he
also bred Luminant, grandam of Shoot a Line. Furthermore both fillies
go back at four generations to the Arches Hall Stud foundation mare, Felsetta.

No British owner-breeder has enjoyed a greater share of success since
the war than Dick Hollingsworth. His distinctive colours of crimson, silver
braid, which he inherited from his father, Sydney, have been carried to
victory in forty-three Group races. Twenty-one of the twenty-three individuals involved (all homebred) trace back to Felsetta through her daughter,
Felucca.

Bireme is one of four individual Group I scorers, the others being Ark
Royal (Yorkshire Oaks), Buoy (Coronation Cup), and Longboat (Ascot
Gold Cup). Although Bireme is Hollingsworth's one and only classic winner,
Sir John Astor's homebred pair, Cut Above (St Leger) and Sharp Edge
(Irish 2000 Guineas), are also members of this family, likewise trained by
Major Dick Hern at West Ilsley.

Jakie Astor, who used to own both Hatley Stud, at his Bedfordshire
home, and Warren Stud, Newmarket, and Dick have been friends since
their school days together at Eton. That Jakie should have bred the half-
brothers, Cut Above and Sharp Edge, was due to an exchange of mares
between the two breeders, an arrangement which turned out to be singularly
one-sided!

A bachelor member of the Jockey Club, Dick Hollingsworth was born
in the last year of the Great War, he and his younger brother, John, being
brought up in Surrey, near Guildford. Their father, Sydney, was a Lloyds'
underwriter, and Dick spent eighteen months with a Lloyds' broker until

the outbreak of war in which he served with the Royal Berkshire Regiment.

In due course Dick returned to the City to pursue his career as a stock-broker while John settled down to farm Arches Hall's arable acres. Before very long there were two bereavements in the family. John died aged twenty-seven in 1949 from an illness contracted in North Africa during the war. Within two years Sydney Hollingsworth was also dead.

So Arches Hall, which is situated above the River Rib, near Ware, between the villages of Standon and Much Hadham, passed to Dick together with a handful of mares that he and his brother had owned in partnership. Amongst them were two of Felsetta's daughters, Bardia, ancestress of Shoot a Line, and Felucca.

Felsetta (Felstead – Ka-Lu-A) was Sydney Hollingsworth's first racehorse; Joe Lawson, then training at Manton, having bought her as a foal in 1933 for 860 guineas. The next year the same combination purchased Raeburn as a yearling. He was to win the Irish Derby in the same year that Felsetta gained one of her two wins in the Atalanta Stakes, Sandown Park. It was really Raeburn who kindled young Dick's interest in racing.

Due to the prevailing wartime conditions, Felucca (by Nearco) ran exclus-ively at Newmarket where she was trained by George Colling at Hurworth House – he and his successor, John Oxley, were Dick Hollingsworth's only two trainers prior to Dick Hern. Felucca's solitary victory was gained over seven furlongs as a three-year-old defeating subsequent Oaks heroine, Hycilla. She was also runner-up that season in the Cambridgeshire carrying 7st 8lbs.

Between 1955 and 1958 Felucca was responsible for three winners of the Park Hill Stakes, the fillies' equivalent of the St Leger. This unique treble comprised Ark Royal, Kyak and Cutter, all saddled by George Colling and ridden by Manny Mercer whose brother Joe was to partner so many of their relations as Dick Hern's stable jockey at West Ilsley.

Although Ark Royal proved the best of the trio on the racecourse (she was runner-up in the Oaks to Triple Crown heroine, Meld), and bred three Group winners in Eagle, Ocean and Hermes, the future development of the family rested with the half-sisters, Kyak and Cutter.

Group winning descendants of Kyak (she survived until she was twenty-nine years of age), bred by Arches Hall Stud, comprise Anchor, Bireme, Buoy, Fluke, Dry Dock, Mariner, Raft and Sea Anchor. Corresponding winners for Cutter are Admiral's Launch, Longboat, Sky Ship, Sloop, Tepukei and Torpid.

Individual honours must be accorded to Ripeck (Ribot – Kyak), whose conception involved her dam in a five-day train journey across Europe to visit the great Ribot then standing in his native Italy. Ripeck is dam of Buoy and Bireme, both Group I winners at Epsom, and grandam of Sea Anchor, who became a leading sire in New Zealand. Buoy and Longboat became sires in Australia.

The most recent Hollingsworth star, Longboat carried off the 1986 stayers' Triple Crown of the Ascot Gold Cup, Goodwood Cup and Doncaster Cup. By the miler Welsh Pageant and his owner's sixth individual Royal Ascot scorer, Longboat is a grandson of Cutter as are Jakie Astor's two classic winners Cut Above and Sharp Edge.

An obvious feature with all these Hollingsworth horses is that their names have a nautical connotation. It all started with Felucca, whom Sydney Hollingsworth named after a particular type of boat found on the Nile. His son Dick adopted the practice more by accident than design. Incidentally Bireme is called after an old-fashioned galley with two banks of oars.

Dick Hollingsworth considers himself extremely fortunate to have had just two stud grooms. They are Roy Ingram, who occupied that position from 1951 until his retirement in 1986, and his long-time assistant, Stephen Lindsey. Both men always realized that the Arches Hall breed are late developers requiring very patient handling. In less sympathetic hands, the family might have been altogether less successful.

Ashley Heath and Warren Hill Studs

(now Warren Park Stud)

NEWMARKET · SUFFOLK

To sell an outstanding horse before his or her true ability becomes manifest is galling in any circumstances. Such has been the unfortunate experience of a comparative newcomer to racehorse ownership in Gerald Carroll. He sold Carroll House a couple of years before he triumphed in the 1989 Ciga Prix de l'Arc de Triomphe and the colt never left Michael Jarvis's stables. Furthermore, at that year's October Yearling Sales, he consigned the 1991 Premio Parioli (Italian 2000 Guineas) winner, Misil.

Gerald Carroll, an industrialist, financier and property developer, whose business headquarters are at Carroll House, Westminster, bought the adjoining Ashley Heath Stud and Warren Hill Stud in 1988 to add to his considerable property interests worldwide which include a 57,000-acre sheep station in Queensland, Australia.

Only eighteen months earlier these two prestigious studs, which are situated opposite Henry Cecil's Warren Place stables overlooking Newmarket (where the Carroll Foundation sponsors the July Cup), together with Fitzroy House stables, had been sold by Greek shipping magnate Captain Marcos Lemos to Clearwood Stud, a New Zealand consortium.

Presiding over the two studs is an imposing house built by Sir George Bullough in the style of a favourite French chateau near Le Touquet. In 1934 Bullough, owner of Longholes Stud, and his son-in-law, Lord Durham of Ashley Heath Stud, had the homebred winners of both fillies' classics, the former with Campanula (1000 Guineas) and the latter with Light Brocade (Oaks).

One of Ashley Heath's claims to fame is as the home of Prince Chevalier. The French Derby winner embarked upon stud duties there in 1947 and remained in residence until 1958 when transferred to Cheveley Park Stud where he died three years later. Sire of Charlottesville, Arctic Prince and Doutelle, he is also maternal grandsire of Brigadier Gerard.

In 1968, two years before the death of Lord Durham, Ashley Heath and Warren Hill Studs were sold separately. Ashley Heath was purchased by Anthony Samuelson, and Warren Hill by Captain Marcos Lemos. Within four years Samuelson, who stood Royal Levee and Some Hand, had sold out to his neighbour who converted both studs into show-places, setting a standard that was only to be surpassed by the great Arab building programme.

Over the next twenty years, Marcos Lemos's blue and white colours (which match the funnels of the family's shipping line, Lemos Pateras Ltd) became increasingly familiar on British racecourses, most of his runners being trained by Clive Brittain at the Lemos-owned Carlburg stables.

Two early reversals would have discouraged a less enthusiastic owner. Within a fortnight during 1966 two of his horses broke a leg – one of them, Grecian Sea, had cost 27,000 guineas as a yearling (just 1,000 guineas less than the record paid for Sayajirao in 1945). Undaunted he then paid 7,800 guineas for a Petition colt at that year's October Sales. Named Petingo, he proved a champion juvenile and a champion three-year-old miler winning the Sussex Stakes and St James's Palace Stakes. Standing under the Airlie flag in Ireland, he was champion sire of 1979, thanks to Troy. The next year his son Pitcairn was champion sire by virtue of Ela-Mana-Mou.

The first two stallions which Marcos Lemos stood at Ashley Heath Stud were Derby runner-up Cavo Doro (bred and ridden by Lester Piggott), another yearling purchase, and homebred Averof. Their stud careers dovetailed exactly. Both went to Ashley Heath in 1975 (Cavo Doro spent his initial season at Someries Stud), and both were exported in 1981, Cavo Doro to Brazil and Averof to South Africa.

Averof (St James's Palace Stakes), by whom Marcos Lemos bred the brilliant South African campaigner Foveros, had been purchased privately 'in utero' from Lord Howard de Walden of Plantation Stud. However, the mare that really did well for Warren Hill Stud was Guiding Light. Bred by the Queen, and a granddaughter of Above Board (dam of Doutelle), she cost 8,600 guineas as a three-year-old at the 1968 December Sales.

Two of Guiding Light's daughters are La Dolce and Princess Zena. The former is dam of Pebbles and the latter is dam of Supreme Leader. Pebbles provided her breeder with a resounding classic triumph in the 1984 General Accident 1000 Guineas. Rather surprisingly Marcos Lemos then sold her to Sheikh Mohammed for whom she excelled as a four-year-old, winning the Breeders' Cup Turf, Dubai Champion Stakes and Coral-Eclipse Stakes, the only filly to win this historic contest.

Supreme Leader, who was third in the General Accident 2000 Guineas and fourth in the Ever Ready Derby, was sold to join the élite band of jumping sires under the Coolmore flag in Ireland. Earlier the Marcos Lemos colours had been carried to another classic victory by Julio Mariner in the 1978 St Leger. Own-brother to one Oaks winner in Juliette Marny and half-brother to another in Scintillate, Julio Mariner had realized top price of 40,000 guineas at the Newmarket October Yearling Sales. The son of Blakeney made little impression as a stallion at Ashley Heath Stud. Eventually he was exported to Holland via Cobhall Court Stud, a jumping establishment in Herefordshire.

The last two stallions at Ashley Heath were Good Times and Precocious, and Lady Tavistock was involved with both of them. It was she who, together with agent Keith Freeman, imported Good Times from Italy where he had won the local 2000 Guineas. Good Times was replaced for the 1990 season by the Tavistocks' homebred Precocious who had been standing at New England Stud on the Cambridge side of Newmarket.

Further changes were afoot at Ashley Heath for the 1991 season. First, Dick Waugh, younger brother of John Waugh, resigned as manager – ten years earlier he had succeeded Philip E. H. Mitchell, now general manager of Prince Khalid Abdullah's Juddmonte Farms. Then, due to a major rebuilding and refurbishment programme, Precocious joined Good Times at Goosemoor Stud in Yorkshire. Only the previous year, Gerald Carroll had taken on Michael Russell, formerly in the employ of Brook Holliday (Sandwich Stud) and Sheikh Mohammed, as bloodstock comptroller and racing manager; his father bred the celebrated Rheingold.

Aston Park Stud

ASTON ROWANT · OXFORDSHIRE

The wheel of fortune so far as thoroughbred breeding is concerned was never better illustrated than by Aston Park Stud. In 1989 Elegant Air emulated his stud companion, Dominion, by becoming leading first season sire. The following April Elegant Air had to be put down on humane grounds suffering from a vertebral cyst.

Aston Park is at Aston Rowant, adjoining the M40, only thirty-nine miles from London and eighteen miles from Oxford. Situated on chalk land in Oxfordshire, it nestles under the picturesque Chilterns whose thickly wooded slopes rise steeply to a height of 800 feet barely half a mile away to the east. On the north side, the tall chimneys of the Chinnor cement works are a familiar landmark.

Dominion's first crop were foals when Anthony and Bernice Cuthbert purchased Aston Park in 1979 from Jeremy Willder, but vacant possession was not available until the following summer. Meanwhile part of the original property, Aston House Stud, was sold to Anthony and Jenny Chapman, breeders of that good stayer Buckley, now a Cobhall Court Stud National Hunt sire.

Originally the Cuthberts, both keen event riders, living a couple of miles away near Tetsworth, intended running Aston Park as a mixed farm. However they changed their minds when Bob McCreery, chairman of the Dominion syndicate, said how keen he was for the stallion to remain there. There was also a very experienced stud groom in Tim O'Rourke. Now at New England Stud, he had been at Aston Park since 1965.

Twice champion sire of two-year-olds (1984/5), Dominion (Derring-Do – Picture Palace) was actually conceived at Aston Park by Derring-Do whom he replaced. Furthermore his maternal grandsire, Princely Gift, was also bred there. It is indicative of his enormous success that Dominion should have five top sons standing in the British Isles – Primo Dominie,

Nomination, Domynsky, Dominion Royale and Governor General.

Aston Park was first utilized for breeding bloodstock by Clarence Hailey Snr, who bought the park of the old Aston Rowant Estate for £4,000 in 1928. A pioneer bloodstock agent and horse photographer, he was obliged to sell after his partner went into liquidation. So in the mid-1930s the stud passed into the hands of Ulsterman, William Barnett.

Head of Messrs W. and R. Barnett Ltd, grain importers from Belfast, William Barnett was invariably referred to as Trigo Barnett after his homebred Derby and St Leger winner of 1929. Trained by Dick Dawson at Whatcombe (where both Derring-Do and Dominion were trained by Arthur Budgett), Trigo was bred, conceived and reared at brother Sam Dawson's Cloghran Stud in Ireland.

Barnett duly transferred his bloodstock from Cloghran to Aston Park where Clarence Hailey Jnr was manager – he later became manager to Lord Rosebery at Mentmore. Amongst those to journey across the Irish Sea were Trigo and his dam, Athasi. Both are buried on the stud and she is depicted on the mare and foal weathervane presiding over the main yard.

The succession of matings between Blandford, sire of Trigo, and Athasi (all three commemorated by races in Ireland), is part of Stud Book folklore. Many of her offspring had Spanish names associated with grain. One of them Harina (= flour) became the grandam of the Aga Khan's celebrated pair, Tulyar and Saint Crespin III.

Nowadays the Barnetts board their stock at nearby Adstock Manor Stud. The star in their midst is Time Charter. Not only is Harina her fifth dam, but she is also by Saritamer. He stood at Aston Park for one season and she is his only progeny of note.

Both William Barnett Snr and Trigo died in 1946 whereupon the stud became the property of Alfred Allnatt. The breeder of Princely Gift, a noted sire of sires, he received much publicity when purchasing 134 animals, including Colombo, from Lord Glanely's executors.

Having been rested for a long time, Aston Park was bought by Richard Willder of Granada Television in 1960. He rebuilt and modernized the premises for occupation by three French-bred stallions, Dicta Drake, Polic (sire of Polyfoto), and Le Tricolore. At that stage Bob McCreery (Stowell Hill) was manager and he has been closely involved ever since and is the breeder of Derring-Do's classic winning son, High Top.

In the early 1970s, Derring-Do, who went completely blind, shared his quarters with Frankincense (by Princely Gift), and Swing Easy, by which time the stud had been taken over by Richard Willder's son, Jeremy.

High Top (2000 Guineas) is one of Derring-Do's three classic winners, together with Roland Gardens (2000 Guineas) and Peleid (St Leger). Dominion himself was third in the 2000 Guineas. After an interim period with Ian Balding at Kingsclere, which coincided with the death of his owner-breeder, Colonel Percy Wright, he excelled in the USA before Bob McCreery repatriated him.

Dominion's sons, Primo Dominie and Nomination, both won the OCL Richmond Stakes. Primo Dominie, who is the only winner of the Coventry, Richmond and July Stakes, now stands at Cheveley Park Stud. Nomination, whose part breeder is Penny van Straubenzee (formerly Mrs Jeremy Willder), is at Limestone Stud. Both did well with their first crop of runners in 1990, as did another Dominion horse in Domynsky.

Elegant Air (by Shirley Heights) was trained by Ian Balding for Paul Mellon, the combination associated with his grandsire, Mill Reef. With his first crop of runners, he sired two Group I winners in Dashing Blade (Three Chimneys Dewhurst Stakes, GPA National Stakes, Gran Premio d'Italia Trofeo Saima), and Air de Rien (Prix Saint Alary), both bred by Littleton Stud.

For the 1991 covering season, Aston Park Stud fielded three stallions with old stager Dominion, and two young sons of top sires in Squill (by Stop the Music), who also does a southern hemisphere season at Gooree Stud in Australia, and Weldnaas (by Diesis).

Aston Upthorpe Stud

ASTON TIRROLD · OXFORDSHIRE

The first property that Sheikh Mohammed owned in Britain was the Duke of Windsor's old bolt hole, Fort Belvedere, which he then sold to Charles St George – the present owner is Galen Weston of Barrettstown Stud Farms. On the other hand, the first stud bought by the Sheikh was Aston Upthorpe and it was here that St George retired Lorenzaccio.

Aston Upthorpe, which Sheikh Mohammed gave to his younger brother Sheikh Ahmed and is home of the latter's champion, Mtoto, is 210 acres of 1,000 acres of farmland and gallops which Sir William Pigott-Brown acquired in the autumn of 1962 from the trustees of Leonard Cundell. The young amateur rider thus became the landlord of his mentor, Aston Tirrold trainer, Frank Cundell, Leonard's nephew.

At Chilton, which is next door to Aston Tirrold on the borders of Oxfordshire and Berkshire, near Didcot, Leonard Cundell trained Noble Star. Owned in partnership with Frank's father, he was a smart stayer during the early 'thirties. A couple of decades later the star of Frank Cundell's Aston Tirrold stable proved to be Noble Star's son Crudwell, the winner of fifty races under both Rules.

William Pigott-Brown's career in the saddle was short and sweet. Twice leading amateur during the early 'sixties, despite considerable weight problems, he gained a memorable victory in the 1961 National Hunt Chase on Superfine. A spectator that afternoon was his 80-year-old grandfather, Gilbert Cotton, who had partnered the winner of the amateurs' Grand National in 1912.

By the time that Aston Upthorpe was sold to Sheikh Mohammed in 1981, William Pigott-Brown had forsaken Aston Tirrold and horses for London and the contrasting business world of pop music and nightclubs. Viewed retrospectively, the nucleus of mares he established with the assistance of the British Bloodstock Agency was very much on target.

As a breeder in his own right, his most important mare was Vivien. By Nearco, she was bought privately from Edward Bee's Cotswold Stud. Her progeny included Virginia Gentleman (Queen Anne Stakes), who became a sire in Australia, and Jakomima. Trained by Peter Walwyn, she carried her breeder's colours to victory in the Musidora Stakes.

Two other mares bred fillies destined to earn renown for owner-breeders. In 1966 to a mating with Crocket, Honeymoon House, Aston Upthorpe's very first mare, foaled Fanghorn. Three years later to a mating with Reform, Golden Plate, a yearling purchase, produced Mrs Moss. Both Crocket and Reform were stallions under BBA management.

In the years ahead, Fanghorn and Mrs Moss became celebrated brood-mares. For Baroness Thyssen, who operated from Daylesford Stud in Gloucestershire, Fanghorn bred her homebred champion sprinter, Double Form. Mrs Moss, whom her breeder named after the wife of the famous motor racing driver, Stirling Moss, has excelled for the Tavistocks at their Bloomsbury Stud.

As well as his own mares, Pigott-Brown also maintained a handful of boarders, amongst them Sweet Molly, dam of that excellent miler Jimmy Reppin. Also kept there were a couple of mares belonging to Beckhampton trainer Jeremy Tree, they being the last of the animals which he had inherited from Mereworth Stud in Kent owned by his uncle, Peter Beatty.

Initially William Pigott-Brown managed the stud himself, but before long his former riding colleague, Dave Dick, had taken over the reins. He also doubled up as manager of nearby Wyld Court Stud, then owned by a consortium headed by Peter de Savary. Today the stud is managed by Robert Acton from Dalham Hall, the nerve centre of the Maktoum racing empire.

From 1971 (the year in which the present stud groom, Frank Berry, arrived at Aston Upthorpe) until 1975, the stud was home to Lorenzaccio, a syndicated stallion under the auspices of the BBA. During that period the conqueror of Triple Crown hero Nijinsky for the Champion Stakes sired that highly successful stallion Ahonoora. He was actually bred by Wyld Court Stud whence Lorenzaccio was switched for a couple of seasons prior to being exported to Australia in 1977.

Since the Pigott-Brown era, Aston Upthorpe has been transformed into one of the best appointed studs in the country. There is now accommodation for three stallions. A wonderful range of buildings, which have been greatly enhanced by the use of Scandinavian larch, includes new stallion and foaling units, an office complex and covering yard.

However, the Maktoums have only ever had one stallion there at any one time. First to take up residence was Maktoum Al Maktoum's Touching Wood. Winner of the English and Irish St Legers and runner-up in the Derby, he came to Aston Upthorpe for the 1984 season having completed his initial season at Dalham Hall. In 1988 his owner moved him out to New Zealand; two years later his son Ashal won the Ascot Gold Cup.

Touching Wood's replacement was 1989 Horse of the Year, Mtoto. Raced by Ahmed Al Maktoum, who had only recently taken over Aston Upthorpe, Mtoto won the King George VI and Queen Elizabeth Diamond Stakes and was beaten a neck when runner-up to Tony Bin in the Ciga Prix de l'Arc de Triomphe. Also successful twice in the Coral-Eclipse Stakes and Prince of Wales's Stakes, the son of Busted was syndicated for £2.8 million. He commenced covering at a fee of £18,000 (1 October).

As well as accommodating the mares visiting Mtoto, Aston Upthorpe (sponsors of the Yorkshire Oaks) is a permanent home for around thirty mares owned by Sheikh Ahmed. As is to be expected, they are a select collection in the best Arab tradition. Amongst the more distinguished are Gesedeh, Hayloft, Ski Sailing and Tralthee. Hayloft, like Aston Upthorpe, used to belong to Sheikh Mohammed. Bred by Limestone Stud, she is dam of Wassl, the first good racehorse to carry Sheikh Ahmed's distinctive yellow colours with black epaulettes.

Banstead Manor Stud

NEWMARKET · SUFFOLK

During 1986 two yearling colts, by Persian Bold and resident Ile de Bourbon, shared the same paddock at Hugo Morriss's Banstead Manor Stud, Newmarket. As Persian Heights and Ile de Chypre respectively, they were to finish first in successive runnings of the Group I International Stakes at York, the former subsequently being disqualified and placed third.

In 1989 the International Stakes (formerly Benson and Hedges Gold Cup, Matchmaker International), was sponsored for the first time by Prince Khalid Abdullah and carried the suffix Juddmonte. It was in the spring of 1987 that the Saudi Arabian owner-breeder purchased Banstead Manor which has become the public half of his breeding operation in the United Kingdom centred on his Juddmonte Farms at Wargrave-on-Thames.

The first of Khalid Abdullah's flag-bearers to take up residence at Banstead Manor was Rainbow Quest in 1988, the stallion having completed his first two covering seasons at Wargrave-on-Thames. His other Prix de l'Arc de Triomphe hero, Dancing Brave, stands at Dalham Hall. Lesser Abdullah stallions are also Newmarket based at Eagle Lane Farm, formerly the Vanian brothers' Dullingham Stud.

Situated at Cheveley opposite White Lodge Stud, Banstead Manor (at the time of the Domesday Book the land belonged to the Benstedes), used to form part of Colonel Harry McCalmont's vast Cheveley Estate where he bred Triple Crown hero Isinglass. In 1925 Henry Morriss acquired the property specifically to stand his 2000 Guineas and Derby winner of that year, Manna. His hopes of emulating Isinglass evaporated when he broke down in Solario's St Leger.

Henry Morriss spent most of his life in China where he was chairman and part owner of the North China Daily News and had substantial interests in Shanghai's bullion broking business. A keen amateur rider he noticed some unusual horses one day whilst returning to China on the Trans Siberian

Railway. He duly acquired a number to race at Shanghai bringing off some noted coups. Unfortunately they were censured by the authorities whereupon he switched his racing allegiance to England.

In 1921 he gave Fred Darling an annual commission to select the best yearling that money could buy. Two years later at Doncaster the great Beckhampton trainer secured Manna (Phalaris – Waffles) for 6,300 guineas. Following that colt's Epsom victory, his owner was invariably referred to as Manna Morriss.

Manna covered his first mares at Banstead Manor in 1926 when the stud produced its first notable winner, Artist's Proof, who joined Manna as a stallion in 1932. When the latter departed to France he was replaced by another homebred in Tai-Yang who had an extraordinary unbeaten record, winning once at three years (Jockey Club Stakes) and once two years later!

As sires Manna is notable for Colombo (2000 Guineas) and Miracle (Eclipse Stakes), whilst Artist's Proof is the maternal grandsire of Petition. Tai-Yang's dam Soubriquet was the stud's foundation mare. Runner-up for Sir Edward Hulton in the 1922 1000 Guineas and Oaks, she cost 12,500 guineas from his executors at the 1925 Newmarket December Sales.

The inevitable mating between Manna and Soubriquet resulted in Pasca, dam of Pasch (2000 Guineas, Eclipse Stakes) and grandam of Pinza (Derby, King George VI and Queen Elizabeth Stakes). The latter, whose sire Chanteur II stood at Banstead Manor, was sold 'in utero' to Fred Darling. Trained by his former head lad, Norman Bertie, he provided Sir Gordon Richards with his one and only Derby winner in 1953.

Two years earlier Manna Morriss died in Shanghai, but not before he too had been accredited with breeding a Derby winner, albeit a substitute affair at Newmarket. In this instance he had acquired the 1940 hero, Pont l'Eveque, 'in utero', but sold him at the end of his two-year-old days to Fred Darling for just £500!

During Manna Morriss's lifetime, the stud was run by his wife. She handed over the reins to their son, Nicky, and when he died in 1963, his eldest son, Hugo, took charge. Both bred runners placed in the Derby, Nicky with Alcaeus, runner-up to St Paddy in 1960, and Hugo with Pentland Firth, who finished third to Roberto in 1972.

Following the sale of Banstead Manor, Hugo maintains a few mares at Lanwades Stud, amongst them Boule de Suif and Scala di Seta. The former is half-sister to three good colts in Intervener, Grey Moss and Barrons Court. Scala di Seta bred two stars in Italy with Stone, 1978 Horse of the Year, and Stouci (Gran Criterium).

The last good performer Hugo bred at Banstead Manor is Persian Heights. Sold as a yearling for 25,000 guineas to Prince Yazid Saud, he won the St James's Palace Stakes before becoming a syndicated stallion at Coolmore.

Stallions have always played a major role at Banstead. Since the Manna Morriss era they have included Chanteur II, Supreme Court, Nearula, Bally-moss, Salvo, Upper Case, Shantung, Wollow, Lombard, Ile de Bourbon and Beldale Flutter. Ile de Bourbon's runners started doing well just as soon as he was exported to Japan in 1987. The very next year came Kahyasi (Ever Ready Derby, Budweiser Irish Derby) followed by the previously mentioned Ile de Chypre. He was bred at Banstead on behalf of his owner, Athos Christodoulou.

Since being acquired by Prince Khalid Abdullah, Banstead Manor Stud has undergone extensive refurbishment and rebuilding under stud manager Simon Mockridge. The public domain, presided over by Rainbow Quest and his close relative Warning, is confined to walking-in mares. That accounts for just 50 acres from a total of 365, of which 140 have only recently been laid down from arable to pasture. One of the principal functions of these pristine paddocks is to provide accommodation for the prince's own mares when visiting Newmarket stallions.

Barleythorpe Stud

OAKHAM · LEICESTERSHIRE

Former chairman of the Thoroughbred Breeders' Association, whose five-year term of office as president runs from 1991 to 1996, David Gibson is the owner-manager of Barleythorpe Stud. So far as the stallions are concerned, this is run in close conjunction with Robert Percival of Glen Andred Stud at Old in Northamptonshire, and Thomas Warner of Red House Stud at Exning on the outskirts of Newmarket.

Until 1974 Barleythorpe was the only stud in Rutland, but since the reorganization of the county boundaries it is now designated as being in Leicestershire. Just outside Oakham at the heart of some of England's finest hunting country, the stud was founded by Lord Lonsdale in about 1870, its proximity to the Cottesmore, the Belvoir and the Quorn doubtless being one of the principal considerations.

An eccentric character, who was universally popular in sporting circles (boxing's Lonsdale Belt is his lasting testimonial), the 5th Earl of Lonsdale (1857–1944) was known as 'The Yellow Earl' after his yellow coach and liveried servants. At one time he leased the animals bred by the National Stud for the duration of their racing careers, amongst them the great Myrobella, dam of Sun Chariot and grandam of Chamossaire.

Hugh Lonsdale laid out Barleythorpe Stud (then spelt Barley Thorpe) with splendid rides of sufficient width to drive a 'horse and two'. Colonel Hall-Walker (later Lord Wavertree) was jointly involved in the scheme and it was their intention to start a National Stud there. However the two men disagreed, whereupon Hall-Walker laid the foundations of the future National Stud at Tully in Co. Kildare.

From 1924 to 1931, Royal Lancer, a colt leased from the National Stud, who had carried Lord Lonsdale's colours to victory in both the English and Irish St Legers, stood at Barleythorpe. Following a couple of intermediate seasons at Tully, he was exported to South Africa in 1933. By that time Barleythorpe was more notable as the home of the Cottesmore kennels than as a thoroughbred stud.

Hugh Lonsdale had bred no horses of any consequence by the time he died in 1944. Having long since vacated the family home of Lowther Castle, he was then living in a rambling Victorian mansion that he had built at Barleythorpe. It was rather an incongruous situation for a man who had inherited 175,000 acres in Westmorland and Cumberland upon succeeding to the title in his twenties.

While Barleythorpe had become dissociated with horses, Highfield Stud in the centre of Oakham had been flourishing under David Gibson's grandfather, George. Due to a scarcity of horse vets in the area, George Gibson had been persuaded by Lord Londonderry to leave Co. Durham, and set up in practice in Oakham. Here he was succeeded in turn by his son, also George, and his grandson, Michael. A former president of the Equine Veterinary Association, Michael is David's younger brother.

One of the horses which George Gibson Snr stood at Highfield was Miracle. Acquired from Lord Rosebery and previously based at his Mentmore Stud, the Eclipse Stakes winner was only a temporary resident in Rutland for in 1942 he was sold to the National Stud in Uruguay. After the war, Gibson bought Barleythorpe and the farms that went with the property. Between the two studs he stood a wide variety of stallions, amongst them Constable, Flush Royal, Kingstone, Seasick, Gustav and Richboy.

The Cesarewitch winner Flush Royal has a particular significance so far as David Gibson is concerned for he gained one of his most important riding successes in the Past and Present Chase, Sandown Park, on Flush Royal's homebred son, Regal Mist. Sire of the Courages' top chasers, Spanish Steps and Royal Relief, Flush Royal is also maternal grandsire of the 1974 Derby winner Snow Knight, a direct descendant of Myrobella. Richboy sired the Cheltenham Gold Cup hero Burrough Hill Lad.

By the outset of the seventies, the whole concept of stallions at Barleythorpe had undergone a radical change. Up till then the horses, which were geared mostly to producing jumpers, were of secondary importance to the veterinary practice with its sophisticated hospital amenities in Oakham. However when David was forced to retire from race riding through injury, he decided to concentrate on running the stud.

He realized immediately that the way forward was to stand commercial horses likely to sire fast, precocious stock. His first two stallion acquisitions were Tribal Chief and Mummy's Pet. With just three seasons at Barleythorpe, where he sired Mrs McArdy (1000 Guineas), before going to

Hamilton Stud *en route* to Japan, Tribal Chief had a very short career in Rutland compared to Mummy's Pet.

Mummy's Pet (Sing Sing – Money for Nothing), retired to Barleythorpe for the 1972 season and he died there in September 1986, aged eighteen. By then he had earned the deserved reputation as England's premier sire of two-year-olds. Bred by the Holland-Martins at their Overbury Stud, Mummy's Pet was a smart sprinter who gained recognition as a sire of sires. His Group winning sons at stud include Runnett, Tina's Pet, Mummy's Game, Aragon, Petorius, Precocious and Reprimand.

The Sing Sing horse stood alongside a number of other successful stallions. They include Mansingh (later transferred to Tom Warner's Red House Stud), Dragonara Palace, Mummy's Game, Free State and Petong. Mummy's Game, who was exported to Italy, had his first crop of foals in 1984, amongst them the remarkable Pen Bal Lady. Bred by David Gibson (Highfield Stud), and sold from Barleythorpe as a yearling for only 5,000 guineas, she was destined to win three Grade I races as a four-year-old on the West Coast of America, earning over half a million dollars.

All these stallions have helped to promote Barleythorpe Stud's reputation for top commercial sires. An added incentive has been to include all routine veterinary fees in the cost of a nomination. For 1991, Mansingh's son, Petong, shares his quarters with two Northern Dancer line stallions in Northern State, an own-brother to Storm Bird, and Mazilier.

Barton Stud

One of a number of studs in the vicinity of Bury St Edmunds, to the east of Newmarket, Barton Stud at Great Barton is owned by the 3rd Lord Fairhaven. Senior steward of the Jockey Club from 1985 to 1989, he lives at Anglesey Abbey in the village of Lode, which is on the other side of Newmarket towards Cambridge.

Ailwyn Fairhaven inherited the title upon the death of his father in 1973. As Major Henry Broughton, the latter had succeeded his elder brother, Huttleston (the 1st Lord Fairhaven) when he died in 1966. It was Huttleston's executors who bequeathed Anglesey Abbey and its celebrated geometric gardens to the National Trust.

Huttleston Broughton, who was born in America, where his father (former Conservative Member of Parliament for Preston) had industrial interests, was created a Baron in 1929. Four years earlier he and his brother had acquired Barton Stud from the executors of newspaper tycoon Sir Edward Hulton. Owner of Warren Tower Stud, Cheveley, Edward Hulton had founded Barton Stud in 1921.

Joint partners in Barton Stud, the Broughton brothers both served in the army during the Second World War. In their absence the stud was leased to the old Aga Khan who stood a succession of stallions there, amongst them Tehran, Dastur, Umiddad and Umidwar. More important was Nasrullah. He retired to Barton Stud for the 1944 season at a fee of £198 before departing to Joe McGrath's Brownstown Stud on the Curragh.

As racing manager to the 1st Lord Fairhaven, Lady Cambridge was involved in the purchase of two notable foundation mares. Both were yearling acquisitions from Beau Parc Stud, Co. Meath, the one, Marilda, being bred by Lady Lambart, and the other, Constantia, being bred by her son, Sir Oliver Lambart.

Marilda, who cost 2,100 guineas in 1949, had an influential daughter in Quenilda. She was responsible for thirteen individual winners, including the multiple scorers Quoit (seventeen races), Quy, the first horse to race for the present Lord Fairhaven, and Quentilian. In 1988 Quenilda's grandson Quinlan Terry carried Lady Fairhaven's colours to victory in the William Hill Cambridgeshire.

Having won races with her three-parts sister, Adelicia, the 1st Lord Fairhaven paid 2,800 guineas for Constantia as a yearling in 1950. She rewarded him by winning the National Breeders' Produce Stakes (then a major contest) and Lowther Stakes, to be rated the second best juvenile filly of her year.

Eight of Constantia's progeny scored. The last of them was Constans. This durable gelding won three consecutive runnings of the Prix de Saint-Georges, despite being hobdayed for a wind infirmity and having a history of breaking blood vessels!

From 1954 to 1989, Barton Stud was managed by Major John Critchley-Salmonson. For a while he doubled up as manager to Sir John Musker at Shadwell Stud and to Major Michael Wyatt at Duke's Stud. In Critchley-Salmonson's opinion, Star Moss (Mossborough – Star of France) was the best horse bred by the Fairhavens in his time. Star of France, who once changed hands for fifty guineas, cost 1,500 guineas at the 1957 Newmarket July sales. The price included her Mossborough filly foal – as French Fern she proceeded to win the Ribblesdale Stakes.

That year (1960) marked the arrival of her own-brother, Star Moss. Winner of the Royal Lodge Stakes, his three-year-old career was restricted through injury to just two starts. In the St Leger he finished runner-up to Ragusa on unfavourably firm ground. Retired to Eve Stud (now Woodditton Stud) and subsequently switched to Barton Stud, Star Moss made little impression as a stallion. Exported to Australia in 1973, he died not long afterwards.

Other stallions to have stood at Barton Stud are Espresso (sire of triple Ascot Gold Cup winner, Sagaro), Klairon, Royalty, Relkino, and the present duo, Night Shift and Charmer. It was to a mating with Klairon that French Fern produced Shangamuzo. A 3,000-guinea yearling, he won the 1978 Ascot Gold Cup as a five-year-old, before becoming a sire in Brazil.

Over the years the Fairhaven family's principal trainers have been the Newmarket stalwarts Jack Waugh, Ryan Jarvis, Bruce Hobbs and Sir Mark Prescott, while additional winners for the 'silver, copper hoop and armlets' have included Summer Day and her son Heave To, Boscage, Calaba and Two of Diamonds.

The public and private sectors of Barton Stud have always been run independently of one another, each benefiting from a strict rotation of paddocks. Prominent with both categories is the American Donald T. Johnson, whose decision to stand Night Shift (Northern Dancer – Ciboulette) there together with a coterie of mares, has ushered in a new era of prosperity for the whole establishment.

Donald Johnson, who stands Giboulee, another son of Northern Dancer at his Crescent Farm in Kentucky, decided to board Night Shift in England because of the concentration of Northern Dancer line stallions back home in the States. It was a novel experiment to bring a nucleus of supporting mares as well, but in the event they were hardly needed. With only his second crop of three-year-olds, Night Shift was second only to Sadler's Wells on the list of leading sires for 1990. The principal contributor was the brilliant filly In the Groove (Dubai Champion Stakes, Juddmonte International Stakes, Goffs' Irish 1000 Guineas).

An earlier winner of the Irish 1000 Guineas is Front Row, one of Barton Stud's star boarders. Her progeny reared on behalf of Mrs F.G.(Doris) Allen include Colmore Row (Norfolk Stakes), an Irish National Stud stallion currently based at Blackmore Vale Stud in Dorset.

For the 1991 season Night Shift was joined by Charmer. Like the previous residents, Royalty and Relkino, he raced for the Dowager Lady Beaverbrook. All these stallions either stand or stood under the management of the British Bloodstock Agency. Upon John Critchley-Salmonson's retirement on 1 January 1990, Joss Collins of the BBA became manager of the stud.

Beech House Stud

NEWMARKET · SUFFOLK

Since Sheikh Hamdan Al Maktoum took over Beech House Stud in the autumn of 1989, it has been utilized as a holding station, a far cry from past glory days. Mares from his Shadwell Stud in Norfolk and Derrinstown Stud in Ireland are based there while visiting Newmarket stallions. From September to November it is the turn of yearlings prior to entering training.

Beech House has a unique place in the development of the thoroughbred during the second half of the twentieth century for it was here that Martin Benson stood Nearco throughout his stud life. He also bred the mare Lady Angela, and her colt foal of 1954 by Nearco was none other than Nearctic, the sire of Northern Dancer.

Originally part of Colonel Harry McCalmont's vast Cheveley Estate, Beech House Stud, which takes its name from a profusion of fine trees, had been sold to Charles Heckford in the early 1920s. Brother-in-law of Newmarket trainer Reg Day, his career as a jockey was disrupted by the Kaiser's war after which he decided to concentrate on stud management.

In 1930 Martin Benson, who had failed to find a suitable property in the home counties, bought Beech House Stud, retaining Heckford as his manager. A bookmaker, who traded as Duggie ('Never Owes') Stuart, Martin Benson spent a great deal of money on improving the amenities at Beech House as well as establishing a band of top-quality mares.

Unable to acquire nominations to the more fashionable stallions of the day, he determined to buy the best horse that was available. In 1934 he paid the Maharajah of Rajpipla £50,000 for Windsor Lad shortly after his Derby victory. The colt proceeded to win the St Leger, Coronation Cup and Eclipse Stakes. Due to ill health, he survived only three covering seasons in Newmarket and was the subject of a disputed insurance claim.

Martin Benson then set about finding a replacement for Windsor Lad and in 1939 he bought Nearco for £60,000, just four days after Federico

Tesio's unbeaten champion had gained a fourteenth victory in the Grand Prix de Paris. The deal, which was negotiated by the British Bloodstock Agency and sanctioned by Benito Mussolini, involved a price equalling the record paid for the 1927 Derby hero, Call Boy.

Nearco (Pharos – Nogara) commenced covering at Beech House in 1940 at a fee of 400 guineas. Subsequently syndicated, his nominations were soon selling for upwards of £2,000. Twice champion sire (1947, 1948), he was also three times leading sire of broodmares (1952, 1955, 1956). His classic winners are Dante, Nimbus, Sayajirao, Masaka and Neasham Belle.

During the war Nearco used to be sent to north Wales after the covering season for safe keeping, although a special air-raid shelter had been constructed for him on the stud. Twenty-two years of age when he was put down in June 1957 suffering from cancer, his burial place on the stud is marked by a striking memorial tablet depicting an open book.

In 1960 Martin Benson sold Beech House to Sir Victor Sassoon. The purchase was made upon the recommendation of Sir Noel Murless who, by then, was Sassoon's bloodstock manager and principal trainer. When he died in 1961, Sir Victor owned around sixty mares and four studs – Beech House and Eve Stud in Newmarket, Thornton Stud in Yorkshire, and Killeen Castle Stud in Ireland.

In the interim he had become one of the country's foremost owners, winning the Derby four times within the space of seven years. Two of those winners were the homebred pair, Crepello (1957) and St Paddy (1960), both trained by Murless. Crepello was out of an oustanding mare in Crepuscule, dam also of Honeylight (1000 Guineas) and Twilight Alley (Ascot Gold Cup).

Both Crepello and St Paddy spent the duration of their stud life at Beech House and each died in retirement, the former aged twenty in 1974 and the latter aged twenty-seven in 1984. The champion sire of 1969, Crepello had four classic winning daughters with Mysterious, Crepellana, Celina and Caergwrle. The best of his sons was the Snailwell Stud celebrity, Busted, sire of Bustino. Most notable of St Paddy's offspring are Connaught, maternal grandsire of champion filly Pebbles, and Jupiter Island.

Following Sir Victor Sassoon's death, his widow continued with Beech House Stud until it was purchased by Louis Freedman of Cliveden Stud exactly ten years later. In the interim Lady Sassoon gradually reduced her bloodstock interests, selling Thornton Stud and eight animals to Lord Howard de Walden.

The sixty head of stock acquired by Louis Freedman, who had already bred an Oaks winner (Polygamy) and was destined to breed a Derby winner

(Reference Point), also made a lasting contribution. It was from this source that his colours were to be carried to victory in four runnings of the Park Hill Stakes, thanks to Attica Meli, Mil's Bomb, Royal Hive and Madame Dubois.

From 1975 to 1989, Beech House Stud was owned by Dr Carlo Vittadini, a Milanese banker, who later installed his daughter, Franca, as manager. A very successful owner-breeder in Italy, whose affairs here were managed by Norwich agent Keith Freeman, Carlo Vittadini owned the 1975 Derby hero Grundy. That year he prevailed over Bustino in a titanic struggle for the King George VI and Queen Elizabeth Diamond Stakes.

Although Grundy never stood at Beech House Stud (he was syndicated to stand at the National Stud before going to Japan), stallions there under the Vittadini flag, which traded as Cotswold Bloodstock, consisted of St Paddy, Abwah, Ribero, Habat, Orange Bay, Imperial Fling, Ardross and Pharly.

Someone who remembers all of them is stud groom Michael McFarling. He has occupied that responsible position since 1963 having first gone to Beech House Stud six years earlier to take charge of Crepello when he came out of training.

Biddestone Stud

BIDDESTONE · WILTSHIRE

Any aspirations that a small breeder has of a Royal Ascot winner are remote to say the least. To have two winners at the meeting is verging on the realms of fantasy, yet this was the singular achievement of John L. Moore of Biddestone Stud in 1988 with Mtoto (Prince of Wales's Stakes) and Powder Blue (Wokingham Stakes).

Against all the odds, John Moore was the only breeder to be accredited with more than one Royal Ascot winner that year. His annual tally as a breeder stood at three individual winners of six races in Great Britain, value £434,420, which placed him second to the Aga Khan. Here the similarity ends as His Highness had twenty-eight winners of forty-six races, worth £636,825.

That season, Horse of the Year Mtoto not only gained a second consecutive success in both the Prince of Wales's Stakes and Coral-Eclipse Stakes, but he also achieved a commanding victory in the King George VI and Queen Elizabeth Diamond Stakes. Finally he was second, beaten a neck by Tony Bin, in the Ciga Prix de l'Arc de Triomphe in which he had finished fourth the previous year.

Having spent the greater part of his working life in the West End of London, John Moore is a solicitor by profession, with specialist knowledge of the law of property and retail property development. For someone with a logical mind, it was strangely out of character to launch into the realms of bloodstock breeding without any prior experience, except as an enthusiastic racegoer.

Two breeders helped initially: Kenneth Lazenby, who bred that exceptionally fast filly From Russia With Love and managed Jim Mullion's shipping interests in the City, and Major John de Burgh of Oldtown Stud, Co. Kildare. Father of Hubie, who now runs the adjacent Derrinstown Stud for Sheikh Hamdan Al Maktoum, John de Burgh had a couple of mares in partnership with John Moore in the early days.

31

John Moore's first two in-foal mare purchases were in 1964. Fair Renown cost 1,000 guineas at Ascot in November and Wharfedale 1,750 guineas at the Newmarket December Sales. As their new owner had no stud of his own at the time, they were boarded out, but that was only a very temporary arrangement.

The decision to acquire Biddestone Manor, near Chippenham, in Wiltshire, from Brigadier Michael Morley (father of trainer David Morley) in the winter of 1969 was greatly influenced by the twenty arable acres opposite. Gradually additional land was purchased and the facilities developed so that it is now a model establishment of 100 acres and twenty-seven boxes.

Wharfedale, who died at the advanced age of twenty-three after producing her last foal, is the grandam of Powder Blue. In winning the Wokingham Stakes, Powder Blue was emulating her fifth dam, Kong, who triumphed back in 1937. Kong was destined to earn renown at Whitsbury Manor as dam of the three-parts brothers, Nimbus and Grey Sovereign.

John Moore was an admirer of the Kong family and he was inbreeding to this mare when mating Wharfedale with the Grey Sovereign horse, Raffingora. The result was another grey, Raffindale. Always regarded as a potential champion by his trainer, Ryan Price, his career here was marred by the virus. However he took on a new lease of life in Australia where he won two Group I events. In the AJC Handicap at Randwick he established a new Australian record time for eight furlongs, and in the VATC Marlboro Cup at Caulfield he set a new course record for seven furlongs. He has had his share of success as a stallion in the southern hemisphere.

One of those breeders who lay far greater emphasis on the bottom (distaff) line than the top (male) line in a pedigree, John Moore always favours buying into a family with plenty of female relatives, preferably owned by breeders operating at the top end of the scale. This *modus operandi* provides a sporting chance of improving the credentials of one's own mare at someone else's expense.

Amazer, dam of Mtoto, was just such a mare. By the little-known French sire, Mincio, and a winner in that country, the nine-year-old was bought through the British Bloodstock Agency for 5,800 guineas from her breeder, Sir Robin McAlpine (Wyck Hall Stud) at the 1976 Newmarket December Sales. Her grandam Zabara (1000 Guineas) was to become the second dam of Circus Plume (Gold Seal Oaks).

Trained by Alec Stewart for Sheikh Ahmed Al Maktoum, Mtoto (Swahili for 'my dear child') realized 110,000 guineas at the 1984 Highflyer Sales. A horse who improved with age, just like his sire Busted, Mtoto replaced

Bustino as their sire's best racing son. Retired to his owner's beautifully appointed Aston Upthorpe Stud for the 1989 season, he was syndicated at £70,000 a share to start covering at a fee of £18,000 (1 October).

Savoureuse Lady, a 190,000-guinea yearling, who won the 1990 Prix Fille de l'Air, Saint-Cloud, is Amazer's twelfth individual winner. Her next two progeny were a Caerleon filly in 1989 and a Niniski colt in 1990. At the age of twenty-four, she foaled a Slip Anchor filly in the spring of 1991 prior to retirement.

Although Amazer's days as a producer are over, John Moore is fortunate in having Mtoto's three-parts sister, Belle Arrivée (by Bustino) back in the stud. Likewise trained by Alec Stewart, Belle Arrivée won a small race as a three-year-old, but she should have a bright future as a broodmare. These are certainly the sentiments not only of her owner-breeder but also his very experienced stud groom, Melvin Rylance. He knows a great deal about top-quality bloodstock, having been stud groom at Robert Sangster's now defunct Swettenham Stud in Cheshire.

John Moore emphasizes just how difficult it is for a commercial breeder to survive in the present economic climate. Always a strong advocate for some form of breeders' prizes, he did gain official recognition for breeding Mtoto. For the 1988 season he was voted TBA Breeder of the Year as well as Leading British-Based Breeder, a unique double in any one year.

Bloomsbury Stud

WOBURN · BEDFORDSHIRE

At the end of the private drive at Woburn Abbey in Bedfordshire overlooking the lake is a life-size bronze by Philip Blacker, the former National Hunt jockey turned sculptor, of a mare who has proved one of the great post-war bargains. Her name is Mrs Moss (Reform – Golden Plate) and she is the cornerstone of the Tavistocks' Bloomsbury Stud.

At the unveiling of this sculpture in the autumn of 1990, Tattersalls' auctioneer, Peter Holmes, described how he had sold Mrs Moss, then a six-year-old in-foal mare, at the 1975 December Sales for 2,100 guineas to Lady Tavistock – the former Henrietta Tiarks. A small winner at Chester, she was consigned by Ralph Fitzjohn from Fedamore House Stud, Co. Limerick.

When it comes to thoroughbreds, truth is often stranger than fiction. Upon closer inspection it transpired that Mrs Moss has a club foot (a minor deformity). Consequently approaches were made to the Irish vendor to take her back, but to no avail. Understandably his reaction was, 'You bought her, she's yours.'

Up till then Henrietta Tavistock had experienced ten inconsequential years as a bloodstock breeder. Looking back, the future Duchess of Bedford recalls that she really bought Mrs Moss on impulse, 'by falling in love with her divine head'. She had never previously bought any horse without first consulting her husband and a veterinary surgeon.

Actually the mare did have two other attractions so far as her new owner was concerned. She is a daughter of Reform, who stood at Sir John Musker's Shadwell Stud in Norfolk, and she is out of a mare by Whistler, a horse bred by the Holland-Martins at Overbury Stud in Gloucestershire. Johnnie Musker and Ruby Holland-Martin were personal friends and two breeders for whom Henrietta had the highest regard.

At that time the Tavistocks were living at Chevington outside Newmarket where they started Bloomsbury Stud. When the Duke of Bedford decided to take up permanent residence in France, Robin and Henrietta Tavistock sold their Suffolk home to Arthur Boyd-Rochfort (who renamed it Tally Ho Stud), moving to Woburn in the spring of 1979. They brought their mares with them and they now occupy the converted range of listed farm buildings dating back to 1780.

Mrs Moss retired from active broodmare service aged twenty in 1989 after nursing her fifteenth foal, an Ajdal filly named Mrs Moonlight. Her record stands at ten individual winning offspring, headed by the stakes winners, Pushy, Jupiter Island, Krayyan and Precocious, who arrived in successive years from 1978 to 1981.

Pushy, the only filly of the quartet, was put into training with Henry Cecil and she proved an exceptional two-year-old, winning Ascot's Queen Mary Stakes and Cornwallis Stakes.

The very first foal actually born at Woburn, Jupiter Island climaxed a brilliant career by collecting the 1986 Japan Cup (Group 1) as a six-year-old in course record time for one and a half miles. Originally sold as a yearling for 10,000 guineas, the son of St Paddy was reacquired by the Tavistocks on the eve of his greatest English success in the Hardwicke Stakes. Altogether he won fourteen races and £750,000.

Sons of Overbury-bred stallions, both Krayyan (by Tower Walk) and Precocious (by Mummy's Pet) excelled as juveniles. Krayyan, a 150,000-guinea yearling (the nomination to Tower Walk cost just £600), won the National Stakes, Sandown Park. The following year Precocious was undefeated in five starts, including the Gimcrack Stakes, Molecomb Stakes and Norfolk Stakes. Sadly he never ran again due to a cracked knee.

For the 1988 covering season, Mrs Moss had the rare distinction of three sons standing in England simultaneously, with Krayyan (Blackmore Vale Stud), Precocious (New England Stud) and Jupiter Island (The Elms Stud). Krayyan, who started off at the Irish National Stud, has since returned to Ireland, while Precocious moved to Ashley Heath Stud where he replaced Good Times only to join the latter at Goosemoor Stud in Yorkshire for the 1991 season.

It was in conjunction with her long standing bloodstock adviser, Keith Freeman, that Lady Tavistock was responsible for importing the Italian 2000 Guineas winner, Good Times, to Britain. He has enjoyed only limited success as a sire, rather like Overbury-bred champion Grundy, another son of dual champion sire Great Nephew.

To the end of 1990, Mrs Moss's descendants have won sixteen Group races. Obviously it is particularly satisfactory that her daughters are also

35

maintaining the tradition in the paddocks. Pushy, who commenced stud life at Mill Ridge Farm in Kentucky, was mated with the great Secretariat to produce Bluebook (Gainsborough Stud Fred Darling Stakes, Princess Margaret Stakes, Prix de Seine-et-Oise). Putupon (own-sister to Precocious) is dam of Pole Position, winner of three Group sprints in France.

Inevitably females from the Mrs Moss family are regarded as gold dust. One of few to have come on the open market is Pushy's first foal, Eye Drop, who cost Maktoum Al Maktoum (Gainsborough Stud) $750,000 as a yearling.

The Tavistocks, whose eldest son Lord Howland is with Tattersalls, get enormous pleasure from their stud which in recent times supports as many as twenty-five mares and their followers of which about one third are boarders, David Sieff and Lord Chelsea both being long-time supporters. For the 1991 season there were five daughters of Mrs Moss.

Bloomsbury Stud, which owes its name to the area of London owned by the Bedford family (the paddocks are named after streets and squares there), has experienced success on the Turf before. The present Marquess of Tavistock's colours, purple-and-white stripes, black velvet cap and gold tassel, originally belonged to the 5th Duke. He bred three Derby winners at Woburn with Skyscraper (1789), Eager (1791) and 'son of Fidget' (1797), the only unnamed colt to win the Blue Riband.

Bottisham Heath Stud

NEWMARKET · SUFFOLK

Robert Cowell, who farms at Kirtling outside Newmarket, had it in mind to sponsor a race should he ever have the good fortune to win a Group I contest, an objective achieved when his homebred filly Sally Brown triumphed in the 1985 Yorkshire Oaks.

Four years earlier, Bob Cowell had gained his first major success as an owner-breeder when another filly, Top Hope, scored on his local course in the inaugural running of the Rockfel Stakes. Upon reflection this event at the Cesarewitch meeting seemed ideal for sponsorship so in 1985 it became the Chevington Stud Rockfel Stakes.

At that time the race was listed, but the following year it was elevated to Group 3 status. From 1987 (that October day racing was actually abandoned due to damage caused by the great storm) the race has been called the Bottisham Heath Stud Rockfel Stakes which reflects Bob Cowell's acquisition of another stud closer to Newmarket.

The Rockfel Stakes for two-year-old fillies over seven furlongs commemorates one who started her racing career in sellers and progressed to win the 1000 Guineas, Oaks and Champion Stakes. Furthermore her one and only foal was Rockefella. It could be said that Bob Cowell, a noted point-to-point rider in his day, has enjoyed a comparable rise to fame in bloodstock circles.

He began by buying foals to sell as jumping stores. One delivered to his Parsonage Farm for an inclusive price of £350 hit the jackpot when as Lucius he triumphed in the 1978 Grand National. By then it was no longer possible to keep a young horse at home for £5 a week, so Bob switched to buying well-bred fillies that could be sold as potential broodmares.

Initially Bob Cowell's adviser was Raymond Barnes, but following his untimely death, David Minton, another local agent, has filled the breach.

37

In conjunction with trainer Michael Stoute, the team has enjoyed remarkable success, first at Chevington Stud on the Bury St Edmunds side of Newmarket, and then at Bottisham Heath Stud at Six Mile Bottom on the London road.

Bob Cowell procured Unsuspected, dam of Sally Brown, in rather a roundabout way. Having originally recommended her as a foal to Ray Barnes who paid 1,700 guineas for the filly on behalf of a client, she failed to make her 1,000 guineas reserve as a yearling. As the first flat horse owned by Bob's father, Cecil, she won eight races.

From 1981 to 1983 Unsuspected produced three star fillies at Chevington in Shoot Clear, Sally Brown and Untold. Fourth to Pebbles in the General Accident 1000 Guineas, Shoot Clear (Waterford Candelabra Stakes) was rated the best of her sex in England as a juvenile.

Sally Brown (Yorkshire Oaks, Ribblesdale Stakes), who was fourth in the Gilltown Stud Irish Oaks, and Untold (Yorkshire Oaks, Hoover Fillies' Mile), who was second in the Gold Seal Oaks, and third in the Gilltown Stud Irish Oaks and Holsten Pils St Leger, shared third top ranking amongst the fair sex at three years.

All three were retained to carry Bob Cowell's colours, grey and maroon quarters with white sleeves, although Untold was sold privately to Sheikh Mohammed after finishing second to Midway Lady in the Oaks upon her seasonal reappearance.

Remarkably Sally Brown and Untold became the first Group winners for their respective sires, Posse and Final Straw, while Shoot Clear was only a second such winner for her sire, Bay Express. All three stallions have since been banished abroad, but at that time they were all located at Newmarket studs.

Bob Cowell's other foundation mare, Port Ahoy, belongs to the same Feola family as Unsuspected's sire, Above Suspicion. Whereas Unsuspected represents a family that excelled for the McGraths at Brownstown Stud on the Curragh, Port Ahoy is half-sister to two mares belonging to Captain Marcos Lemos, then of Warren Hill Stud – La Dolce, dam of Pebbles, and Princess Zena, dam of Supreme Leader.

Their success was all in the future when Bob Cowell bought Port Ahoy as a yearling for 15,500 guineas from Marcos Lemos, she being by his outstanding flag-bearer, Petingo. Having scored twice as a juvenile, she too produced two very smart fillies of comparable ability. They are Top Hope, the Rockfel Stakes heroine, and Pretty Pol. By her victory in the Premio Carlo Porta in Milan in 1985, she concluded a memorable year for their breeder as between them, Pretty Pol, Sally Brown and Untold won eight races, half of them Group affairs – a fantastic achievement for a stud with only half a dozen mares.

As he owned two such daughters, Bob Cowell sold Port Ahoy that November, carrying to Mill Reef, in a private transaction with Robert N. Clay of Three Chimneys Farm in Kentucky. There is a prejudice against chesnut sons of Mill Reef and the resulting colt, Turmalin, did nothing to change popular belief.

In March 1987 Bob Cowell bought Bottisham Heath Stud from local trainer Ian Matthews, and he moved his stock there from Chevington that autumn. Also making the move was his young stud manager Stephen Kemble, who came to Chevington from Egerton Stud where he used to ride out the great Brigadier Gerard. Previously Stephen (who went to the same school, Pangbourne College, as his employer) was in Ireland with Arthur Moore, for whom he rode twenty-six jump winners, and Vincent O'Brien.

Today Bottisham Heath is a modern private stud whose previous wind-swept terrain has been transformed by the planting of hundreds of trees and shrubs. Adjacent to the late Ruth, Lady Halifax's old Swynford Paddocks Stud, it was founded by Lord Matthews (Ian's father) in 1975. Ian has since acquired most of Nidd Hall Stud (now Nidd Park Stud), near Harrogate in Yorkshire, from Guy Reed.

Brook Stud

The Theatre and the Turf shared in an extraordinary success when April the Fifth, owned and trained by Tom Walls, won the 1932 Derby. Tom Walls staged a succession of farces at the Aldwych Theatre which played to packed houses every night. Equally popular were the series of smash hits, including *Rose-Marie*, at the Drury Lane Theatre in the 1920s under the direction of master impresario Sir Alfred Butt.

Earlier Alfred Butt, who started work as a clerk in Harrods (he was knighted for his services as Director of Rationing at the Ministry of Food during the Great War), had taken over the management of the Gaiety Theatre upon the death of George Edwardes. With Ballykisteen Stud, Edwardes founded one of the most important commercial studs in Ireland. Butt for his part was responsible for putting Brook Stud firmly on the map.

Alfred Butt acquired Brook Stud at Cheveley in 1934 following the death of Sir Richard Garton, who had stood his July Cup winner Sir Cosmo there. The stud, which takes its name from a stream that runs through the property, had actually been founded a few years earlier by Archie Falcon. A Newmarket racing correspondent turned professional backer, this Yorkshireman had previously sold Woodditton Stud to Sir Victor Sassoon.

An enthusiastic owner, who loved the ambience of racing and enjoyed a tilt at the ring, Alfred Butt bought Brook Stud to stand Orpen whom he had purchased at the dispersal of Sir John Rutherford's bloodstock in the spring of 1932. The previous year Orpen had finished second in the Derby and St Leger and third in the 2000 Guineas. Subsequently runner-up in the Ascot Gold Cup, Orpen, who was a rig, failed as a sire.

Initially Alfred Butt was somewhat unlucky with his bloodstock. Two mares that he sold were to excel in Ireland. Having no stud of his own at the time, he sold Straight Sequence cheaply to Sir Percy Loraine and she became the foundation of his breeding operation based at Kildangan Stud. Then, with the advent of the Second World War, he disposed of Serena and her daughter, Solar Flower, to Joe McGrath for whom they became the cornerstone of his famous Brownstown Stud Farm on the Curragh.

However the war did provide Alfred Butt with the opportunity of two fortuitous purchases. One was the adjoining Lensfield Stud, which became the public part of Brook Stud, and the other was the mare Quick Arrow from the French breeder Leon Volterra, king of the French theatre and music hall. Stranded in Newmarket after the fall of France, Quick Arrow was to produce Oaks heroine Steady Aim, third dam of Danzig. She was Butt's only classic winner although he did breed Fraise du Bois II, winner of the Irish Derby.

As well as winning the Oaks in 1946, Alfred Butt also owned a brilliant juvenile that season in the homebred Petition (Fair Trial – Art Paper), whose dam had cost just 250 guineas. Rated second only to Tudor Minstrel on the Free Handicap, he won the New (now Norfolk), Richmond, Gimcrack and Champagne Stakes. Unfortunately he injured his back when charging the tapes in Tudor Minstrel's 2000 Guineas but recaptured his form to win the Eclipse Stakes at four years.

Petition spent the duration of his stud life at Brook Stud either under long-serving stud groom Ernest Prentice, or his son Jack who succeeded him. The son of Fair Trial, who died there aged twenty in 1964 (two years after the death of Alfred Butt), was the champion sire of 1959 thanks to the brilliant grey filly, Petite Etoile. He also sired two very influential sons in Petingo and March Past. Ironically Petingo is a great, great-grandson of Straight Sequence.

In due course Petition was replaced by two top American-breds in Royal Record II and Amber Rama, each of whom was banished to Japan. However on the other side of the coin, the Brook Stud Company, with veterinary surgeon Professor E. Brayley Reynolds and journalist Eric Rickman joining Kenneth Butt on the board of directors, became a major force at the Newmarket October and Houghton Sales. In 1959, 1968 and 1970, Brook Stud was the leading vendor of yearlings at the October dispersal.

Two mares to make a marked contribution were Daring Miss and Pristina. Daring Miss, already dam of the own-brothers Gay Time, Elopement and Cash and Courage, had an influential daughter in Jaffa. She bred Jacinth (grandam of Jaffa Line), whom Kenneth Butt procured from the William Hill Studs as a yearling. Rated the top two-year-old of 1972, she was runner-up in the 1000 Guineas and was one of sixteen mares when David Harris operated Brook Bloodstock PLC under the government's business expansion scheme.

Pristina, a homebred daughter of Petition, produced three top fillies in as many years with Mange Tout, Hecla and Rose Dubarry. More recently Brook Stud is responsible for another good filly in Shebeen, who gained four Group wins. Another mare to make her mark is Mamzelle, dam of Gwent and Haneena.

A former chairman of the Thoroughbred Breeders' Association and the Newmarket Stud Farmers' Association, Kenneth Butt was in his seventies when selling Brook Stud as a going concern to chartered accountant and president of the ROA David Harris, in July 1981. At that time Philip E.H. Mitchell became manager of both Brook Stud and Lord Hartington's Side Hill Stud. His successor is bloodstock agent Will Edmeades.

After an interim period without a stallion, Brook Stud had a new resident for the 1983 season in Kalaglow. A grey by Kalamoun, he won the King George VI and Queen Elizabeth Diamond Stakes and Coral-Eclipse Stakes as a four-year-old. Syndicated by the BBA for £5 million, he has proved a prolific sire of winners. With Never So Bold having been sold to Cheveley Park Stud during 1989, Kalaglow gained two new stud companions for 1991 in Shavian and Statoblest. Their arrival coincided with a major refurbishment programme which involved extending the stallion accommodation from two to four boxes, all the work being done to the highest specification.

A Kris half-brother to the Ascot Gold Cup hero, Paean, Shavian was a top three-year-old miler, winning the St James's Palace Stakes and Beefeater Gin Celebration Mile for his owner-breeder, Lord Howard de Walden. Statoblest (King George Stakes, Palace House Stakes) is a dual Group winning sprinter by the ultra successful Ahonoora.

Burton Agnes Stud

DRIFFIELD · NORTH HUMBERSIDE

When Marcus Wickham-Boynton died on 19 December 1989, less than two weeks after all ten mares from his famous Burton Agnes Stud at Driffield in the old East Riding of Yorkshire had been dispersed at the Newmarket December Sales, the future of the stud, in the short term at least, was assured.

Earlier in the year Wickham-Boynton had announced that as from the beginning of 1990 the stud would be leased for an interim period to William Macauley. One of many students of bloodstock to have experienced a year of yearling preparation at Burton Agnes under stud groom George Taylor, William, whose family used to own Eyrefield House Stud on the Curragh, had been running Barry Hills's Roehoe Stud in Nottinghamshire.

Meanwhile the Burton Agnes Estate was inherited by a schoolboy, twelve-year-old Simon Cunliffe-Lister. Simon, whose mother is a daughter of the former Conservative leader of the House of Lords, Lord Whitelaw, is a distant relation of the eighty-five-year-old previous owner (a third cousin twice removed) which should ensure that the great Elizabethan house remains a family home and not a museum.

Interestingly this mellow brick house has never been bought or sold on the open market, but has simply passed from one family to another whenever a male line became extinct. Members of the Wickham-Boynton family have lived there continuously since 1654. Open to the public, it contains a treasure trove of antique furniture and oriental china together with French impressionist and modern paintings.

Situated on the edge of the Yorkshire Wolds, next door to Sledmere Stud and only a few miles from Bridlington on the east coast, Burton Agnes, the 'broad village' with 2,000 acres of prime arable land, owes the second half of its name to Agnes de Albermarle. She witnessed a legal document concerning the property in 1175 and part of the original Norman manor dating back to that period has been preserved for posterity.

In the normal course of events, Burton Agnes would have been left to Marcus's elder brother, Henry, but sadly he died in August 1942. Within three months their father, Thomas, was also dead. However it was not until 1947 that Marcus inherited the estate from his mother.

It was really Thomas Wickham-Boynton who started breeding horses at Burton Agnes. Together with his lifelong friend Henry Cholmondeley, manager of Sledmere, he won seventy-eight King's Premiums for stallions awarded by the Hunters' Improvement Society. Thomas submitted his first yearlings to Tattersalls' Doncaster Sales in 1921. Amongst the first TB stallions at Burton Agnes were By Jingo (Ascot Gold Cup), Spion Kop (Derby) and Winalot.

By the time Marcus Wickham-Boynton returned home after the war, the place was in a dilapidated state and the stud was virtually non existent. Although he stood both Nepenthe and Fair Copy for Lord Derby for a while, Marcus, who would spend three months a year supervising his cattle ranch in Kenya, decided upon a change of direction.

Convinced that the location was too remote from Newmarket to attract a horse of the highest class, Marcus set about reorganizing the establishment for the production of top-quality commercial yearlings. He had an excellent training behind him. Having worked at the French National Stud (Haras du Pin) and for the celebrated trainer Atty Persse, he had spent ten years as estate and stud manager to the late Lord Carnarvon at Highclere.

In the 1950s and 1960s Burton Agnes dominated Tattersalls' premier yearling sales – in 1958 these September Sales were transferred from Doncaster to Newmarket where they became the Houghton Sales and then the Highflyer Sales. During these twenty years the stud headed the vendors' table seven times and was never out of the first three, an unprecedented achievement in modern times.

With a knowledge of bloodstock that was only matched by his own business acumen, Marcus Wickham-Boynton built up a broodmare band that was the envy of all his contemporaries. Certain Burton Agnes families gained worldwide recognition, and although an English classic winner eluded them, they produced a galaxy of talent. Since the stud was reformed in 1941, it has been responsible for over 240 individual winners of more than 700 races.

Notable of the colts have been Prescription, Die Hard, Just Great, Soysambu, Anselmo, Derring-Do, Recupere, Kneller and Great Marquess. A fine miler, Derring-Do (Queen Elizabeth II Stakes), is much the most important, although at only 1,200 guineas, he was the cheapest yearling in the 1962 consignment. A noted sire of sires, his two most consequential sons have been High Top (2000 Guineas) and Dominion.

Last of the top domestic winners bred by Marcus Wickham-Boynton are the half-brothers Kneller and Great Marquess, respective winners of the 1988 and 1990 Jockey Club Cups for Charles St George. Sadly Kneller, who also won the Doncaster Cup, died from peritonitis soon after his Newmarket victory. Both colts were trained by Henry Cecil, a former Burton Agnes student.

In the past many of Wickham-Boynton's retained fillies were trained at Warren Place by Henry Cecil's predecessor, Sir Noel Murless. One of them, Varinia, should have been partnered by Lester Piggott in the 1966 Oaks. However in the event Piggott chose to ride Valoris on whom he won with Varinia in third place. It was this incident that caused the permanent split between Murless and his retained jockey.

On balance Burton Agnes probably fared better with fillies than colts. High on the roll of honour are Key (Nassau Stakes), Even Star (Irish 1000 Guineas), Collyria (Park Hill Stakes), Borana (Pretty Polly Stakes), Lucyrowe (Coronation Stakes, Nassau Stakes, Sun Chariot Stakes), and Connaught Bridge (Yorkshire Oaks, Nassau Stakes).

Latterly Marcus Wickham-Boynton raced on a more parochial scale with the occasional filly in training at Malton with either Bill Elsey or Peter Easterby. However, as winners like the American pair White Mischief and Bonshamile showed, Burton Agnes still had an international reputation.

Buttermilk Stud

BARFORD ST. MICHAEL · OXFORDSHIRE

In a David and Goliath confrontation, the accolade of Leading Breeder in the British Isles for 1969 was conferred upon Mrs Leonard Scott. Owner, with her late husband, of Buttermilk Stud, she prevailed over Lord Rosebery by just £62! Whereas Buttermilk was represented by only two individual winners, the Rosebery tally accrued from twenty-four members of the Mentmore breed.

That season Buttermilk Stud was responsible for Horse of the Year Park Top. Her victory in the King George VI and Queen Elizabeth Stakes climaxed a remarkable era for this small private stud in north Oxfordshire. In 1967 and 1968, Luciano, an exact contemporary to Park Top, was voted Horse of the Year in Germany, and in 1970 Precipice Wood triumphed in the Ascot Gold Cup.

These are amazing achievements by any standards, but the true perspective only becomes apparent in the knowledge that Mrs Scott only had four mares at the time and that the most she ever paid for a mare was 700 guineas, which is absolutely unbelievable. Furthermore she always did most of the work herself aided by Kitchener Haynes, her stud groom for more than thirty years.

Situated at Barford St Michael, five miles to the south of Banbury, between Deddington and Chipping Norton, Buttermilk was utilized both by the Royalists after the Battle of Edgehill as well as by Cromwell's parliamentary forces. Recently the only intruder to this haven of rural England noted for the indigenous Hornton ironstone, has been the American airforce base at nearby Upper Heyford.

It was entirely through the good offices of an AA patrolman that Joan and Leonard Scott (he was an uncle of former *Daily Telegraph* racing correspondent Peter Scott) first discovered Buttermilk when they were searching for a suitable farm to turn into a small stud. They bought the property in 1934. At first they stood a couple of modest stallions in Cranford Cross and Galantry Bower, but it was not until after the war that they really started breeding from their own mares.

The foundation mare was Academia. Purchased unseen through blood-stock agent Major Patrick Honner of Shamrock Stud for £400, this grey made a lasting contribution through her daughter, Grecian Garden. Mated with Mossborough, by whom Mrs Scott bred six colts, all winners, Grecian Garden produced the own-brother and sister, Spartan General and Spartan Queen, both of whom did well for Sir Freddie Laker, owner of Woodcote Stud.

Versatile Spartan General, who ran in the Derby and St Leger, and was runner-up in the Champion Hurdle, became a champion sire of jumpers in which sphere his half-brother Precipice Wood also excelled. Successful at Royal Ascot at three (King George v Stakes) and four years (Ascot Gold Cup), Precipice Wood gave Mrs Rosemary Lomax the distinction of being the first lady to train a Gold Cup winner when defeating the previous year's Derby winner, Blakeney.

Precipice Wood had a smart own-brother in Coed Cochion. He was likewise raced by Bobby McAlpine at whose Emral Stud Precipice Wood died aged fourteen in 1980. Coed Cochion also scored at Royal Ascot (Queen Alexandra Stakes), but he died in Ireland during his initial stud season.

Precipice Wood and Coed Cochion were by Lauso who stood at Willie Stephenson's Tudor Stud in Hertfordshire. He was one of few men to train both a Derby winner (Arctic Prince) and a Grand National winner (Oxo). It was a couple of Arctic Prince mares acquired at successive New-market December Sales that provided Mrs Scott with her greatest achievements as a breeder.

She bought Nellie Park, dam of Park Top, for 480 guineas in 1961, and Light Arctic, dam of Luciano, for 300 guineas in 1962. In due course she obtained 500 guineas for Park Top as a yearling (having tried unavailingly to sell her 'in utero'), and 1,550 guineas for Luciano as a foal.

Park Top was trained by Bernard van Cutsem for the Duke of Devonshire, being by Kalydon, who stood alongside Lauso at Tudor Stud, and had been bred and trained by van Cutsem. A great racemare, Park Top scored thirteen times and excelled at Ascot. In addition to the 'King George', she won the Hardwicke, Ribblesdale and Cumberland Lodge Stakes. She also won the Coronation Cup. Like so many top females, Park Top failed in the paddocks. Eventually Andrew Devonshire returned her to Buttermilk where she died in May 1989 at the age of twenty-four.

Luciano, on the other hand, proved a tremendously successful sire in Germany – he had retired to Gestut Harzburg for the 1970 season having displaced Orsini as the record post-war stakes earner in that country. His ten victories (six Group I), included the Deutsches Derby and two runnings of the Aral-Pokal.

Unlike the majority of commercial breeders, Mrs Scott was never influenced by fashion when it came to producing bloodstock. Of course she could have made much more money by breeding fast, precocious stock. Instead she preferred to rear middle-distance and staying horses. Interestingly neither Park Top nor Luciano ever ran as two-year-olds.

While Joan Scott was never in a position to ignore financial considerations altogether (in buying stock she favoured an in-foal mare so as to recoup as much of the initial outlay as quickly as possible), she always utilized the services of classically bred stallions standing at a comparatively modest fee.

She had a particular liking for the great Stanley House tap-roots. Significantly both Mossborough (Nearco – All Moonshine) and Kalydon (Alycidon – Lackaday) are descendants of Hyperion's grandam, Serenissima. In fact All Moonshine is half-sister to Hyperion.

Mrs Leonard Scott died aged eighty-eight in February 1991. Five years previously she had sold Buttermilk Stud to a neighbouring farmer, Angus Irvine, a former stockbroker and amateur rider. In the interim, Buttermilk was developed as a conference centre, although Joan Scott, who is fully entitled to be regarded as the most successful 'small' breeder of her generation, remained in residence.

Cheveley Park Stud

NEWMARKET · SUFFOLK

The 1980s saw enormous foreign investment in Newmarket stud land spear-headed by the Arab legions. The focal point of their involvement centred on Sheikh Mohammed's Dalham Hall Stud. However, right opposite, on the other side of leafy Duchess Drive, David and Patricia Thompson have been proudly flying the flag for Britain at Cheveley Park Stud.

David Thompson, founder of the food conglomerate, Hillsdown Hold-ings, and his wife, Patricia, who started the Hoopers' department store chain, are great enthusiasts and their patriotic red, white and blue colours have become a familiar sight. Together with horses owned independently by David, their son Richard and various partners, the Thompsons had as many as eighty horses in training at the start of the decade (spread between twenty trainers) and sixty broodmares.

For the 1991 season Cheveley Park controlled seven stallions of which Music Boy, Never So Bold, Primo Dominie and Prince Sabo were actually located at the Newmarket headquarters. Of the remainder, Tina's Pet and Scottish Reel were based as Wood Farm Stud in Shropshire, and Nordance was in Ireland at Oak Lodge Stud, Co. Kildare.

When the Thompsons purchased Cheveley Park in 1975, the intention was to run it as part stud and part training centre. Here Music Boy, who had already won the Gimcrack Stakes, was prepared to win the King George Stakes as a three-year-old. Incidentally Goodwood's prestige sprint was also won by Tina's Pet and Primo Dominie, the latter scoring from Prince Sabo!

Music Boy, whose dam Veronique is half-sister to Rocky Royale, a useful handicapper raced by Patricia Thompson's late father, Claude Henchley, was a yearling bargain at Doncaster in 1974 at 1,800 guineas. The colt raced for Ken Mackey, a business colleague of David Thompson and a partner in the stud until his death in 1983.

49

This sprinter, whose progeny includes Cheveley Park-bred Mattaboy (Middle Park Stakes), has proved one of the most prolific winner getters imaginable. Appropriately enough he has pride of place in the stallion yard, occupying the box built specially by Colonel Harry McCalmont for his 1893 Triple Crown hero, Isinglass. Also successful in the Ascot Gold Cup and Eclipse Stakes, his earnings of £57,455 constituted a record until eventually surpassed by Tulyar in 1952.

Homebred Isinglass remained here throughout his stud life. His sons include John O'Gaunt, sire of Swynford. Subsequent Derby winners to grace these quarters are Spearmint (1906), Captain Cuttle (1922) and Psidium (1961). In 1919 Phalaris, grandsire of Nearco, embarked upon his stud career at a fee of 200 guineas.

In the Cheveley Park office there is an historical document showing that Aethelstan, the first King of England, owned the property in Anglo Saxon times and bred horses here, since when several medieval reigning monarchs have owned parts of the estate.

The aesthetic qualities of the present stud are owed more to the Duke and Duchess of Rutland in the early part of the last century. The 5th Duke won four classics, homebred Cadland winning the 2000 Guineas and Derby in 1828. His wife is commemorated by Duchess Drive, the beautiful tree-lined avenue connecting the stud with Newmarket.

Between 1921 and 1942, Cheveley Park was owned by local trainer Robert Sherwood, who had as many as seven stallions standing there simultaneously. He left the stud to his secretary, Albert Stafford-Smith, whose son Richard was manager when it was purchased by the Thompsons. Stallions during the Stafford-Smith era included Colombo, King's Bench, Hook Money, Prince Chevalier, Zimone, Psidium, Derring-Do and Forlorn River.

As a grandson of Derring-Do, Primo Dominie, the only juvenile ever to complete the Coventry, July and Richmond Stakes treble, provides a sense of continuity. He excelled with his first crop of runners in 1990; so too did Prince Sabo. The 1987 covering season was certainly action packed as both Scottish Reel and Nordance also embarked upon their stallion careers at that time.

That August the Thompsons recruited Chris Richardson as managing director of their breeding enterprise (Michael Stoute is also a director). Younger brother of Tim Richardson, who manages Stavros Niarchos's Haras de Fresnay-le-Buffard in Normandy, Chris had been in charge of the same owner's Spring Oak Farm in Kentucky.

For the next couple of years Chris busied himself with the modernization and refurbishment of two adjoining studs which had just been acquired, thereby providing a total of 600 acres of prime stud land. They were Brook Holliday's Sandwich Stud and Mrs Ann Sutton's Strawberry Hill Stud.

By January 1990, which coincided with the retirement of Cheveley Park's long-standing stud groom/manager, Alan Baker, the jigsaw was complete. Cheveley is the public stud with additional accommodation for half the private mares. The other half is divided between Sandwich Stud and the Parrishs' Indian Creek Farm in Kentucky. Sandwich also has a marvellous new yearling yard with every conceivable amenity for sales preparation. Strawberry Hill is basically an isolation unit.

Time was when Cheveley Park's broodmare band was noted for quantity rather than quality. That assessment has long since required a reappraisal as the quality of yearlings consigned to the Highflyer Sales bears witness. With a nucleus of top mares (including Salsabil's own-sister, Nearctic Flame), the objective is to produce high-class yearlings for the commercial market.

Chris Richardson, who has also handled the racing side together with his wife Annie since 1990, has the assistance of Andrew Snell as stud groom at Cheveley Park and John Marsh as assistant manager at Sandwich. The promotion of the stallions is the responsibility of James Beazley, and local bloodstock agent David Minton is a consultant.

Childwick Bury Stud

ST. ALBANS · HERTFORDSHIRE

When Jim Joel sold all his broodmares at the 1986 Newmarket December Sales, it was the most important dispersal since James Dewar's in 1954. However the 92-year-old veteran owner-breeder was not giving up racing. Indeed the following April he won the Seagram Grand National with Maori Venture and the year after his unbeaten High Estate was officially rated the leading juvenile of his generation.

Highlight of the sale at 720,000 guineas was Fairy Footsteps, heroine of the 1981 1000 Guineas, whose half-brother, Light Cavalry, had won the preceding year's St Leger. Their dam, Glass Slipper (sold here as a barren mare), is half-sister to Royal Palace, hero of the 1967 2000 Guineas and Derby. Their third dam, Picture Play, triumphed in the 1944 1000 Guineas.

Picture Play was one of the first foals that Jim Joel bred following the death of his father, Jack Joel, in 1940. She was a great-granddaughter of the famous Childwick Bury Stud foundation mare, Absurdity. Bred by John Musker of Westerham Hill Stud (later transferred to Shadwell Stud) in 1903, this mare by Melton had cost 310 guineas as a yearling at Tattersalls' in Knightsbridge.

Jack Joel and his younger brother, Solomon, were nephews of Barney Barnato. When their uncle died, they continued running the family business of Barnato Brothers and the Johannesburg Consolidated Investments Company, Jim eventually succeeding his father as chairman. Before long both Jack and Solly were racing on an extensive scale, the former being presented with the famous 'black, scarlet cap' when Sir Richard Sutton forsook the turf.

From 1887 Jack Joel kept his breeding stock at Northaw House, Potter's Bar, to which the remarkable Sundridge retired in 1905. Despite being unsound of his wind, he progressed from selling plater to top sprinter, ten of his seventeen victories being for Joel who had bought him as a four-year-old for 1,450 guineas. Commencing at a fee of nine guineas, he was champion sire of 1911 when his son Sunstar became the first of Jack Joel's two Derby winners.

Four years earlier Jack Joel had acquired Childwick Bury Stud, near St Albans, in Hertfordshire, from its founder, Sir John Blundell Maple, the furniture magnate. Amongst the stallions he stood at Childwick Bury (named after his Cesarewitch winner) was Triple Crown hero Common.

Altogether Jack Joel bred the winners of eleven classics from three foundation mares. From Yours came Our Lassie (Oaks) and Your Majesty (St Leger); from Absurdity, Jest (1000 Guineas, Oaks), Black Jester (St Leger) and Humorist (Derby); and from Doris, Sunstar (2000 Guineas, Derby) and Princess Dorrie (1000 Guineas, Oaks). Another was Oaks heroine, Glass Doll.

Many of them have tombstones at Childwick Bury. In the main yard are monuments to Humorist, Sunstar and Doris. Named by Solly Joel after his daughter, he gave Doris to his brother as he had no stud of his own at the time. On the other side of the coin, Jack presented Rosaline to a children's charity – sold for £25, she bred the Oaks winner Rosedrop, dam of Gainsborough.

All eight of Jack Joel's classic winners were recorded between 1903 and 1921, but he never enjoyed comparable success again. One of the contributing factors must have been his bringing back to the stud horses below the classic ideal – back in 1913 he had paid a record £45,000 for Prince Palatine, but he never came up to expectations.

When Jim Joel inherited the stud during the early part of the war, it was in a state of decline. He determined therefore to cut out the dead wood and concentrate on the Absurdity family which had served the stud best over a long period. So it was to a mating with Donatello II that her granddaughter Amuse (by Phalaris) produced Picture Play.

The most brilliant horse bred by Jim Joel is undoubtedly Royal Palace (Ballymoss – Crystal Palace). One of the first batch of horses Jim Joel sent to Sir Noel Murless instead of Ted Leader, Royal Palace was a champion at three and four years, winning the 2000 Guineas, Derby, King George VI and Queen Elizabeth Stakes, Eclipse Stakes and Coronation Cup.

Retired to Egerton Stud as the joint property of Jim Joel, Lady Macdonald-Buchanan and Lord Howard de Walden, Royal Palace appeared to have all the credentials to make a top stallion, but apart from the Queen's Dunfermline (Oaks, St Leger), he sired little of consequence. He was the oldest surviving winner of an English classic when put down at the National Stud in March 1991 aged twenty-seven.

53

Ironically his close relative Welsh Pageant (Tudor Melody – Picture Light), who was conceived at the National Stud, proved an infinitely superior progenitor. One of the leading milers of his generation, he spent the duration of his stallion life at Woodditton Stud (1972–1984), where he excelled, although his solitary classic winner is Gerald Oldham's homebred Zino.

Welsh Pageant's dam Picture Light is by another 2000 Guineas winner in Court Martial whom Jim Joel bought for £60,000 from his owner-breeder, the 2nd Lord Astor. The champion sire of 1956 and 1957, he was exported to the USA in 1958. The next season he was replaced at Childwick Bury by his son Major Portion (Sussex Stakes), who was the last stallion to stand there.

Additional Group 1 winners bred by Jim Joel are Connaught (Eclipse Stakes), who was runner-up in the Derby, West Side Story (Yorkshire Oaks), who was beaten a short head for the Oaks, and Pandofell (Ascot Gold Cup), whom he sold for 600 guineas at the end of his two-year-old career.

A much respected figure, Jim Joel attributes the success of Childwick Bury Stud to the Phalaris male line and the female family of Absurdity. Although he has finally severed all connections with breeding, he lives in the stud house overlooking the main yard (painted in special Childwick green) and maintained in immaculate condition. For three months of the year the paddocks are occupied by the Joel string of jumpers as they enjoy their summer holidays under the eye of agent Peter Doyle.

Cliff Stud

In 1982 Henry Cecil formed a bloodstock company in partnership with his then wife, Julie, and their great friend and yearling spotter Tote Cherry-Downes, to take over the lease of Cliff Stud from her father, Sir Noel Murless. That October, Henry's twin brother, David, arrived home from America to become manager of the stud. There was drama in store.

The following autumn, Cliff Stud consigned a Riverman colt to the Highflyer Sales which became known as the celebrated case of lot 116. Suffice to say that Tattersalls' decision to resubmit this yearling two days after he first went through the ring was vindicated in the High Court. As Sulaafah, the colt won two Group races in Germany and is now a stallion at Hart Hill Stud in Dorset.

Cliff Stud, which is situated 500 feet above sea level on the edge of the glorious North Yorkshire Moors, is just outside the picturesque village of Helmsley and is part of Lord Feversham's Duncombe Park Estate. No distance away is Hambleton where Noel Murless embarked upon his training career.

Noel Murless moved south to Beckhampton in 1948, but he did not sever his Yorkshire connections altogether. Only the previous year he had leased Cliff Stud (originally known as Helmsley Stud) following the death of its founder, William Thorpe, who lived in Scarborough, in February 1946.

A Nottingham lace manufacturer, William Thorpe laid out the stud with the help of his trainer, Matthew Peacock, and it was completed by the outbreak of war. A prominent owner in the north, his best homebred winner was Oxonian. He was included in the 1946 dispersal sale divided between Helmsley in March and Stockton in July when nineteen lots realized 15,400 guineas.

By then Noel and Gwen Murless had already assembled a few mares of their own, two purchases having been made at Newmarket in 1942. Congo cost 130 guineas in September and Cuddlededee cost just forty-five guineas in December. It was Cuddlededee's son, Closeburn, by the savage Bellacose, who provided Murless with a first major success as a breeder by winning the 1947 Stewards' Cup. However it was Congo, also by Bellacose, and a half-sister to Nimbus and Grey Sovereign, who became the Murless foundation mare.

Amongst Congo's descendants are Lowna (Molecomb Stakes), her son Gospill Hill (Blue Riband Trial Stakes), and Adios (Royal Lodge Stakes). All three were trained at Warren Place, the latter pair being owned by the Canadian Garfield Weston of Barrettstown Castle Stud in Ireland. In 1988 Lowna's granddaughter, Miss Demure, won the Update Lowther Stakes.

Noel Murless trained the winners of nineteen English classics. Unique amongst them is Caergwrle whom his wife bred and who carried her colours of royal blue, lemon cross-belts, to victory in the 1968 1000 Guineas. Caergwrle, who is buried at Cliff, is half-sister to the top miler St Chad (Wills Mile, Jersey Stakes, Hungerford Stakes), who became a successful sire in Ireland. Their grandam, Cheetah, was bred by the Queen.

One of Noel Murless's principal patrons was Sir Victor Sassoon. Following his death in 1961, Lady Sassoon gradually reduced her husband's considerable bloodstock interests. Beech House Stud was sold to Louis Freedman of Cliveden Stud, and Eve Stud was bought by Murless himself who renamed it Woodditton Stud.

It had been the custom to send the pick of the Sassoon yearlings to be reared at Cliff Stud where Murless regarded the limestone land as second to none for producing bone in young stock and infinitely superior to the land at another Sassoon property in the same part of Yorkshire, Thornton Stud, near Thirsk.

Consequently a very distinguished number of Sassoon-breds spent their formative years at Cliff. With the notable exception of Crepello, they include St Paddy, Twilight Alley, Sweet Moss, The Creditor and Sucaryl. Another star was George A. Pope Jnr's Mysterious, winner of the 1973 1000 Guineas and Oaks.

When David Cecil took over Cliff Stud all the original owners were patrons of his brother's stable – the office administration is still conducted from Warren Place. At that time Daniel Wildenstein was one of the principal owners and his first crop of Cliff foals included the great Steinlen. This son of Habitat was America's champion grass horse of 1989, winning the Breeders' Cup Mile and Arlington Million as a six-year-old entire.

Subsequently Henry Cecil and Daniel Wildenstein parted company, but as Wildenstein was anxious to keep his young stock in Yorkshire, he asked David to find suitable alternative accommodation. The outcome was that David now has charge of all the Wildenstein weanlings which are either born in England, Ireland, or the USA.

These are reared at Guy Reed's Copgrove Hall Stud, near Burton Leonard (once the home of Major Lionel Holliday), the fillies having originally been located at the same owner's Nidd Hall Stud, now Ian Matthews's Nidd Park Stud. Some of Wildenstein's breeding stock are also kept at Sledmere Stud which David manages for the Sykes family. Copgrove Hall and Sledmere are within a forty-mile radius of Cliff Stud where Bill Lawton was stud groom for about twenty years.

The new Cliff Stud has already been associated with two European Oaks winners in Filia Ardross (1989 Preis der Diana) and Rafha (1990 Prix de Diane Hermes). The former was bred there by Charles St George (Blue Bear Stud) and the latter by Prince Faisal (Nawara Stud), both Warren Place patrons. As a daughter of Thornton resident Kris, Rafha has really helped to put Yorkshire back on the bloodstock map.

It was whilst working in the USA that David Cecil first had his attention drawn to the benefits of shed rearing yearlings, a system he has perfected with great success. He and his brother Henry are also enthusiastic breeders of Murray Grey cattle and the twins sponsor the Cecil Cup at the local Ryedale Show. They have also produced numerous winners at major shows up and down the country.

Cliveden Stud

TAPLOW · BERKSHIRE

Derek Powley has been stud groom to the Freedmans at Cliveden Stud since April 1972. When he arrived there the previous November, the weaned foals included fillies by Reform and Busted. The former was Polygamy, heroine of the 1974 Oaks, and the latter was Great Guns, grandam of the 1987 Ever Ready Derby winner, Reference Point.

In the interim Derek Powley had been looking after the resident stallion, I Say. One of the first horses owned by Louis Freedman, a director of Land Securities, I Say had won the 1966 Coronation Cup having finished third to Sea Bird II in the Derby. It was I Say's success that motivated his owner into becoming involved with bloodstock breeding.

Louis Freedman became one of the biggest owner-breeders in the country within a remarkably short space of time. In December 1966 he purchased Cliveden Stud on the banks of the River Thames at Taplow, near Maidenhead, following the death of the 3rd Lord Astor. Then in August 1971 he acquired Beech House Stud at Newmarket from Sir Victor Sassoon's widow.

Each was a very different transaction. At Cliveden neither the great house, synonymous with Nancy Astor and now owned by the National Trust, nor any of the stock were included. Most of the mares and fillies were sold by sealed bid and dispersed in the USA, with the majority of horses in training being purchased by Lord Rotherwick of Cornbury Park Stud.

While Louis Freedman and his wife Valerie moved from Haslemere to Cliveden where they built a new house, their ownership of Beech House was short lived – in 1975 they sold the property to Dr Carlo Vittadini, a fellow patron of Peter Walwyn's stable where Polygamy was trained. However the Beech House bloodlines have made a lasting contribution. Furthermore it established Freedman as a major patron of Sir Noel Murless's stable where Henry Cecil trained Reference Point.

Reference Point certainly set the record straight so far as Cliveden was concerned. Waldorf Astor (the 2nd Viscount) bred the winners of eleven classics, all descendants of one of three foundation mares, Conjure, Popinjay and Maid of the Mist, five Oaks winners, Sunny Jane (1917), Pogrom (1922), Saucy Sue (1925), Short Story (1926) and Pennycomequick (1929) being equally matched by five Derby seconds, Blink, Buchan, Craig an Eran, Tamar and St Germans.

In 1967 stud manager Michael Bramwell and Walter Nightingall, who trained I Say but died not long afterwards, bought Louis Freedman two yearling fillies. They were Lucyrowe (Coronation Stakes, Nassau Stakes, Sun Chariot Stakes) and Seventh Bride (Princess Royal Stakes). In the Nassau Stakes, Lucyrowe defeated Seventh Bride by a short head.

A 1,550-guinea yearling, Seventh Bride produced Polygamy as her first foal. Beaten a short head by the Queen's Highclere for the 1000 Guineas, she was to gain compensation in the Oaks. The next year her own-sister, One Over Parr, won the Cheshire and Lancashire Oaks. Sadly Polygamy died without ever having a foal. Bramwell's predecessor as manager was Major Carey Foster, MRCVS, and he bought an influential mare in Tina II. Her daughter, Guillotina, is dam of One Way Street and grandam of Ever Genial, all Group winning fillies.

A key member of the present Cliveden team is breeding expert Peter Willett. It was upon his recommendation that the mare Byblis was procured for 5,700 guineas at the 1967 Newmarket December Sales. Consigned by Hugh Leggatt of Pirnie House Stud in Roxburghshire, she became the third dam of Reference Point.

Reference Point's dam Home on the Range (Habitat – Great Guns) is just one example of the Freedmans' extraordinary flair in naming their animals. Winner of the Sun Chariot Stakes, she is by Habitat and at one time there were no fewer than six of his daughters in the Cliveden brood-mare band.

Top of the International Classification at both two and three years, Reference Point gained Group I successes in the Ever Ready Derby, King George VI and Queen Elizabeth Diamond Stakes, Holsten Pils St Leger and William Hill Futurity. These achievements were all the more meritorious as he underwent a sinus operation in March of his three-year-old days. Prior to Epsom, Louis Freedman sold a quarter interest in the son of Mill Reef to a syndicate headed by Lord White, chairman of the Derby sponsors, Hanson Industries.

It was disappointing that Reference Point did not remain in training as a four-year-old. Instead he retired to Dalham Hall Stud where he covered his first mares in 1988 at a split fee of £70,000. On his own admission, Louis Freedman is emotional and sentimental about his horses and he just could not bear the mental and physical strain of keeping his star in the limelight for another season.

Following Reference Point, whose own-sister, Shottermill, died without ever seeing a racecourse, the emphasis at Cliveden has switched to Beech House bloodlines. The original package included ten shares in Crepello, his brilliant daughter The Creditor, together with a number of future winners in Freedman's distinctive yellow colours with black spots, amongst them Abwah. He was destined to sire Absalom, the Dunchurch Lodge Stud horse.

Notable of the fillies taken over from Lady Sassoon were Attica Meli and Mil's Bomb. Both proceeded to win the Park Hill Stakes, as did two of their respective relations, Royal Hive in 1977 and Madame Dubois in 1990. The latter also won the Ciga Prix de Royallieu. Meanwhile descendants of The Creditor have produced two Royal Ascot winners with Queen Midas (1987 Ribblesdale Stakes) and Private Tender (1990 King Edward VII Stakes).

A year to the day on which Reference Point won the Ever Ready Derby, Louis Freedman stepped down as manager of the stud in favour of his younger son, Philip, the new chairman of the TBA. It must have been particularly galling for him when Reference Point's dam, Home on the Range (twelve), died in March 1990 carrying a dead colt by Kris. However with two mares producing Group 2 winners that season with their first foals, Cliveden remains very much in the classic firmament.

Copgrove Hall Stud

COPGROVE · NORTH YORKSHIRE

Time was when Guy Reed was just about the biggest owner-breeder in the country. A Yorkshireman, born and bred, he owned two studs within striking distance of Harrogate, Nidd Hall at Ripley, and Copgrove Hall, about five miles distant next to Burton Leonard. He was also Sam Hall's landlord at Spigot Lodge, the historic Middleham training establishment.

Guy Reed's operation revolved around his homebred stallion, Warpath (Sovereign Path – Ardneasken), whom he had acquired 'in utero' at the 1968 Newmarket December Sales for 14,000 guineas from Sir David Wills's Hadrian Stud. He bred a profusion of winners by this grey stallion, notably Shotgun, who finished fourth in Shergar's Derby.

Ardneasken, whose dam is half-sister to the Rockefella brothers, Gay Time, Elopement and Cash and Courage, proved an excellent foundation mare. Another of her sons, Dakota, carried Guy Reed's colours into fourth place in the King George VI and Queen Elizabeth Diamond Stakes, prior to becoming a champion sire in Poland.

One of Ardneasken's daughters, Siouan, is dam of Apache. The most recent good winner bred by Guy Reed, he just failed to emulate Dakota in winning the St Simon Stakes. Both Shotgun and Apache were trained by Chris Thornton, Sam Hall's successor at Spigot Lodge. Ardneasken died aged twenty-four in July 1988.

Warpath, who did exceptionally well with his jumpers (he twice won the TBA's annual award as the leading British-based sire of the steeplechase winners), had died in May of the preceding year – in fact on the very same day that Nidd Hall Stud's original stud groom, Jack Dobson, was buried. Dobson's counterpart at Copgrove Hall, Howard Smith, used to look after Warpath.

This period was a watershed for Guy Reed. In April 1987 he consolidated his breeding activities by selling the greater part of Nidd Hall Stud to Newmarket trainer Ian Matthews, who has since retired. His father, Lord Victor Matthews, formerly owned Bottisham Heath Stud at Newmarket.

In the autumn of 1985, Nidd Hall Stud had become home for a significant number of yearlings managed by David Cecil for Paris fine arts dealer Daniel Wildenstein. Previously they had been under his care at Cliff Stud, but fresh pastures were sought when Henry Cecil, who had installed his twin brother at Cliff, and Wildenstein went their separate ways.

For an interim period, the Wildenstein fillies were based on eighty acres at Nidd Hall (that part of the property belonging to Ian Matthews continues to trade as Nidd Park Stud), with the colts at Copgrove Hall Stud. Here Guy Reed developed an entirely new stud complex on 250 acres.

In 1988 Guy Reed finally sold Nidd Hall and the remaining acres there, by which time all his own bloodstock was based on the paddocks surrounding his Copgrove Hall home. He had bought the house and fifty acres following the death of Major Lionel Holliday in 1965. Meanwhile Holliday's grandson, Anthony Gillam, had started another stud on the other half of the Copgrove Hall Estate.

Lionel Holliday, who was the leading breeder of his generation, founded the original Copgrove Stud in 1939, and he kept a nucleus of mares there, the weanlings being sent to his principal establishment, Cleaboy Stud, in Co. Westmeath.

Amongst the winners bred at Copgrove Stud during Tony Gillam's time was that good miler Brook. His breeder, Tommy Stack, partnered Red Rum to the third of his Grand National victories and Tony Gillam had been one of that horse's earlier trainers. Tommy Stack was also a partner in The Brianstan when this stallion retired to Copgrove Stud for the 1972 season.

At present, Guy Reed maintains a private broodmare band of twelve at Copgrove Hall Stud of which seven are members of the Ardneasken family. However by far the most important aspect of the operation are the blue-blooded Wildenstein yearlings. Surprisingly Daniel Wildenstein, whose bloodstock empire trades as Dayton Limited in Europe and Allez France Stables in the USA, has never owned his own stud. In the past he has leased studs, but nowadays he maintains all his stock as boarders.

The majority of his broodmare band is based in Kentucky, divided between Three Chimneys Farms (Robert Clay), Claiborne Farm (Seth Hancock), and Clovelly Farms (Robin Scully). There are also mares in Ireland (Coolmore), France (Haras de Clarbec), and England (Sledmere). Prior to Souren Vanian's financial troubles, there was also a number at Hadrian Stud. Incidentally, Pawneese, to whom Dakota was placed in the 1976 'King George', is a permanent boarder at Sledmere.

Having raced such star fillies as Allez France, Pawneese, Flying Water and All Along, Daniel Wildenstein has one of the finest collections of mares in the world outside Arab ownership. His 1990 complement totalled seventy-six with a comparable number of horses in training. Most of them incorporate the word blue (or its French equivalent) in the name, Wildenstein's French racing colours being royal blue with light-blue cap. It is also the practice to name all the animals with the same first letter as the dam.

On whichever side of the Atlantic they have originated, all Wildenstein foals are transferred to Copgrove as weanlings. The American ones are usually flown over from Lexington to Stanstead, via New York, in two batches during October. By that time the previous crop of yearlings has departed to France where Elie Lellouche is now the principal handler.

Thus far David Cecil has reared a host of Group/Grade winners for Daniel Wildenstein up in Yorkshire. The most celebrated is American champion Steinlen, who was reared at Cliff Stud. However the 1990 racing season in France yielded two homebred stars in the Group 1 winners, Epervier Bleu (Prix Lupin), and Pistolet Bleu (Criterium de Saint-Cloud). They will not be the last Wildenstein winners to bring reflected glory to Copgrove Hall Stud.

Cotswold Stud

LOWER SLAUGHTER · GLOUCESTERSHIRE

Mary James of Cotswold Stud has been one of the pioneers in England of selling substantial numbers of yearlings annually at auction on the American agent system. This technique, which had already been perfected by a handful of leading breeders in Ireland, involves taking a yearling over from the vendor for an intensive course of pre-sales preparation (usually a minimum of ten weeks) and presentation.

Significantly much of Mary James's considerable success in this specialized field has been with American-bred animals. During the 1980s her operation expanded to such an extent that she became Tattersalls major consignor. Cotswold Stud headed the Highflyer Sales numerically in both 1988 and 1989 when also the top domestic stud on aggregate.

In 1989 she had responsibility for a record seventy-eight yearlings altogether. Remarkably every single one reached the sales-ring. The twenty-nine catalogued at the Highflyer Sales were all sold for a grand total of 2,110,500 guineas. Top price and the highest ever for a Cotswold yearling was the 370,000 guineas paid for a colt belonging to Dancing Brave's first crop.

Not surprisingly it sent shock waves through the bloodstock industry when the news broke in March 1990 that the company trading as Cotswold Stud had gone into receivership. However the trouble had no reflection on the running of the stud which had been cross guaranteed with an outside manufacturing business that ran into financial difficulties.

Originally known as Manor Farm, Cotswold Stud was founded during the Second World War by Edward Bee, a much respected owner-breeder under both Rules. A farmer, who spent many years growing maize and tobacco on an extensive scale in Rhodesia, he bred two horses who became leading sires in Australia, Coronation Boy and Better Boy.

Better Boy was an own-brother to Our Betters (My Babu – Better So).

64

Sold as a yearling for 3,700 guineas and the best racehorse that Ted Bee ever bred, she was one of the leading two-year-old fillies of 1954, winning the Lowther Stakes before enhancing her reputation in the USA.

Ted Bee invariably had some useful jumpers in training. When he died in 1966 he bequeathed an Irish-bred three-year-old, by Vulgan, to his niece Peggy (formerly Mrs David August, now Mrs Miles Boddington), who inherited his racing colours. As The Dikler he was destined to win her the 1973 Cheltenham Gold Cup. Coincidentally his regular partner had been Barry Brogan, Mary James's first husband.

Cotswold Stud was bought in 1980 from Frank Haydon of hackney renown. This consisted of fifty acres at Manor Farm on the edge of the picturesque Gloucestershire village of Lower Slaughter, below Stow-on-the-Wold. Frank Haydon had started Idiot's Delight on his distinguished stud career here – soon the pair of them were relocated nearby at Hurstwood Stud, Adlestrop.

The commercial yearling market is just about as competitive a business as one could imagine. Mary James's meteoric rise from obscurity to the top echelons has been nothing short of sensational, the more so when one considers that she only embarked upon selling yearlings (the first two appeared at the 1981 Newmarket October Sales) to pay for her event horses.

Ironically the yearling business blossomed to such an extent that there was never time to devote to eventing! Along the way there has been help from many people, not least of whom is stud groom Anna Jordan, while her loyal band of clients has included James Wigan of London Thoroughbred Services, the American breeders Marshall Jenney and George Strawbridge, Lord Huntingdon and Michael McCalmont.

It was Lord Huntingdon, then William Hastings-Bass, who trained the James's first homebred winner, Granny's Bank (Music Boy – Sweet Eliane). The first top winner they bred was a partnership affair, Shulich gaining a Group I victory in the 1985 Gran Premio di Milano Trofeo Lancia from Floors Stud-bred Welnor.

Since then there have been numerous top performers reared at Cotswold Stud. Two of them, Braashee, who won the 1990 Prix Royal-Oak (French St Leger), and Ghariba, who finished fourth in the General Accident 1000 Guineas, were bred by James Wigan from the mare Krakow – she is now back at West Blagdon. Other celebrities include Sapience, the St Leger runner-up, Top Class, who finished third to Nashwan in the 'King George', and Saratogan, an ante-post favourite for the 2000 Guineas. From the 1988 Highflyer draft came three particularly fast juveniles in Ozone Friendly, Robellation and Routilante.

With Cotswold Stud going from strength to strength, an additional seventy acres on the Cheltenham side of Lower Slaughter were acquired to augment the acreage and facilities at Manor Farm. Fortunately Mary James was able to purchase this block of land in 1990 and it is from here that she plans to live and work in the future.

Notwithstanding the financial dramas of 1990, Mary James was still one of the leading lights at that year's sales. That season she had seventy horses through her hands with over thirty yearlings consigned either to the Newmarket Highflyer and October Sales or Goffs' Cartier Million Sales at Kill in Ireland. These were all prepared for sale from a rented yard at Lord Hartington's Side Hill Stud at Newmarket. Despite the recession, a Reference Point colt from the same family as Shulich realized 340,000 guineas at the Highflyer dispersal.

Since the summer of 1990, Mary James has been acting as stud and racing manager to Jocelyn Hambro at Waverton Stud which is just five miles distant from Lower Slaughter. The following January they entered into a partnership whereby Cotswold Stud and Waverton Stud would be run in conjunction – she was able to retain the name Cotswold for her own piece of land. It is from these two studs that Mary James has been preparing her 1991 yearlings.

Crimbourne Stud

WISBOROUGH GREEN · WEST SUSSEX

Since the spring of 1990, Crimbourne Stud has been owned by Sir Eric Parker, whose colours were carried to a magnificent victory in the following year's Seagram Grand National by the appropriately named Seagram. Deputy chairman and chief executive of the Trafalgar House Group, his predecessor was Lord Victor Matthews. His son Ian is the former Newmarket trainer who owns Nidd Park Stud in Yorkshire. Trafalgar House is an enormous conglomerate with interests ranging from the *QE2* and The Ritz, to John Brown and Ideal Homes.

It is Eric Parker's intention to run Crimbourne as a commercial yearling operation, selling the colts and retaining some fillies. His involvement with jumping and the flat is curiously reminiscent of the stud's founder, John U. Baillie, owner of the 1959 Whitbread Gold Cup winner, Done Up. Parker bought Crimbourne from John Bird who had inherited the stud when his uncle John died in August 1989.

John Baillie, a stockbroker and keen amateur rider in his day, will always be remembered in racing circles for running a campaign that eventually succeeded in getting the Verdict family accepted within the pages of the *General Stud Book*. Having been officially labelled 'Half-Bred', they finally gained admission to Volume 36, which Weatherbys published in 1969.

Verdict had made a lasting impression upon John Baillie, when, as an undergraduate at Cambridge, he had seen her win the 1923 Cambridgeshire. He determined that should he ever start breeding racehorses it would be with one of the family. At the 1939 July Sales, he bought a yearling grand-daughter, by Noble Star out of Versicle, for 410 guineas.

Officially described as black, a colour which has never been popular with the racing fraternity, Firle, as the filly was named, proceeded to win six races during the war. By then Verdict was already a noted broodmare, her progeny including Quashed, winner of the 1935 Oaks as well as the

Ascot Gold Cup, and Thankerton, who had finished third in the 1936 Derby.

Initially John Baillie boarded his mares, first with Geoffrey Freer, the Jockey Club handicapper who is commemorated with a race at Newbury, and then with banker John Glyn – they owned studs in Gloucestershire and Oxfordshire respectively. Then in 1954 he bought Crimbourne at Wisborough Green, not far from Lavington Stud in West Sussex where Ron Woodruffe was to serve for so long as stud groom.

Foaled between 1944 and 1960, Firle's six daughters all scored. Amberley bred that durable gelding Colour Blind, who won sixteen races in John Baillie's colours, but the key figure proved to be Lavant (by Le Lavandou), whose ten winning offspring included two champion sprinters in So Blessed and Lucasland.

So Blessed was bought as a yearling for 8,900 guineas by Sir David Robinson, then the largest owner in the country. An outstanding three-year-old, he won the July Cup, King George Stakes and Nunthorpe Stakes. Later bought by Lord Howard de Walden to stand at his Thornton Stud in Yorkshire, So Blessed was based there from 1970 to 1979 when exported to Japan, like so many other sons of Princely Gift.

John Baillie bred an exceptionally good filly to So Blessed in Duboff. Successful in the Sun Chariot Stakes at three years and the Child Stakes at four years, she made another spectacular appearance at Newmarket when realizing 100,000 guineas at the 1976 December Sales *en route* to Hesmonds Stud, also in Sussex.

The continuing success story so far as Lavant's male descendants are concerned revolves around her great-grandson, Petorius, a product of Stackallen Stud in Ireland. By Mummy's Pet out of The Stork, he won the Temple Stakes (dead-heat) and Cornwallis Stakes, before becoming a prolific sire of winners at Tara Stud, Co. Meath. The Stork was bred at Crimbourne by the little-known Club House (own-brother to Reform), who stood locally at Southdown Stud.

Raced by John Baillie himself, Lucasland excelled as a four-year-old, winning the July Cup and Diadem Stakes. Although she produced a useful daughter in Lucent (Lingfield Oaks Trial Stakes), the two most recent celebrities from the family originate through her unraced half-sister, Luckhurst. Mated with the handicapper Owen Anthony (who stood locally at Sladelands Stud), she foaled Stumped.

Sold for 7,000 guineas as a yearling and 110,000 guineas at the Newmarket December Sales two years later for export to the USA, Stumped emulated Duboff by winning the Child Stakes (formerly Falmouth Stakes). Just to maintain the family sequence, Stumped's outstanding daughter, Sonic Lady, won the Child Stakes in both 1986 and 1987 for Sheikh Mohammed.

One of a host of star mares in the Dalham Hall galaxy, Sonic Lady, who had cost the Sheikh $500,000 as a yearling, proved the champion three-year-old filly in Europe during 1986 when she won three Group 1 events: the Goffs' Irish 1000 Guineas, Prix du Moulin de Longchamp Ecurie Fustok and Swettenham Stud Sussex Stakes; she was also third to Midway Lady in the General Accident 1000 Guineas.

John Baillie had his own definite ideas about breeding bloodstock. His two priorities were to breed from winning mares that belonged to a dominant female line. The Verdict family certainly fell into that category and the fact that he was quite prepared to use unfashionable stallions like Lucero (sire of Lucasland), Owen Anthony and Club House, showed that he was considerably more enterprising than many of his contemporaries.

There was no fanfare of trumpets when the last four remaining mares from the old Crimbourne Stud appeared at the 1989 Newmarket December Sales. Two were offered as the property of Bunny Bird – Lucent, who had proved disappointing in the paddocks, in foal to Shareef Dancer, and her unraced daughter, Laser Beam, due to Aragon. Between them they realized a derisory 13,600 guineas. Perhaps Sir Eric Parker will steer Crimbourne back to further glory.

Dalham Hall Stud

NEWMARKET · SUFFOLK

A visit to Sheikh Mohammed's Dalham Hall Stud is just as likely to be
on the agenda of a sightseeing tour of Newmarket as the National Horse-
racing Museum or Hyperion's statue. Quite apart from having some of
the most impressive stud buildings in the world, Dalham Hall also accommo-
dates the finest collection of stallions in Britain and is the nerve centre
of the most extensive racing and breeding empire in the country.

Sheikh Mohammed Bin Rashid Al Maktoum is the third of the Maktoum
'racing' brothers, sons of the late Ruler of Dubai who died in the autumn
of 1990. His two elder brothers are Sheikh Maktoum Al Maktoum (Gainsborough Stud) and Sheikh Hamdan Al Maktoum (Shadwell Stud). Whereas
they both have additional studs in Kentucky, Sheikh Mohammed concentrates his operation exclusively on this side of the Atlantic.

Under the collective title of Darley Stud Management, he runs Dalham
Hall as his flagship under the supervision of Alec Notman, together with
the additional Newmarket studs of Derisley Wood, Hadrian, Rutland,
Someries (most of the land but not the title), Warren, White Lodge and
Church Hall Farm. There are also three studs in Ireland with Kildangan,
managed by Michael Osborne, MRCVS, former director of the Irish
National Stud, Old Connell and Ragusa, all in Co Kildare.

Also under the Darley banner is Aston Upthorpe Stud, owned by Sheikh
Mohammed's younger brother, Sheikh Ahmed. The other key figures in
the organization are Darley Stud directors Robert Acton, general manager
and formerly assistant director at the National Stud, and Anthony Stroud,
the racing manager. Between them they have responsibility for around
500 horses in training and 300 mares and their followers, not to mention
the stallions.

Ironically it was by the merest chance that Sheikh Mohammed came
to own Dalham Hall Stud in the first place. Back in September 1981 pro-

tracted negotiations by Stavros Niarchos to purchase the stud from James Philipps failed at the eleventh hour when the vendor learned that the Greek shipping tycoon intended dispersing the stock. The very next month, Sheikh Mohammed bought the place as a going concern.

Until November 1970 Dalham Hall had been known as Derisley Stud. At that time Jim Philipps owned two studs, Dalham Hall at Gazeley, four miles south-east of Newmarket, and Derisley Stud off Duchess Drive, both managed by Dick Waugh. When his two stud grooms reached retirement age simultaneously, Jim Philipps decided to sell the old Dalham Hall Stud which name he promptly bestowed upon Derisley Stud.

The former Dalham Hall Stud was bought by Patrick McCalmont, a condition of sale being that it was renamed Gazeley Stud. Jim Philipps's father, the 1st Lord Milford, had bought the property in 1928 specifically to stand his very first racehorse, Flamingo, winner of the 2000 Guineas and runner-up in the Derby. He was to stand a succession of stallions there.

Milford purchased the present Dalham Hall Stud following the death of Sir Alec Black in 1942. It was then one of five studs which had constituted his Compton Park Stud situated between Wooditton Road and Duchess Drive. Now another three of those studs, Derisley Wood, Hadrian and Someries (the land, but not the name) are likewise owned by Sheikh Mohammed. In splendid isolation is Major Michael Wyatt's Dunchurch Lodge Stud which adjoins Dalham Hall.

During the 1960s, three former Charles Engelhard celebrities, Romulus, Indiana and Tin King, retired to stand at the then Derisley Stud – all three eventually wound up in Japan. They had been preceded there by Lord Milford's homebred Honeyway. In due course he was replaced by his illustrious son, Great Nephew, another colt of his own breeding.

A champion sprinter, who stayed well enough to win the Champion Stakes, Honeyway was a double rig when first put to stud. Returned to training, he overcame his fertility problems to become an influential sire. He had an outstanding son in Great Nephew (Prix du Moulin de Longchamp), who was beaten a short head for the 2000 Guineas, while the best of his daughters was probably the 1000 Guineas heroine, Honeylight.

Great Nephew, who spent the duration of his stud life at the new Dalham Hall Stud, died aged twenty-three in 1986. For some inexplicable reason he was never really fashionable despite being twice champion sire, in 1975 and 1981, by courtesy of his Derby winning sons, Grundy and Shergar.

Both Honeyway and Great Nephew are buried at Dalham Hall. The latter was foaled in 1963, just a year after Lord Milford died. By then his son, Jim Philipps, had taken control of the two studs, which instead of producing stock to run in their breeder's colours, had been redirected towards producing yearlings for Tattersalls' sales.

Soon Dalham Hall was top of the list of commercial yearling studs. Its draft at the 1975 Houghton (now Highflyer) Sales saw seven lots sold for a record aggregate (369,000 guineas) and a record average (52,714 guineas). 202,000 guineas was obtained for a Mill Reef colt (Million), then the highest price ever paid at a thoroughbred auction in Europe.

The greatest optimist could not have foreseen the speed with which Sheikh Mohammed was rewarded for his purchase of Dalham Hall Stud and all its bloodstock. One of ten mares involved in the package was Oh So Fair, carrying to Kris. The resulting offspring was Oh So Sharp. She became only the fourth member of her sex this century to win the fillies' Triple Crown, following Pretty Polly (1904), Sun Chariot (1942) and Meld (1955).

During the present decade, the focus of attention at Dalham Hall has switched to stallions. For 1991 there was a dazzling collection comprising Dancing Brave, Machiavellian, Old Vic, Polish Precedent, Reference Point, Shareef Dancer and Soviet Star. Between them they had won twenty Group I races in Europe, including seven classics. The only Sheikh Mohammed flag-bearers amongst them are Old Vic, Polish Precedent and Soviet Star, all yearling acquisitions.

Derisley Wood Stud

NEWMARKET · SUFFOLK

In March 1986 Derisley Wood Stud and neighbouring Hadrian Stud, owned by the Vanian brothers, Souren and Garo, went into liquidation. The future of the two studs was settled predictably enough on the last day of September when they were bought by Sheikh Mohammed whose Dalham Hall Stud adjoins both properties.

That season Souren Vanian had operated Derisley Wood as a stallion station with walking-in mares only, a customary procedure in the USA but not in this country. The stallions involved were Blazing Saddles, Claude Monet, Glint of Gold, Legend of France, Magic Mirror, Posse, Siberian Express, Valiyar and Wattlefield.

Despite the financial difficulties behind the scenes, the experiment was deemed a success. Having acquired the stud's own shares in the stallions from the receiver, Souren Vanian then transferred most of the stallions to Dullingham Stud which had only recently been built on an arable plot a few miles away as a yearling annexe for Derisley Wood.

That arrangement under Bill Johnson, who had been stud manager at Derisley Wood since 1964, lasted for two more seasons (1987, 1988) when the Dullingham premises were purchased by Prince Khalid Abdullah's Juddmonte Farms. As Eagle Lane Farm, it has continued to operate as a stallion station with Rhydian Morgan-Jones as managing director and Alan Walker as manager.

Bill Johnson was once stud manager to Sir David Robinson, the TV rentals magnate who was better known as a prolific buyer of yearlings than as a breeder. He first went to Derisley Wood about six months after the stud was bought by film director and distributor Irving Allen in August 1957.

The vendor on that occasion was Mrs F.J. Barlow. She had stood a couple of stallions in Sir Cosmo, who started stud life at Brook Stud, and Grandmaster. Both horses won the Free Handicap, the latter having cost 12,000 guineas at the 1945 Newmarket December Sales. To Sir Cosmo, Mrs Barlow bred the smart two-year-old Cosmohone.

When Irving Allen purchased Derisley Wood, half the land was arable. The only stallion in residence was a grey son of Nasrullah standing at a comparatively modest £248. At that stage he had two fairly undistinguished crops of runners and his owner was asked to find alternative accommodation for him.

The stallion was none other than Grey Sovereign who was destined to earn fame and not a little fortune at the now Gazeley Stud. Ironically there was never to be a replacement of equivalent stature. Four years elapsed before Derisley Wood became a public stud again. The first arrival was Ascot Gold Cup hero Pandofell and he was followed by the sprinters Galivanter and Sammy Davis.

None of that trio lasted long, Pandofell being exported to Russia, but there was an interesting new recruit in Midsummer Night II. Winner of the Cambridgeshire for owner-breeder Paul Mellon, he sired top miler Jimmy Reppin (Sussex Stakes), sire of a marvellous mare in Reprocolor. To Jimmy Reppin, Irving Allen bred Motionless, who was placed in both the English and Irish 1000 Guineas.

A series of other stallions took up residence at Derisley Wood in Irving Allen's time, amongst them Acer, Court Fool, Jolly Jet, Dubassoff, Double Jump and My Swallow. None of them did particularly well, Double Jump and My Swallow having headed the Two-Year-Old Free Handicap in 1964 and 1970 respectively.

My Swallow was a particular disappointment. Third in a vintage 2000 Guineas to Brigadier Gerard and Mill Reef, and the only one to beat the latter as a juvenile, he became the very first winner of the French quadruple crown for juveniles – the Prix Robert Papin, Prix Morny, Prix de la Salamandre and Grand Criterium. That season Irving Allen paid David Robinson £400,000 for his champion. Unfortunately My Swallow never repaid the outlay and by 1978 he had been banished to Japan.

Irving Allen had the unusual distinction of owning two winners of the Stewards' Cup. He scored with homebred Patient Constable in 1966 and Royal Smoke in 1969. The former had failed to reach her reserve as a yearling, while the latter came to stand at Derisley Wood but proved totally infertile.

Their owner also had Fittocks Stud at Cheveley which was utilized for yearlings and in the grounds there was a fully equipped private cinema. However Irving Allen is probably best remembered in bloodstock circles as the instigator of the Newmarket School of Stud Management, forerunner to the courses now run by the National Stud and the TBA.

When Irving Allen sold Derisley Wood to the Vanians in the autumn of 1979 to return to California, it looked as though the stud was entering a new period of prosperity. An Armenian entrepreneur with extensive motor and transport interests in the Sudan, Souren Vanian was a familiar figure on French racecourses.

He had owned Manado, the top two-year-old of his generation in France, and was the breeder of Comtesse de Loir. Soon he would achieve Royal Ascot glory with two colts bought in training – Critique (Hardwicke Stakes) and Valiyar (Queen Anne Stakes). Valiyar became a Derisley Wood stallion, as did another Royal Ascot winner Posse (St. James's Palace Stakes), sire of Sally Brown.

At their zenith the Vanians owned sixty mares at Hadrian Stud (bought from Sir David Wills in 1981) with another seventy at their Manado Stud in New South Wales, Australia, all of them imported from England or Ireland.

One of the major contributory factors to the downfall of the Vanian brothers' operation was an outbreak of virus abortion in the spring of 1985. Twenty foals were lost at Hadrian where Daniel Wildenstein and Daniel Prenn both suffered casualties with their boarders. This was the main reason why Souren Vanian converted Derisley Wood into a stallion station on American lines. His long-term plan was for as many as twenty horses with a nationwide shuttle service of horseboxes to collect all the visiting mares.

Dunchurch Lodge Stud

NEWMARKET · SUFFOLK

Major Michael Wyatt of Dunchurch Lodge Stud, Newmarket, knows just how fickle bloodstock breeding can be. Time and again he has retained fillies with all the credentials to make broodmares and they have disappointed. Conversely many with apparent shortcomings have been culled only to excel in the paddocks. He describes the experience as 'character building'!

Chairman of the Jockey Club's Race Planning Committee, Michael was born at Dunchurch Lodge, near Rugby, the home of his grandfather, Major Harold Cayzer. Vice chairman of the Clan Line, he hunted with the Pytchley and had horses in training with Sir Cecil Boyd-Rochfort at Freemason Lodge, Newmarket.

When Harold Cayzer died on a business trip to South Africa in February 1948, his daughter Mary and her husband, Brigadier Wilfred Wyatt, decided to move their small Dunchurch Lodge Stud to Newmarket should a suitable property become available. Three months later Lord Fitzwilliam was killed in an aeroplane crash over France and the Wyatts were able to buy his picturesque Rockingham Stud with its thatched roofs in Duchess Drive from his executors. The original Dunchurch Lodge is now a staff training college for the GEC Group.

At the 1948 Newmarket December Sales, the Wyatts bought the mare Trial Ground, in foal to Hyperion, for 7,200 guineas. Mated with Precipitation, who stood at neighbouring Someries Stud under Boyd-Rochfort's management, the following year, Trial Ground produced the St Leger winner, Premonition. Joint-favourite with Pinza for the Derby, Premonition was involved in two controversial episodes. Disqualified after finishing first in the Irish Derby, he then narrowly beat his pacemaker Osborne for the Winston Churchill Stakes, Hurst Park. The outcome was that his trainer was fined £100 by the stewards for failing to give Roy

76

Burrows (the rider of Osborne and Premonition's lad) explicit riding instructions.

Premonition, the first stallion to stand at the new Dunchurch Lodge, was a stud failure. So too were Flying Slipper (Nassau Stakes) and Nectarine (Lingfield Oaks Trial Stakes), two of the Wyatts' best homebred fillies, both by the great broodmare sire Nearco. Ironically their unraced own-sister, Sarie, rendered yeoman service for Mrs Jane Levins Moore in Ireland.

The family had originated at Dunchurch Lodge when Harold Cayzer purchased the grandam Dalmary (Blandford – Simon's Shoes) as a yearling from the National Stud for 800 guineas in 1932. Not only did Dalmary win the Yorkshire Oaks, but she also became one of the most important foundation mares in the General Stud Book.

Dalmary's penultimate foal, Rough Shod, established an omnipotent branch of the family in the USA, many of its members, like Thatch, being trained by Vincent O'Brien. Two of Rough Shod's descendants are the close relatives Nureyev and Sadler's Wells, two key stallions of the late 80s and early 90s.

The best Dunchurch Lodge-bred performer belonging to the Dalmary line was her grandson, Tudor Era. Sold to race in the USA, he became a top grass performer there and finished first in the 1958 Washington DC International only to be relegated to second place. Michael Wyatt still has representatives of this family, but its more notable winners, such as Governor General, Ala Hounak, Sudden Love, Galunpe and Negligent, have all been for other breeders.

Harold Cayzer's second foundation mare was Gold Rush (Gold Bridge – Gold Race), who cost 2,000 guineas as a yearling in 1942. Dam of the very speedy Gamble in Gold (Lowther Stakes), she has likewise wielded enormous influence beyond the confines of Dunchurch Lodge.

The grandam of Whistling Wind and Magic Flute, Gamble in Gold's greatest gift to posterity has been as the third dam of the Tavistocks' renowned broodmare Mrs Moss. Alas there has been no comparable bonanza back at the Dunchurch Lodge camp although the female line still flourishes there. Persian Boy, who made his name in Japan, is probably the most significant home winner.

Michael Wyatt became chairman of the Dunchurch Lodge Stud Company upon the death of his mother, Mrs Mary Munro, in 1969. By that time Derrick Candy had become the family's principal trainer and Michael continues to have horses in training at Kingstone Warren with his son, Henry.

At that time Dunchurch Lodge, under the management of Frank Chapman, had two local appendages with Chippenham Lodge Stud, towards

Ely, which was sold to the late James McAllister, and Duke's Stud at Ashley which Michael Wyatt bought when he left the army and which he still owns.

For a brief period in his dotage, Premonition stood at Dunchurch Lodge alongside his replacement, Roan Rocket, who had spent his initial covering season at neighbouring Derisley Wood Stud. Roan Rocket, who was owned in partnership with old Tommy Frost (his son Thomas is still involved there), made his mark as a sire. Mated with Premonition's three-parts sister, Queen of Arisai, he sired Catherine Wheel. Winner of the Nassau Stakes and Musidora Stakes and third in the 1000 Guineas, she was sold cheaply as a yearling to the late Tom Blackwell of Langham Hall Stud.

Whereas Roan Rocket was the leading three-year-old miler of his generation, his successor, Absalom, another grey, was a sprinter. The winner of Group races at two, three and four years, he has done particularly well with his juveniles, amongst them Dead Certain, the champion two-year-old filly of 1989. Standing no more than 15.2 hands high, Absalom is a rarity amongst thoroughbred stallions in so far as he is an infinitely better sire than his own sire, Abwah. His grandsire Abernant was always rated by Sir Noel Murless as the fastest he ever trained.

Following the sale of the Someries Stud acres in December 1990, Dunchurch Lodge Stud is the only stud in the block of land between Duchess Drive and Woodditton Road, which used to form Sir Alec Black's Compton Park Stud, not now owned by Sheikh Mohammed. The others are Dalham Hall, Hadrian and Derisley Wood.

Egerton and Lordship Studs

NEWMARKET · SUFFOLK

In 1985, two years before she died aged ninety-two at her Northamptonshire home, Cottesbrooke Hall, Lady Macdonald-Buchanan sold her famous Egerton and Lordship Studs to Malcolm Parrish. The new owner, who is a businessman based in France where he has a number of horses in training, then rested the paddocks and completely renovated the two properties which were operational again by the 1990s.

Catherine Macdonald-Buchanan inherited the Lavington and Westerlands Studs in West Sussex upon the death of her father in 1935. He was the one and only Lord Woolavington, the Scottish whisky magnate who was born James Buchanan. Contrary to his advice that she should retain only four yearlings per year, his daughter very soon owned two more studs, this time in Newmarket.

They were Lordship and Egerton which are situated on opposite sides of the Cambridge road, the former being acquired in 1937 and the latter in 1942. Each had strong associations with the Royal family. Lordship was bought from Lord St Davids, the breeder of Feola, and it was from Egerton Stud (purchased from the Princess Royal's husband, the 6th Earl of Harewood) that Richard Marsh trained King Edward VII's three Derby winners, Persimmon, Diamond Jubilee and Minoru.

Between them Sir Reginald and Lady Macdonald-Buchanan (he died in 1981) became two of the most prominent owner-breeders in the country. Initially they patronized Fred Darling's stable at Beckhampton, then his successor, Sir Noel Murless, who moved to Newmarket, as well as the former Beckhampton stable jockey Sir Gordon Richards. Lady Macdonald-Buchanan utilized her father's 'white, black hoop and armlets, red cap with gold tassel', while her husband's 'black, white hoop and armlets' had obvious connotations with the family's most celebrated brand of whisky.

Egerton House Stud, as it was then called, has a long involvement with stallions. One of the more interesting names historically is Anmer, the King's horse who was brought down in the 'suffragette' Derby of 1913. Prior to the Second World War, Egerton was leased to the old Aga Khan who stood his Derby winners, Bahram and Mahmoud, there until both were exported to the USA in 1940.

So far as the Macdonald-Buchanans were concerned, Egerton pursued its traditional role as a public stud. At first Lordship was used as a base for weaned foals and yearlings, as well as mares from Lavington which were visiting Newmarket stallions. Coincidentally the very first mare to foal at Lordship was Mary Tudor II in 1938 – the resulting colt foal by Hyperion was none other than Owen Tudor.

An erratic performer, Owen Tudor won substitute races for the Derby and Gold Cup on the July Course at Newmarket, just behind Egerton Stud. His stud innings was long and honourable. Located at Egerton in all but his first four seasons (he started off at neighbouring New England Stud), he died in 1966 aged twenty-eight. His progeny range from a great sprinter, Abernant, to a great stayer, Elpenor (Gold Cup). In between were the brilliant miler Tudor Minstrel, and top middle-distance performer Right Royal V.

Abernant, who was homebred at Lavington Stud, is fully entitled to be regarded as one of the fastest horses of all time. He and Tudor Minstrel were bred on very similar lines, for they shared the same third dam in Sledmere-bred Lady Josephine. Tudor Minstrel was homebred by James Dewar, another Scottish whisky manufacturer, at his Homestall Stud in Sussex.

Unlike Tudor Minstrel, Abernant failed to establish an important male line. Retired to Egerton Stud in 1951 where he died at the age of twenty-four in 1970, he excelled with fillies. His solitary classic winner is Abermaid, but he features as maternal grandsire of two more Guineas heroines in Humble Duty and Caergwrle. He is also maternal grandsire of Derring-Do. Abernant's own male line rests almost exclusively with his grandson Absalom, the Dunchurch Lodge Stud resident.

The Macdonald-Buchanans never had another horse at Egerton of the same calibre as either Owen Tudor or Abernant. By comparison their counterparts were a motley collection with Acropolis, Major Portion, Royal Palace, Brigadier Gerard, Estaminet, Final Straw and Jalmood. Both Royal Palace and Brigadier Gerard were particular disappointments as they were outstanding racehorses.

The only homebred member of the group is Estaminet who wound up in Australia. He traces back to Abernant's half-sister, Fille du Regiment.

Their dam Rustom Mahal had two filly foals, as did Owen Tudor's dam, Mary Tudor, so there were only very limited opportunities to propagate their distaff families.

In 1949 the Macdonald-Buchanans fielded the favourite in both the 2000 Guineas and the Derby won by Nimbus. Abernant was beaten a short head at Newmarket, and Royal Forest finished fourth at Epsom. Royal Forest, whose dam, Tudor Maid is an own-sister to Owen Tudor, became a champion sire in Brazil.

During the period from the mid-1950s to the mid-1980s when all the mares were centred on Lordship Stud rather than Lavington, such winners emerged as Philip of Spain (sire of King of Spain), Port Merion, Parthenon, Relay Race, Estaminet, Carnoch, Amboise, Marching On and Forward Rally. It was Sir Mark Prescott, who had taken over as number one trainer from Jack Waugh, who saddled Lady Macdonald-Buchanan's last major winner, Forward Rally, in the 1986 Zetland Gold Cup at Redcar. By that stage the family had bred no less than 500 individual winners worldwide.

Post-war managers at Egerton and Lordship comprise Brigadier Bowden-Smith (who was joint master of the Pytchley with Sir Reginald Macdonald-Buchanan), Michael Oswald, who became manager of the Royal Studs, Jack Waugh, Fred Day and Henry Plumptre. In all that time the only two stud grooms at Egerton were Jack Podmore and Bill Cornish. Between them they taught many an aspiring stud manager the rudiments of the business. Following the sale of Egerton when it ceased to stand stallions, Bill Cornish went as stud groom to Nunnery Stud in Norfolk.

Eydon Hall Farm

Few breeders have climbed the international bloodstock ladder as far and as fast over the last two decades as Gerald Leigh. He has progressed from boarding a few animals with former royal jockey the late Harry Carr at his Genesis Green Stud (now owned by Walter Swinburn, Snr) to creating the glorious Eydon Hall Farm on the Oxfordshire-Northamptonshire border, north of Banbury.

In the interim, Gerald Leigh, a former property developer and proprietor of Hamptons, the estate agents, owned Cayton Park Stud, Wargrave-on-Thames. Now part of Juddmonte Farms, he bought this stud from Mrs Gerald Trimmer-Thompson of March Past fame in January 1973 and sold it to Prince Khalid Abdullah in the summer of 1979.

James Delahooke, who had been managing Cayton Park, then took over as general manager to Khalid Abdullah. James had been a director of the local Stud and Racing Services and it was one of his colleagues, Martin Burdett-Coutts, who bought Gerald Leigh his first 'serious' mare, Miss Petard. She cost 64,000 guineas at the 1973 Newmarket December Sales in the year that she won the Ribblesdale Stakes.

Miss Petard was one of five mares that Khalid Abdullah acquired from Gerald Leigh in the Cayton Park package. Meanwhile her daughter Kiss became one of three original Cayton Park mares which were transferred in due course to Eydon Hall Farm. The others were Canton Silk and Chappelle Blanche.

Situated in the best part of the Bicester country adjacent to the Grafton, Eydon Hall was originally a hunting lodge built by the Reverend Francis Annesley. During the summer of 1983, Gerald Leigh bought the house and 600 acres from Lady Ford – she is a niece of Nancy Astor of Cliveden renown, and a cousin of Khalid Abdullah's first trainer, Jeremy Tree.

Gerald Leigh has transformed Eydon Hall Farm (he prefers the connotation farm to stud) into a magnificent establishment for the breeding and rearing of young thoroughbreds. Not only are there all the usual amenities associated with a top-class private stud, and with 300 acres of post-and-rail paddocks, there is an enviable ratio of acres to horses, but there are also the prerequisites for making and breaking yearlings, with comprehensive grass and all-weather gallops.

The fact that Gerald Leigh keeps a third of his broodmare band at Mill Ridge Farm in Kentucky is indicative of the balance of power so far as the stallions are concerned, but the initial difficulty he experienced in procuring nominations to top stallions over here was largely rectified with a block purchase of shares from the executors of William Hill (Whitsbury Manor and Sezincote Studs).

Amongst them were two shares in Habitat and he has exerted a profound influence at Eydon Hall. He is the sire of Miss Petard's daughter Kiss, who is the dam of Casey (1985). The very first foal born at Eydon Hall, she carried her breeder's colours, 'brown, beige chevrons, brown cap', to victory in the Kikuka Sho Park Hill Stakes.

The mating of Canton Silk with Habitat resulted in the top filly Brocade. Successful in the Prix de la Forêt (Group I) and Bisquit Cognac Challenge Stakes, Brocade had as her first offspring the Shirley Heights filly Free at Last – she ran fourth in the 1990 General Accident 1000 Guineas and is a graded winner in California as a four-year-old.

Only the previous season homebred Markofdistinction had occupied the same position in the General Accident 2000 Guineas on only his second racecourse appearance. In 1990 the son of Known Fact proved the champion miler of Europe, winning the Queen Elizabeth II Stakes at the Festival of British Racing following wins in the Trusthouse Forte Hungerford Stakes and Queen Anne Stakes. Then sold for stallion duties in Japan, Markofdistinction is so named because of a scar on his off-fore knee, the result of a kick which prevented his sale as a yearling.

Markofdistinction's dam, Ghislaine, is one of only three foals that Gerald Leigh bred from Cambretta, the others being the Group scorers Pluralisme and Only. He bought Critique's own-sister, Cambretta, for $200,000 in 1979, and sold her for $1 million in 1982. The best price obtained at auction so far is the $2.6 million paid for a Nijinsky colt at Keeneland in July 1985.

Not many Eydon Hall mares have been acquired as yearlings, but Infamy is a notable exception. This grey daughter of Shirley Heights, who cost 100,000 guineas from Hesmonds Stud at the 1985 Highflyer Sales, triumphed in the Cheveley Park Stud Sun Chariot Stakes and Gordon Richard EBF

Stakes before landing the Grade 1 Rothmans' International at Woodbine in Canada.

Gerald Leigh's colours were carried to another Grade 1 victory in North America when Bequest, whose dam Quest was a foal purchase there, won the Santa Barbara Handicap, Santa Anita, in March 1991. Bred in partnership with Whitsbury Manor Stud, this Sharpen Up mare will join Gerald Leigh's other Kentucky based mares at Mill Ridge Farm.

It is stud policy to keep fewer than twenty mares on both sides of the Atlantic with colts being offered for sale either as weanlings or yearlings – an increasing number change hands privately at home. Gerald Leigh, who is much more American orientated than other breeders, emphasizes the need to be flexible and he considers culling to be an integral priority. He favours a young broodmare band and will invariably sell a mare just as soon as he has two or three of her daughters.

Of all the personalities involved with Eydon Hall Farm, either directly or indirectly, Gerald Leigh is fulsome in his praise for manager Terry Campbell, who was also his right-hand man at Cayton Park. Not only does he foal all the mares but he is involved in every stage of their development until going to the sales or into training. Retained fillies are divided between Luca Cumani and Guy Harwood. The occasional filly owned in partnership with Sven Hanson (they share dual Oaks heroine, Fair Salinia) is placed with Michael Stoute. Although boarders are not part of the general scheme of things, there is a nucleus of mares owned by Athos Christodoulou, another of Guy Harwood's patrons.

Floors Stud

KELSO · ROXBURGHSHIRE

A handful of great country houses in Britain have thoroughbred studs. Amongst them are Woburn Abbey, where the Tavistocks' Bloomsbury Stud shares the grounds with a safari park, Lord Carnarvon's Highclere Castle, complete with Egyptian artefacts, and the Duke of Roxburghe's Floors Castle, the largest inhabited castle in Scotland. All these ancestral homes are open to the public.

Floors, which overlooks the Borders' town of Kelso in Roxburghshire, is the only private stud in Scotland engaged in breeding top-quality bloodstock. Many good horses, particularly jumpers, have been raised in the vicinity of the Tweed Valley, but Floors has adopted the mantle of the late Hugh Leggatt's Pirnie House Stud, on the other side of Kelso, as a fully fledged commercial enterprise.

Guy David Innes-Ker, 10th Duke of Roxburghe, was only nineteen years of age when inheriting the title and the extensive Floors Estate of over 50,000 acres upon the death of his father in 1974. A member of the Jockey Club and one time senior steward, he had started a small stud at Floors in 1947 with the object of breeding runners for his own silver and green colours.

The 9th Duke, known as Bobo Roxburghe, was also a teenager when succeeding to the title. His two principal trainers were Matthew Peacock and his son Richard from Middleham. The latter trained two of his best homebreds in Erudite (Free Handicap) and Sweet Story (Yorkshire Cup, Northumberland Plate).

Guide was another good winner and this half-brother to Ballymoss stood at Floors throughout his stud life. By the time of his demise aged twenty-one in 1970, he had been replaced by Sweet Story, a close relative to that noted sire of sires Sovereign Path. Popular and convenient with the hunting fraternity in the Buccleuch and Jed Forest country, both Guide and Sweet Story made their mark as jumping sires.

85

By the mid seventies, the emphasis at Floors Stud, which still had the inestimable services of stud groom Paddy Sullivan (his successor is Barry Hosie), had changed dramatically. The new Duke was intent on establishing a commercial yearling operation following the traditional course of retaining only the occasional filly to preserve a particular bloodline.

Whereas Lord Lovat's son, Simon Fraser, once had a rather grandiose scheme for producing bloodstock up at Beaufort Castle in Inverness-shire, which never came to fruition, Guy Roxburghe quickly made his mark as a serious breeder thanks to the purchase of the mare Norfolk Light for 12,000 guineas at the 1977 Newmarket December Sales.

Prior to selling Norfolk Light for 23,000 guineas at the same venue five years later (in the interim her half-sister Yanuka had finished third in the 1000 Guineas), Roxburghe mated her with Welsh Pageant to breed Welnor. A 25,000-guinea yearling at the 1982 Newmarket October Sales, he excelled in Italy as a three-year-old winning the Derby, Gran Premio d'Italia and Premio Emanuele Filiberto.

The preceding December, Welnor's own-sister Pageantry had been sold in Park Paddocks due to Dominion for 12,500 guineas. At the time she was carrying Just Class, who proceeded to win three Graded races in the USA. Fortunately Floors Stud already had another December Sales purchase who was to scale greater heights, at least in commercial terms.

In 1980 the mare Vaguely (Bold Lad IRE – Vaguely Mine) was acquired for 28,000 guineas from Sir John Astor's Warren Stud. From a half-sister to the St Leger hero Provoke, she belonged to the same illustrious Cliveden family as that fine stayer Trelawny.

Five years later Floors Stud sold Vaguely's Shirley Heights colt at the Highflyer Sales for 110,000 guineas to join the Newmarket stable of Robert Armstrong. Tragically his wife, Mary, a cousin of Guy Roxburghe, died four years later, by which time Shady Heights, as the colt was called, had proved top class.

Runner-up to Ajdal in the William Hill Dewhurst Stakes and one-time ante-post favourite for the Ever Ready Derby, Shady Heights encountered all sorts of problems as a three-year-old. However the ensuing season he finished in the frame in eight Group races, winning the International Stakes (upon the disqualification of Persian Heights) and Tattersalls' Rogers Gold Cup. Upon the conclusion of his five-year-old career, Shady Heights departed for a predetermined stud career in Japan.

Vaguely has had four foals of racing age since Shady Heights. The two colts, Classic Memory and Rahif (own-brother to Shady Heights), realized 260,000 guineas and 380,000 guineas at the 1988 and 1989 Highflyer Sales respectively. Both fillies have been retained. The first, Dimmer, won the listed BBA Atalanta Stakes, one of two wins at Sandown Park.

A minor winner herself at two and three years, Vaguely set the pattern of additional mares at Floors as her pedigree is far superior to her racecourse accomplishments. The most expensive acquisition so far at 140,000 guineas is Exotic, a half-sister to Full Dress II (1000 Guineas). Her first runner, Arita, scored twice for her owner-breeder as a juvenile. He is optimistic that lightning can strike in the same place twice as Exotic represents another of the great Cliveden families.

Guy Roxburghe is currently involved with about a dozen broodmares and a significant portfolio of stallion shares. Two mares are owned in partnership with Lord Hartington. He is also joint owner with Christopher Heath of Argentum's half-sister Pipsqueak – she went into training at Beckhampton with Roger Charlton.

The Duke of Roxburghe thinks it might be financially advantageous to board all his animals at Stoker Hartington's Side Hill Stud, but Scotland's premier baronet says that would never compensate him for the pleasure of having them at home. Who knows they might even become a tourist attraction!

Fonthill Stud

HINDON · WILTSHIRE

Below the Wiltshire village of Tisbury, home of two famous equine artists – Snaffles, who died there, and Susan Crawford – is Lord Margadale's Fonthill House. One of comparatively few country houses to have been built since the last war, it is situated at the centre of the Morrison family's 10,000-acre Fonthill Estate.

Eighty of these acres are devoted to Fonthill Stud where Set Free (Worden II – Emancipation) earned a unique place in the annals of the Turf during the 1970s. She is the first mare to be accredited with two winners of the Oaks (Juliette Marny and Scintillate) and a winner of the St Leger (Julio Mariner). Only six other mares have bred three classic winners, all in the last century when competition was modest by comparison.

More than two centuries ago a member of the Morrison clan ventured south across the border from Scotland where they now own a substantial part of the beautiful island of Islay on the west coast. It was from here that John Morrison, the first and only Lord Margadale, heir to a nineteenth-century haberdashery fortune, took his title in 1964, the year Set Free was foaled.

A great lover of the countryside, he has devoted his life to politics and hunting. Conservative member of parliament for Salisbury from 1942 to 1964, he was master or joint master of the South and West Wilts from 1932 to 1965. While his two younger sons, Sir Charles and Sir Peter (knighted in 1990), also became MPs, his eldest son James now runs the estate and the stud farm from his home in Hindon. Like his father he is a member of the Jockey Club.

John Margadale made his entrée into racehorse ownership at the Newmarket July Sales of 1952. Here he bought an unraced two-year-old, Fellermelad, and a yearling filly (Caol Ila) from the executors of James V. Rank. Both were by Rank's own horse, Scottish Union, and they were sent to his trainer, Noel Cannon, whose Druids Lodge yard was no distance from Fonthill at Middle Woodford.

Each was successful the following season, Fellermelad providing Margadale's newly registered colours with a win on their début at Newbury in April. With twelve foals in fourteen years, Caol Ila (Gaelic for Sound of Islay) did well for Fonthill Stud. Her son Whisky Poker was a particular favourite achieving the last of seventeen wins as a ten-year-old.

Whisky Poker was trained at Beckhampton by Jeremy Tree who had taken over the Margadale horses upon Noel Cannon's death in 1959. His expanding broodmare band had been established with the acquisition of yearling fillies. The *coup de grâce* had been enacted four years earlier, Emancipation having cost 1,900 guineas at the Newmarket October Sales.

Consigned by her breeder, William Hill, from his Whitsbury Manor Stud just over the county boundary into Hampshire, Emancipation scored at two and three years despite troublesome rheumatics in her shoulder. In due course she produced a superior daughter in Spree. She won the Nassau Stakes and was second in the 1000 Guineas (to Hula Dancer) and Oaks (to Noblesse).

Ironically it was to be Spree's inferior half-sister Set Free, a winner at Newbury on her three-year-old début, who was to earn all the accolades for Fonthill. However, because her first three offspring bore a closer resemblance to giraffes than racehorses, James Morrison and his wife Clare (sister to Mrs Toby Balding) decided to mate her with that well-proportioned little horse Blakeney, in whom they owned a share.

It proved a magic combination. Set Free was the very first mare he ever covered and the result was Juliette Marny. Equipped with blinkers, she won the 1975 Oaks and Irish Guinness Oaks and three years later her own-brother, Julio Mariner, won the St Leger. The top-priced yearling (40,000 guineas) at the October Sales, Julio Mariner was retired to the Ashley Heath Stud of his owner, Captain Marcos Lemos. After two seasons as a National Hunt sire in Herefordshire, he was exported to Holland.

Jim Morrison, who had taken over his father's bloodstock interests in 1972, the year that Juliette Marny was foaled, saw his colours carried to a second Oaks victory by the half-sister, Scintillate. Conceived at Whitsbury Manor by Sparkler, she was then sold to Sheikh Hamdan Al Maktoum for whom she bred the German Group scorer, Alshinfarah.

Juliette Marny, whose useful own-brother Saviour became a sire in India, bred a smart Mill Reef filly in the retained Jolly Bay (Pretty Polly Stakes, Newmarket). Two more of her offspring are North Briton, who was sold cheaply to Bill Gredley of Stetchworth Park Stud, and a Known Fact filly sold for 300,000 guineas at the 1985 Highflyer Sales.

Barren in 1989 for the first time in twenty-one years, Set Free is now retired under the eye of Fonthill stud groom Cyril Iggulden. As he has been there since 1965, he has known each and every one of her seventeen foals – nine are winners, seven of them by Blakeney.

A very experienced man with thoroughbreds, Cyril Iggulden once supervised the training of that fine chasing mare Thataway. Incidentally Fonthill has a link with top-level jumping as Lord Margadale used to stand the HIS stallion Blunderbuss and he sired the 1954 Cheltenham Gold Cup hero, Four Ten.

With a permanent band of between half a dozen and a dozen mares, Fonthill Stud extends to sixteen well-sheltered paddocks. Varying from greensand to a mixture of clay and chalk, they receive regular dressings of liquid sea-manure and are supplied by three different sources of spring water. As an appendage to a large agricultural estate combining arable with dairy and sheep, all the fodder and forage for the horses are home grown.

Accommodation amounts to three separate yards including the old stone-built hunter stabling on the edge of the park. The practice has invariably been to send weaned foals to be reared as yearlings at Blackhall Stud, Co Kildare, a procedure followed by both Juliette Marny and Julio Mariner. However no one is giving Ireland any credit for Set Free's unique record!

Gainsborough Stud

WOOLTON HILL · BERKSHIRE

With a stoically English name that is indelibly written into the annals of the Turf, Gainsborough Stud is owned by Sheikh Maktoum Al Maktoum. The new Ruler of Dubai and Deputy Prime Minister of the United Arab Emirates, he is the eldest of the four Arab racing brothers, followed by Sheikh Hamdan, Sheikh Mohammed and Sheikh Ahmed.

The stud is named after the Triple Crown hero of 1918, homebred by Lady James Douglas, who became the first lady to own a winner of the Derby, albeit a substitute affair at Newmarket. The horse took his name not from the famous artist but from the town in Lincolnshire, close to Limestone Stud.

Lady James Douglas, who was born in France into the Hennessy cognac family, married, as her second husband, Lord James Douglas, a younger son of the eighth Marquess of Queensberry. In 1910 she bought some agricultural land at Woolton Hill, south of Newbury, which she converted into a stud with the assistance of John Porter of Kingsclere.

Lady Douglas's trainer was Alec Taylor at Manton. In addition to Gainsborough, he saddled Bayuda to win the Oaks for her in 1919. She also bred Rose of England, heroine of the 1930 Oaks for patriotic Lord Glanely, and she became the foundation mare of Mrs Florence Nagle's Westerlands Stud. Lady Douglas died in 1941 when Harwood Stud, as the place was then called, was sold to Herbert Blagrave.

Gainsborough, who died aged thirty in 1945, is buried there. Having embarked upon stud life at a fee of 400 guineas in 1920, he was twice champion sire during a long and distinguished career. He gained immortality as the sire of Hyperion, one of the truly great progenitors of the twentieth century and champion sire on six occasions. Another of Gainsborough's sons, Solario, was also champion sire.

Herbert Blagrave, an all-round sportsman, who owned considerable property in Reading, was unique amongst his contemporaries as an owner-trainer-breeder. A licence holder from 1928 until his death in 1981, aged eighty-two, he ran a strictly private stable at Beckhampton Grange, opposite the more famous Beckhampton House establishment. He and his wife, Gwendoline, are commemorated at the Salisbury June fixture by the Herbert and Gwen Blagrave Memorial.

The great majority of Blagrave runners in the maroon and light blue hoops were homebred, and for over half a century he had a fine record at Ascot. The best he bred was probably Chinese Cracker (Ribblesdale Stakes), who was an unlucky second in the 1951 Oaks. Her half-brother China Rock became a champion sire in Japan. Ironically he sold Supertello as a yearling and he proceeded to win the Ascot Gold Cup. Another to be sold was champion hurdler, Anzio.

Herbert Blagrave, who ran Harwood Stud in conjunction with Mount Prospect Stud, Co. Kildare, to which weaned foals were sent every year, enjoyed a great deal of success with older horses, having the happy knack of keeping them sweet and in love with racing. He also had a penchant for French-breds and acquired a number from his friend Leon Volterra of the Haras du Bois Roussel.

One of them, Atout Maitre, became Blagrave's first stallion at Harwood Stud, taking up residence in 1941. He was succeeded in turn by Roi de Navarre, Tudor Minstrel, Match III and Reliance II. Sadly Match (King George VI and Queen Elizabeth Stakes) died from an impacted bowel after only three covering seasons. He was immediately replaced by his three-parts brother Reliance II (Prix du Jockey Club). Both horses were syndicated through the British Bloodstock Agency.

Michael Goodbody has been manager at Gainsborough Stud since 1973 when stud groom Stanley Digweed was just about to retire – he had worked there since 1920, the year that Gainsborough retired to stud. Goodbody succeeded Michael Forsyth-Forrest (a nephew of Gwen Blagrave), who also doubled up as manager at Highclere Stud to the late Lord Carnarvon.

The year before he died, Herbert Blagrave sold the property to James McCaughey, a jumping enthusiast from the Midlands. As a nucleus of Bla-grave's own mares remained in residence trading as Harwood Stud Ltd, the name of the stud was changed to Gainsborough. Sheikh Maktoum Al Maktoum was not inclined to alter the title yet again when taking over in the autumn of 1981.

Since that time the stud has been completely modernized, but with tradi-tional stabling rather than with American barns which predominate today. This blends in with the most up-to-date and luxurious administrative offices from which Michael Goodbody supervises the Sheikh's extensive racing and breeding empire (former jockey Joe Mercer is racing manager) on both sides of the Atlantic.

Initially Maktoum Al Maktoum was much the most successful of the brothers on the racecourse with the classic winners Touching Wood (St Leger, Irish St Leger), Shareef Dancer (Irish Sweeps Derby), Ma Biche (1000 Guineas) and Shadeed (2000 Guineas), not to mention such top sprinters as Green Desert, Lead on Time and Cadeaux Genereux.

None of these horses has ever stood at Gainsborough Stud as it is strictly a private establishment for its owner's own broodmare band. By the 1990s this had expanded to around 130 head. About half are maintained at Woodpark Stud, Co. Meath, which Sheikh Mohammed gave to his brother in the spring of 1989, with the remainder divided between Gainsborough Stud and Gainsborough Farm in Kentucky – this is also the home of Shadeed. Weaned foals from Woolton Hill are sent to Woodpark.

Since paying a record 730,000 guineas for Greenland Park (carrying Fitnah) at the 1981 Newmarket December Sales, Sheikh Maktoum Al Maktoum has invested heavily in fillies. In 1984 Maysoon cost 540,000 guineas. Placed in both fillies' classics, she was an appropriate winner of the Gainsborough Stud Fred Darling Stakes.

Garrowby Stud

GARROWBY · YORK

Throughout the present century, Yorkshire, historically the cradle of the Thoroughbred, has been losing ground to Newmarket as the centre for bloodstock breeding in the United Kingdom, an irreversible decline with the enormous Arab involvement in Newmarket during the 1980s and into the present decade.

Although studs like Burton Agnes and Sledmere have long since forfeited their place at the top of the commercial league table, Yorkshire continues to produce top-class horses. Since the war they have been responsible for four English classic winners with Shirley Heights (Garrowby Stud), winner of the Derby, Caergwrle (Cliff Stud) and Mrs McArdy (Westow Hall Stud), both winners of the 1000 Guineas, and Peleid (Swinton Grange Stud), winner of the St Leger.

Shirley Heights is the first Derby winner to be accredited to a Yorkshire stud since Dante scored in a substitute race at Newmarket in 1945. His status as Yorkshire bred rests upon the fact that his joint breeders are the present Lord Halifax and his late father (who died in 1980) of Garrowby Stud which lies on the western edge of the Yorkshire Wolds. They founded the stud jointly in 1962 on the family estate.

One has to concede that Shirley Heights is by no means Yorkshire 'born and bred'. Conceived at the National Stud by the great Mill Reef, he was actually foaled at Lady (Ruth) Halifax's Swynford Paddocks Stud on the outskirts of Newmarket, where he was reared for the first four months of his life before departing to Garrowby as a weanling.

Ruth Halifax, who died in 1989, was a very successful breeder in her own right as she was entitled to be. Her paternal grandfather was the 5th Earl of Rosebery and her maternal grandfather was the 17th Earl of Derby, two of the most eminent breeders of the present century. Following the sale of Swynford Paddocks in 1977, Ruth Halifax established her own Low

94

House Stud on the Garrowby Estate, the policy being to offer foals at the Newmarket December Sales.

Converted from a neglected farmstead, previously called Cheesecake Farm, Garrowby Stud was started from scratch by the present Lord Halifax (then Lord Irwin) and his father, Charles. Although a nucleus of mares was acquired at the 1963 Newmarket December Sales, it was the simultaneous gift of Ruth Halifax's homebred Daylight that proved significant.

Daylight, one of fourteen winning offspring from the 1000 Guineas third, Light of Day, became the dam of Grey God (Joe Coral Northumberland Plate) and the grandam of Bedtime. This Bustino gelding carried Peter Halifax's light blue and chocolate colours to four Group wins and was runner-up in the 1984 Japan Cup.

Whereas Bedtime was trained by Major Dick Hern, Shirley Heights (Mill Reef – Hardiemma) was entrusted to John Dunlop. He looked to have classic potential in winning the Royal Lodge Stakes and so it proved, the colt bringing off the English and Irish (Sweeps) Derby double. Sadly a strained tendon during preparation for the St Leger prevented him from staying in training as a four-year-old. He covered his first mares at Sandringham in 1979.

Although not fashionably bred on the distaff side, Shirley Heights (syndicated by the BBA for £1.6 million) has proved a classic progenitor. Two of his best sons are Darshaan (Prix du Jockey Club), sire of Aliysa, and Slip Anchor, who emulated his sire and grandsire in winning the (Ever Ready) Derby.

According to John Johnson, who has been stud groom at Garrowby since the stud was founded, the facilities there were hardly adequate for yearlings when Shirley Heights was foaled in 1975. Consequently most of the young stock were submitted for sale as foals. However as Shirley Heights was one of only two colts that year, it was decided to retain him! Present policy is to sell the majority of yearling colts and retain the fillies.

The Halifaxes were not so fortunate with Hardiemma. Having purchased her at the 1973 December Sales, carrying to Upper Case, for 12,000 guineas, they sold her at the same venue three years later for 15,000 guineas, in foal to Mill Reef. The resulting filly then realized an Irish auction record of 250,000 guineas in the year that her own-brother won the Derby.

Fortuitously Hardiemma, who once belonged to Robert Acton of Dalham Hall Stud, left behind a fine broodmare prospect in Bempton. She is responsible for three Group winners in as many years with Gull Nook (Ribblesdale Stakes), Mr Pintips (Ormonde Stakes), runner-up in the 1990 Irish St Leger, and Banket (Princess Royal Stakes). Both Gull Nook, a three-parts sister to Shirley Heights, and Banket are now Garrowby broodmares.

Blakeney is another National Stud stalwart to do well for the Halifaxes. The sire of Bempton, he is also responsible for the retained Mountain Lodge. Bred by the present Lord Halifax, she carried his colours to victory in the 1983 Jefferson Smurfit Memorial Irish St Leger as well as the Tote Cesarewitch. The three-parts sisters, Lake Naivasha and Hymettus, are also smart homebred Blakeney fillies.

Garrowby's proximity to Burton Agnes has proved significant as it was the late Marcus Wickham-Boynton who gave the stud Mountain Lodge's ageing grandam Eyewash. From the same source came Maurine, dam of Belper. This Busted gelding won a multitude of races for Lady Sarah Fitzalan Howard who named him after her uncle – both had the misfortune to lose the sight of an eye.

So far the best winner that Garrowby has bred to Shirley Heights is the useful stayer, El Conquistador, now a National Hunt stallion at Hart Hill Stud in Dorset. A 290,000-guinea yearling in 1984, he is the Halifaxes' highest-priced yearling to date.

With a remarkably high percentage of winners to foals, Garrowby Stud ranks as one of the most successful privately owned studs in the country. The Halifax runners always have a big following locally at York and nothing gives them greater pleasure than a winner at the festival meeting in August.

Gazeley Stud

NEWMARKET · SUFFOLK

Owned by Patrick McCalmont, chairman of the Newmarket Stud Farmers' Association, Gazeley Stud is situated between Dalham and Gazeley. Dalham was described by John Betjeman as 'the loveliest village of west Suffolk'. Prior to 1970 when the late James Philipps sold the stud to the present owner, it was known as Dalham Hall Stud.

The original Dalham Hall Stud was part of a 4,000-acre estate which had belonged to Cecil Rhodes, but the stud dates back to the nineteenth century and at one time Lily Langtry, the Jersey Lily, kept mares here. It was resurrected for stud purposes by Jim Philipps's father, the 1st Lord Milford. He bought it in 1928 to stand Flamingo, winner of that year's 2000 Guineas.

Flamingo was joined there by his year junior three-parts brother Horus, winner of the King Edward VII Stakes, both colts having been yearling purchases from Worksop Manor Stud in the 1920s. Each spent the duration of his stallion life at Dalham, Flamingo siring Lord Milford's homebred Flyon, hero of the 1939 Ascot Gold Cup.

Lord Milford, whose fortune was derived from shipping (founder of the Court Line) and insurance, was able to buy Lady Peregrine, dam of Flamingo and Horus, at the dispersal of Sir John Robinson's bloodstock in 1929. The mare subsequently produced Horus's own-sister, Honey Buzzard. She is dam of Honeyway who in turn sired Great Nephew, both stalwarts of the new Dalham Hall Stud.

After returning from the war, Jim Philipps, who died in 1984, took over the running of the old Dalham Hall Stud where he stood three stallions bred by Federico Tesio: Nakamuro, Naucide and Nicolaus. However of far greater consequence was Grey Sovereign (Nasrullah – Kong). He was owned by Lincolnshire farmer and breeder Jack Measures.

Having spent five seasons at Derisley Wood Stud, Grey Sovereign remained at Gazeley Stud from 1958 to 1970. Transferred to Keith Freeman's Bergh Apton Stud, outside Norwich, he died there in 1976 having just attained his twenty-eighth birthday. When Tattersalls built their modern sales emporium, Keith Freeman re-erected the old sales ring through which Grey Sovereign was sold as a yearling and this marked his last resting place.

Grey Sovereign became a noted sire of sires. His most influential son was Zeddaan, sire of Kalamoun, both winners of the French 2000 Guineas. Zeddaan was conceived at the old Dalham Hall Stud as was Money for Nothing, dam of another major sire of sires in Mummy's Pet.

Just as soon as Pat McCalmont had concluded negotiations for the purchase of what is now Gazeley Stud, he set about finding a suitable stallion. His choice fell upon Hotfoot (Firestreak – Pitter Patter). In fact he bought him prior to the 1970 Champion Stakes in which he finished third to Lorenzaccio and Nijinsky.

Also runner-up in the Irish 2000 Guineas, Hotfoot was still covering mares at the advanced age of twenty-five in 1991. Longevity runs in the male line as his sire Firestreak lived to twenty-four and his grandsire Pardal to twenty-two. The highlight of Hotfoot's stud career came in 1977 when his sons Tachypous and Hot Grove finished second in the 2000 Guineas and Derby respectively.

Tachypous has a particular significance to Gazeley Stud as he was bred and raised there, his dam being the celebrated Stilvi. The comparatively rare combination of a brilliant race-filly and an equally brilliant progenitor, she won four Group sprints. Owner George Cambanis was anxious that Stilvi should be boarded at a Newmarket stud and, as Bruce Hobbs had also trained Hotfoot, Gazeley Stud was an obvious choice. Tachypous (Greek for fleet of foot) was her first foal, but she produced four more black-type winners in Tromos (William Hill Dewhurst Stakes), who headed the International Classification at two years, Tyrnavos (Irish Sweeps Derby), Tolmi (Coronation Stakes), and Taxiarchos.

After standing at various locations in this country, Tachypous was dispatched to the Cambanis-owned family stud in Greece. Meanwhile Tyrnavos (named after the Greek village where Ouzo originates) stood alongside Hotfoot from 1981 to 1985 when exported to Japan. Tromos died after just two covering seasons in the USA and Taxiarchos became a sire in South Africa.

Another of Stilvi's progeny to hit the headlines is Tenea. A cracked bone in a knee restricted her to one racecourse appearance as a two-year-old. At the following year's Newmarket December Sales she was sold by George Cambanis's widow, Lenior, for 1,020,000 guineas to a Niarchos/Sangster syndicate. Tenea was the first thoroughbred millionaire at auction in Great Britain or Ireland.

For the 1988 season Hotfoot was joined at Gazeley Stud by the well-named Sizzling Melody (Song – Mrs Bacon) and once again Pat McCalmont acquired an interest during the horse's racing career, in this instance upon the conclusion of his two-year-old days. Successful in three Group sprints and runner-up to Ajdal in the William Hill Sprint Championship, Sizzling Melody was trained by Lord John Fitzgerald, formerly assistant to Bruce Hobbs. Song was a great commercial success and Sizzling Melody has the credentials to do likewise.

For a number of years Pat McCalmont, whose father owned The Tetrarch, was a partner with his late mother, June, and two brothers, Hugh and Michael, in Martinstown Stud, Co. Limerick. Amongst the good winners bred there was Hotfoot's son, Free State (Waterford Crystal Mile). He stood at Barleythorpe Stud before being exported to South Africa.

Hadrian Stud

NEWMARKET · SUFFOLK

As it is now used exclusively as an annexe for mares visiting the Dalham Hall stallions, Hadrian Stud is one of Sheikh Mohammed's properties which has virtually lost its own identity.

About 1930, Grimsby trawler king, Sir Alec Black, founded the Compton Park Stud on two arable farms situated between Woodditton Road and Duchess Drive. They were known as Ditton Lodge Farm and Derisley Wood Farm, 840 acres which now also include Sheikh Mohammed's Hadrian and Derisley Wood Studs, as well as most of the land belonging to the old Someries Stud.

At the outset of the thirties, Alec Black bred two classic winners in Brown Betty (1000 Guineas) and Colombo (2000 Guineas). The latter raced for Lord Glanely. He had already won the St Leger with the Alec Black-bred Singapore, who had been reared at Compton Stud (now Sandley Stud) in Dorset.

Sir Alec's novel idea of ranching his horses never really materialized as ill health forced him to reduce his involvement in breeding and in 1932 Ditton Lodge and a substantial number of mares were sold to Lord Glanely. Bearing in mind their joint bloodstock involvement, it was coincidental that both Black and Glanely died on 28 June 1942.

In 1947 Sir David Wills (knighted in 1980) acquired that part of the Compton Park Stud which had been named Hadrian Stud by a Mr A.A. Lyons during the war. For more than thirty years his stud manager was Lieutenant-Colonel Douglas Gray. Subsequently Director of the National Stud, he transformed Hadrian into one of the best-appointed private studs in the Newmarket area.

David Wills's early involvement in ownership saw his blue and white colours carried into second place in three Newmarket classics – by Growing Confidence in the 2000 Guineas, and by Unknown Quantity and (homebred) Subtle Difference in the 1000 Guineas. Then in 1953 he hit the jackpot.

That season Happy Laughter, whom trainer Sir Jack Jarvis had procured as a yearling for 3,500 guineas, was rated the leading member of her sex after winning the 1000 Guineas. It was a remarkable achievement as she had not long undergone an operation for severe sinusitis. Unfortunately Happy Laughter was an abject failure in the paddocks.

An altruistic member of the tobacco family, David Wills established a top-quality broodmare band, but all of a sudden he decided to curtail his activities, consigning most of his stock to the 1958 Newmarket December Sales.

Top price of 11,000 guineas was paid for the barren mare, Auld Alliance, whose two-year-old Tomy Lee had been making a name for himself in the USA. The next year he became the first British-bred winner of the Kentucky Derby since Omar Khayyam (bred by Worksop Manor Stud) in 1917.

Hadrian Stud's 1958 crop of foals included two significant fillies. One, Plaza, became dam of 1969 St Leger hero Intermezzo. The other was Tomy Lee's half-sister, Due Respect, destined to become the grandam of 1980 Kentucky Derby heroine, Genuine Risk.

Typical of David Wills's luck, Auskerry, a grandson of Auld Alliance, failed to come up to classic aspirations after winning the Hyperion Stakes, Ascot. His interests in stallions fared no better, Right Boy, Tutankhamen and Sallymount all being major disappointments. However Rocket, a colt of his own breeding, was to excel as a sire in Germany.

Much of the emphasis at Hadrian Stud during the sixties and seventies revolved around boarders. They yielded a real star in Noblesse. The easiest Oaks winner in living memory, she is ancestress of two Khalid Abdullah celebrities in Rainbow Quest and Warning, both now resident at his Banstead Manor Stud.

Bruce Hobbs succeeded Jack Jarvis as David Wills's principal trainer and three fillies with whom he did well were the yearling purchases Hecla, Rotisserie and Sleat.

Hecla had finished runner-up to Mill Reef in the Imperial Stakes, Kempton Park. At stud they combined to produce a colt (Teddington Park) who topped the 1975 Newmarket October Yearling Sales at 75,000 guineas.

In 1981 Hadrian Stud was bought by Souren and Garo Vanian, who already owned the adjoining Derisley Wood Stud. Most of David Wills's mares had been sold at the preceding year's December Sales. The few that he kept, including Sleat, were dispatched to his St Clare Hall Farm, near Bury St Edmunds.

Although Sleat (Sun Chariot Stakes) has bred nothing of note for her owner, her daughters have done well for others – Just You Wait is dam of Reprimand, now a National Stud stallion; Kristana is dam of Ozone Friendly; and Little Loch Broom is dam of Soft Currency. The last named was bred by Peter and Catherine Player of Whatton Manor Stud in Nottinghamshire. Peter, who succeeded Douglas Gray as manager of Hadrian Stud in January 1971, continues to supervise the Wills's mares which are now permanent residents at Whatton in the Vale.

During the Vanian era, which lasted until they ran into financial difficulties in 1986, Hadrian Stud provided a base not only for their own sizeable broodmare band but also for a nucleus of mares owned by Daniel Wildenstein.

Amongst the Wildenstein boarders were All Along and Pawneese, and two distinguished producers in Seneca, dam of Sagace, and Southern Seas, dam of Steinlen. Carrying the GB suffix, Steinlen, who triumphed in the 1989 Breeders' Cup Mile at Gulfstream Park, was foaled at Hadrian prior to his dam visiting the Derisley Wood resident Glint of Gold.

Now that so many of the top-class mares booked to the Dalham Hall horses congregate at Hadrian Stud, there should be many more important winners bred there, but it will be very much a case of reflected glory only.

Hascombe Stud

NEWMARKET · SUFFOLK

Invariably accidents to racehorses involve the good ones, as Sir Philip Oppenheimer and his son, Anthony, know only too well. In November 1990, Sally Rous sustained fatal injuries on a return flight from New York after finishing second in the Budweiser Breeders' Cup at Aqueduct. Five months later Welney died at Newmarket after fracturing his pelvis on the gallops.

Both were scheduled to remain in training with Geoffrey Wragg as four-year-olds for the 1991 season. Ironically they were the Oppenheimers' most recent homebred Group winners. Sally Rous had excelled over seven furlongs as a three-year-old, winning the Jersey Stakes and Jameson Irish Whiskey Challenge Stakes; Welney, who was later gelded, had won the Rokeby Farms Mill Reef Stakes as a two-year-old.

Hascombe Stud, which is situated a couple of miles outside Newmarket, opposite Sandwich Stud, between the villages of Cheveley and Ashley, was purchased by Philip Oppenheimer in November 1965. Former chairman of the Diamond Trading Company, a subsidiary of De Beers, sponsors of the King George VI and Queen Elizabeth Diamond Stakes, he had previously kept some mares with his old friend Nicky Morriss at neighbouring Banstead Manor Stud. The operation was labelled Hascombe and Valiant Studs after his daughter, Valerie, and his son, Anthony — he is a former chairman of the Thoroughbred Breeders' Association.

Now extended to 160 acres, Hascombe Stud, with its ornate thatched roofs, was bought from the executors of Sir Adrian Jarvis, he having inherited the property from his father, John, the first baronet, in 1950. At the time Adrian Jarvis had not been keen on racing and would probably have dispersed the stud but for Tessa Gillian (Nearco – Sun Princess). From that year's crop of foals, she won the Molecomb Stakes and was runner-up in the 1000 Guineas.

Tessa Gillian was own-sister to Royal Charger, the best horse bred by Jimmy Jarvis. Third to Court Martial and Dante in a vintage 2000 Guineas, he was sold for £50,000 to the Irish National Stud *en route* to the USA where he started a male dynasty.

Jimmy Jarvis had founded Hascombe Stud (named after his home near Godalming) in 1936. Sun Princess, who was destined to become the foundation mare, was acquired privately two years later at the Deauville yearling sales from her breeder, the Aga Khan. She was by Solario out of Mumtaz Begum, dam of Royal Charger's three-parts brother, Nasrullah.

Tessa Gillian bred two smart colts for Adrian Jarvis in Test Case (Gimcrack Stakes) and Gentle Art (Richmond Stakes). In 1955 the mare produced twins, one of whom, Courtessa, was culled, prior to breeding top sprinter D'Urberville. Later the Oppenheimers procured his three-parts sister, Lora, as a yearling for 28,000 guineas. For them she bred three fillies, the intermediate of them being On the House, who triumphed in the 1982 1000 Guineas and Sussex Stakes. That was a memorable Goodwood for the Oppenheimers as Dancing Rocks, another homebred filly, defeated Oaks heroine Time Charter for the Nassau Stakes.

Sir Philip Oppenheimer has always had his horses trained in Newmarket, first by Charlie Elliot, the great Boussac stable jockey, then by Humphrey Cottrill, Harry Wragg and the latter's son, Geoffrey. A pioneer in exploiting his horses overseas, Harry Wragg trained Pelerin to win the Grosser Preis von Baden.

Pelerin, by Royal Charger's very influential grandson, Sir Gaylord, also won the Hardwicke Stakes and John Porter Stakes after finishing fourth in the 1980 Derby. The subject of lengthy litigation after his sale to the USA, Pelerin is almost certainly the leading colt bred by the Oppenheimers.

The Hascombe broodmare band is usually around the twenty mark and the oldest established of their female families is also proving one of the most successful. Back in 1959 the mare Stop Your Tickling was acquired privately from Airlie Stud. To a mating with the Banstead Manor resident Ballymoss she foaled Miba. She was one of the top staying fillies of her generation and so too was her daughter, African Dancer (Park Hill Stakes), who was third in the 1976 Oaks. She in turn is responsible for On Show, dam of two Group 2 winners in diminutive Inchmurrin (Child Stakes) and Welney.

Although the Oppenheimer colours, black, white and red, have been victorious at Royal Ascot, one particular race there, the Coronation Stakes, has proved a real bogey affair. In 1979 Buz Kashi actually finished first at the expense of One in a Million, only to suffer disqualification, whereas

Sea Lichen, Dancing Rocks, Inchmurrin and her three-parts sister, Guest Artiste, have all been placed.

Both On the House and Guest Artiste are by Be My Guest, and the Oppenheimers owned another excellent miler by the same sire in Most Welcome. Purchased from his owner-breeder, the late Eric Moller, after finishing third to Reference Point in the 1987 Ever Ready Derby, Most Welcome won the Juddmonte Lockinge Stakes as a five-year-old before being syndicated to stand at Meddler Stud, Newmarket. He will have his first crop of runners in 1993.

Another major star for the Oppenheimer camp was the 1978 King George VI and Queen Elizabeth Diamond Stakes hero, Ile de Bourbon, in whom Sir Philip owned thirty per cent. After seven seasons at Banstead Manor, he was exported to Japan. No sooner had he departed than his runners started to do well, amongst them Petite Ile. Heroine of the 1989 Jefferson Smurfit Memorial Irish St Leger, she had been sold by Hascombe Stud, 'in utero'.

Newmarket studs certainly seem to distribute their share of long-service medals and Hascombe is no exception. John Thomson joined Sir Adrian Jarvis as stud groom in June 1947 and retired as manager in September 1986. He died four years later, just before the retirement of stud groom Jack Cates – he had been there for over forty years. The present manager, Walter Cowe, is brother to Jim, stud manager to Prince Khalid Abdullah at Juddmonte Farms, Wargrave-on-Thames.

Heatherwold Stud

BURGHCLERE · BERKSHIRE

All too often the death of an eminent breeder results in the dispersal of his or her breeding stock. Fortunately when Lady Sefton died in 1980, Captain and Mrs Peter Longton, who had boarded the Sefton animals at their Heatherwold Stud, were able to buy them from the executors at a probate valuation thus maintaining this nucleus of mares in one hand. The transaction was to yield a dividend beyond all reasonable expectations.

Mrs Longton, who has persevered with the stud following the death of her nonagenarian husband in the autumn of 1989, keeps about a dozen mares of her own which descend from Lord Sefton's foundation mare, Nassau (Nasrullah – Meraline). She had cost 2,100 guineas as a yearling from Banstead Manor Stud back in 1948.

Heatherwold's postal address is Burghclere in Berkshire, but it is actually a few miles south of Newbury on the edge of Watership Down in Hampshire. It was here that the Longtons started breeding operations in a small way in 1959 with the inestimable assistance of their long-serving stud manager, Mrs Ann Jenkins. The name of the stud is owed to the pre-war owners, Heatherwold Dairies in Newbury.

Elisabeth Longton is Norwegian and her decision to start a stud in England was motivated by the filly Cecilie whom she bred in her native country. Raced by her uncle, Sir Thomas Fearnley, Cecilie proved one of the best performers ever in Scandinavia. Her seventeen victories from five furlongs to two-and-a-half miles, included the Derby, Gold Cup, and three runnings of the Eclipse Stakes equivalent.

The doyen of Norwegian racing, Thomas Fearnley is commemorated by the Fearnleylopet, a major race at Ovrevoll. Elisabeth Longton's daughter, Mrs Lars Christensen, is a prominent owner in Norway, she and her late husband winning the 1977 Oslo Cup with Brave Tudor. Not long ago

Mrs Longton set up a trust fund to ensure the continuance of the Heather-wold Cup, a two-year-old race at Ovrevoll on Derby Day.

Initially the Longtons had horses in training with Major Peter Nelson in Upper Lambourn. Outstanding amongst them was the luckless Final Court. One of the leading two-year-olds of 1955, he was beaten a short head and a head for the Middle Park Stakes. Final Court never recaptured his juvenile form and it transpired that he had been the victim of dopers.

Heatherwold Stud established a reputation second to none for boarders. Ideally situated with its proximity to Lambourn and all the other training stables on the Berkshire and Wiltshire Downs, it soon became recognized as a centre for both flat horses and jumpers requiring a change of scenery. Just about every one of Fred Winter's many celebrities enjoyed a sojourn with the Longtons.

By the 1990s the permanent broodmare band was in excess of thirty, of which nearly two thirds were owned by outsiders, many of them foreign nationals. One of the first owner-breeders to avail himself of the stud's amenities was the late Sir Brian Mountain. Also a patron of Peter Nelson's stable, he owned a top mare in Victorina, heroine of the Stewards' Cup.

The first winner of Group status bred by Heatherwold Stud was Sir David Robinson's Old and Wise (Prix Thomas Bryon), a leading two-year-old in 1970. Three years later the stud gained a new dimension with the arrival of Lady Sefton's mares from the family stud at Croxteth, outside Liverpool, following the death of her husband. They included Antigua (Hyperion – Nassau).

The last of the Hyperion mares, Antigua (Galtres Stakes), put down in December 1979 aged twenty-one, produced three winners for Heather-wold Stud in Derrylin, Fiesta Fun and Treasure Hunter. Derrylin scored three consecutive Group victories for Lady Sefton before becoming a suc-cessful sire in England – for an interim period he stood in Italy. Treasure Hunter, who topped the 1980 Newmarket October Sales, won the North-umberland Plate as an eight-year-old entire.

Antigua was mated with Welsh Pageant to produce two distinguished Heatherwold broodmares in Anegada and Fiesta Fun. The former is dam of John French (Gordon Stakes). He was bought as a yearling by Charles St George and so too was Saumarez (Rainbow Quest – Fiesta Fun), one of his sire's first crop who cost 45,000 guineas at the 1988 Highflyer Sales.

Saumarez won two races for St George before being sold for a reputed $400,000 to continue his three-year-old career in France. Switched from Henry Cecil to Nicolas Clement, the Rainbow Quest colt proceeded to win three French Group races with brilliant victories in the Ciga Prix de l'Arc de Triomphe (in the customary star-studded field) and Grand Prix de Paris Louis Vuitton. He was then retired to start covering at Haras du Quesnay in 1991.

Fiesta Fun, dam of Saumarez, was a two-year-old when Lady Sefton died. Racing in the colours of Spike Kirby, MR CVS, who acted as veterinary adviser to Heatherwold Stud, she scored four times and was placed third in the Yorkshire Oaks (Group I), and Hoover Fillies' Mile.

Spike Kirby and his partner, Edward Kessly, are commercial breeders aiming for the Highflyer Sales. They have done well over the years with the progeny of two American-bred mares, Bold Flawless, dam of Life at the Top (Waterford Candelabra Stakes), and Allegedly Blue. Life at the Top was one of a draft of six yearlings (all of whom won) that Heatherwold sold for 1.3 million guineas at the 1987 Highflyer Sales when the stud was the fourth leading vendor.

Neither Mrs Longton nor her late husband ever sought publicity for their stud, its continued success as a boarding establishment being owed to personal recommendation. For a number of years Elisabeth Longton has had the occasional horse in training at Beckhampton, first with Jeremy Tree and then with Roger Charlton, but the great majority of the animals she breeds are consigned to Tattersalls' yearling sales. The Heatherwold draft is always turned out in immaculate order. That reflects the dedication of stud manager Ann Jenkins, and her staff headed by stud groom Ian Bailey, who used to be head lad to Peter Makin at Ogbourne Maisey.

Hesmonds Stud

EAST HOATHLY · EAST SUSSEX

The Greek shipping families are not involved in racing to the same extent as the Arabs, but they have made a significant contribution. Stavros Niarchos has studs in France (Haras de Fresnay-le-Buffard) and the USA (Spring Oak Farm), where he bred Miesque. Captain Marcos Lemos, former owner of Ashley Heath and Warren Hill Studs in Newmarket, is the breeder of Pebbles.

Less well known, but an influential breeder none the less, is their compatriot, Peter Goulandris, of Hesmonds Stud in East Sussex. Chairman of the Hellenic Foundation, Peter is based in London from where he controls the Capeside Steamship Company Ltd, the family shipping interests also having headquarters in Athens and New York.

Peter, who shuns publicity, shared a love of shipping and racing with his late father George Goulandris. Before the Second World War, George had horses in partnership with his cousin, George Cambanis (who also came from the island of Andros) and both were prominent members of the Greek Jockey Club. More recently George Cambanis owned that great filly Stilvi.

George Goulandris and his brother, Constantin, were also involved in racing and breeding in France where they had the Haras de la Louviere in Normandy. In 1962 George won the Oaks and Prix Vermeille with Monade, the grandam of Sadeem. Nowadays Peter Goulandris concentrates on Hesmonds while his cousin Chryss runs La Louviere where Le Glorieux was bred – this trades as Petra Bloodstock.

A friend of Claude Harper, founder of the London Bloodstock Agency, George Goulandris always consulted the agency's Raymond Barnes about horses and it was through him that Peter acquired his first notable performer, Shoemaker. Trained by Peter Walwyn to finish runner-up to Blakeney in the 1969 Derby, Shoemaker retired to La Louviere, but died from laminitis after only three seasons.

In 1971 Peter Goulandris bought Hesmonds Stud, which is situated between East Hoathly and Halland, adjacent to the London–Eastbourne road, from the widow of Lieutenant-Commander Dawson Miller. A Lloyds' broker (his nephew, Sir Peter Miller, became chairman of Lloyds), Dawson Miller had horses in training locally with Auriol Sinclair and bred Irish Oaks heroine Garden State.

Peter Goulandris's mother was also a patron of the Lewes stable. When Peter was searching for a stud manager, he chose Jimmy McNaught. The former National Hunt jockey, who had ridden for his mother, took up his new appointment in the autumn of 1977.

Since then Hesmonds Stud has been extended to 500 acres (about ten times its original size) to become one of the largest and most successful commercial yearling studs in the country. From 1978 to 1990, 113 yearlings have aggregated over 10 million guineas at the Highflyer or equivalent sales where it has been the top UK vendor on six occasions.

Jimmy McNaught arrived at an exciting time. At the previous year's December Sales Hesmonds Stud procured the top-priced filly Duboff for 100,000 guineas, while the following year was the turn of the week's second most expensive filly, Triple First, at 118,000 guineas. Both were high-class race fillies with victories in the Sun Chariot Stakes to their credit.

In the interim Peter Goulandris's green and blue colours had been carried to victory in the William Hill Middle Park Stakes and Mill Reef Stakes by Formidable whom Ray Barnes had purchased as a yearling for $60,000. Later Formidable took up residence at Lavington Stud, amongst his sons being the stallions Chilibang, Efisio, Forzando and Reasonable, the last bred by Petra Bloodstock.

Whereas Duboff has proved a disappointing matron, Triple First has been exactly the reverse. Mated with Derby winners, she has produced two runners placed in the Gold Seal Oaks. In 1986 Maysoon (by Shergar) was third to Midway Lady to whom she had finished runner-up in the General Accident 1000 Guineas; next year Three Tails (by Blakeney) was third at Epsom to Unite. Both Highflyer yearlings, they cost the Maktoum brothers 540,000 guineas and 290,000 guineas respectively.

The best colt bred by Hesmonds is probably Terimon (Bustino – Nicholas Grey). This grey cost the Dowager Lady Beaverbrook, who raced the sire, top price of 140,000 guineas at the 1987 Newmarket October Sales. Twice winner of the Earl of Sefton Stakes and placed in a succession of top races, Terimon finished runner-up to Nashwan in the 1989 Ever Ready Derby at 500–1. Two more top colts are Pas de Seul (Prix de la Forêt) and My

Top (Derby Italiano). Both stood in Ireland before departing overseas, the former to Japan and the latter to Italy.

Just recently another Hesmonds filly has been holding centre stage. Acquired 'in utero' from Stackallen Stud, Infamy was sold as a yearling for 100,000 guineas to Gerald Leigh of Eydon Hall Farm. The grey by Shirley Heights won the Cheveley Park Stud Sun Chariot Stakes at three years and the Rothmans' International at Woodbine in Canada as a four-year-old.

Hesmonds Stud, which has sold thirty-nine six-figure yearlings to 1990, also provides a significant number of animals to race in Peter Goulandris's own colours. His principal trainers are Francois Boutin in France and Peter Walwyn at Lambourn. The colts are invariably those that failed to make their reserves.

Nowadays Hesmonds Stud is divided into two parts. The main stud buildings and administrative offices are at Annandale Farm which is where the mares and foals are based. The yearlings, which are the responsibility of David Walters, an international show judge, are concentrated at Tourles Farm on land that comprised the original stud. The total of 400 stud acres incorporates thirty-seven paddocks and some 120 boxes, with four American barns as well as traditional stabling.

Hesmonds Stud's quest for top mares continues unabated. At the 1990 December Sales, Princess Pati (Gilltown Stud Irish Oaks), carrying to Sadler's Wells, was bought for 750,000 guineas, more than twice the price of any other lot catalogued.

Highclere Stud

Highclere Stud, owned and managed by the 7th Earl of Carnarvon, a great stalwart of the Thoroughbred Breeders' Association, has an idyllic setting. In a sheltered bowl between Sidown, the highest point in Hampshire, and Beacon Hill, it is at Burghclere, five miles south of Newbury adjacent to the busy A34 which has recently been rerouted through the periphery of the estate.

Dominating the property is Highclere Castle, which was rebuilt in the 1840s by Sir Charles Barry, architect of the Houses of Parliament, set in glorious parkland laid out by Capability Brown. Highclere has been in the Herbert family since the eighteenth century. It was General Henry Herbert who was created Earl of Carnarvon by George III for quelling the Gordon Riots, caused by opposition to a bill of equal rights for Catholics in 1780.

The systematic breeding of thoroughbreds at Highclere dates back to the turn of the present century under the 5th Earl, the present Lord Carnarvon's grandfather. The famous Egyptologist, many of whose artefacts from the Valley of the Kings can be viewed by the public at the castle, bred Valens, runner-up to Bayardo in the 1909 St Leger.

Both Valens and Robert le Diable, a yearling acquisition at Deauville, stood at Highclere. Winner of the Doncaster Cup, Robert le Diable was an inconsequential sire, but he left an indelible mark at the family stud with Wild Arum, dam of Highclere's most famous broodmare, Malva, who never measured more than 15 hands.

The 6th Earl inherited Malva, three times a winner and then in her first stud season, upon the death of his father in 1923. An irregular breeder, prone to frequent attacks of colic, she produced three distinguished sons in Blenheim (1927, by Blandford), King Salmon (1930, by Salmon Trout), and His Grace (1933, by Blandford). Porchey Carnarvon always maintained that it was preferable to sell and regret than to keep and regret. Consequently all three colts achieved renown in other colours. Blenheim won the 1930 Derby for the Aga Khan, King Salmon won the Coronation Cup and Eclipse Stakes for Sir Richard Brooke, and His Grace dead-heated in the Coronation Cup for James V. Rank.

A 4,100-guinea yearling, Blenheim joined Carnarvon's trainer, Dick Dawson, at Whatcombe – he had also handled Blandford. In due course the Aga Khan sold Blenheim and his Derby winning son, Mahmoud, to the USA, where they exerted a profound influence. Before departing, Blenheim sired Mumtaz Begum, dam of Nasrullah, and Donatello II, sire of Alycidon and Crepello.

His Grace actually stood at Highclere, which between the wars was home to the Aga Khan flag-bearers Diophon (2000 Guineas), Salmon Trout (St Leger), and Felicitation (Ascot Gold Cup). However during that period Porchey Carnarvon was preoccupied with riding as an amateur, the stud being run by his resident land agent, Marcus Wickham-Boynton.

Since the last war, stallions at Highclere have included Chanteur II, Darius, Pandofell, Queen's Hussar, Homing, Troy, and the present residents Teenoso and Sharrood. Both Chanteur and Queen's Hussar became champion sires, the former thanks to 1953 Derby winner, Pinza, and the latter in 1972 by virtue of champion miler Brigadier Gerard.

Tragically Troy died from a perforated gut after only three covering seasons. His replacement is Teenoso. Another star to have completed the Derby and King George VI and Queen Elizabeth Diamond Stakes double, he was part of the package deal which Sheikh Mohammed negotiated for White Lodge Stud in 1989.

Queen's Hussar, who also sired the Queen's Highclere (1000 Guineas, Prix de Diane), dam of Height of Fashion, was bought as a yearling by Porchey Carnarvon from his trainer, Atty Corbett, winning the Sussex Stakes and Lockinge Stakes as a three-year-old. However Queen's Hussar was an unraced two-year-old when Henry Carnarvon, who is the Queen's racing manager, bought the dam Jojo.

Jojo was purchased privately for £2,000 from George Stephens, the breeder of Queen's Hussar, to replace a mare that had died young. In 1979 the present Lord Carnarvon was presented with Highclere Stud by his father who survived for another nine years. By then Jojo had had sixteen foals, one of her twelve winners being Hiding Place (Nell Gwyn Stakes). No less than seven of her sons became stallions, amongst them Little Wolf (Ascot Gold Cup), and Smuggler (Yorkshire Cup), who was exported to New Zealand.

It was only after buying Jojo that Henry Carnarvon realized that his grandfather had bred her fifth dam, Jongleuse. To reintroduce the Malva family at Highclere, Minstrel Girl was acquired from Herbert Blagrave's Harwood Stud (for a time both studs were managed by Captain Michael Forsyth-Forrest), and this line has produced such smart performers as Kittyhawk and Matinée.

Lord Carnarvon's most judicious purchase in recent years is undoubtedly Rosia Bay (High Top – Ouija). She cost 6,200 guineas as a three-year-old from Lord Derby. Prior to being sold for $600,000 at Keeneland in November 1988, this half-sister to Teleprompter bred two stars to National Stud stallions in Ibn Bey (by Mill Reef), and Roseate Tern (by Blakeney).

One of few notable chesnut sons of Mill Reef, Ibn Bey won Pattern races in five countries, one of four Group 1 victories being gained in the 1990 Jefferson Smurfit Memorial Irish St Leger before becoming a stallion in Japan. Successful in the Aston Upthorpe Yorkshire Oaks and placed in the Oaks and St Leger, Roseate Tern was sold by her owner-breeder at the 1989 Newmarket December Sales for 1.1 million guineas, the second highest price ever paid for a filly in Park Paddocks.

Highclere is a modern public stud specializing in the sale of commercial yearlings – a recent star is Arranvanna (1991 Premio Regina Elena). Also partners in the business are Carnarvon's younger son, Harry Herbert, who runs a bloodstock promotion company from an office in Highclere Park, and his daughter, Carolyn, whose husband, John Warren, is the Newmarket-based bloodstock agent. Messrs Herbert and Warren are jointly involved with Kennet Valley Thoroughbreds, a successful racehorse ownership syndicate.

stock Manor Stud where homebred High Line was foaled, reared and has spent his entire stud
. (*Pascal Bouclier*)

gmering Park Stud. Lavinia, Duchess of Norfolk, and stud groom Alfred Goulder, with Castle
oon and her 1988 filly, Moon Festival. (*Trevor Meeks*)

Aston Park Stud where Dominion has proved such an admirable replacement for his own sire, Derring-Do. (*Peter Greenland/TCA*)

The refurbished stallion boxes at Banstead Manor Stud. (*Tim Hannan/TCA*)

Night Shift, the Barton Stud resident, who was the leading British-based sire of 1990. (*Laurie Morton*)

e great Nearco spent the duration of his stallion career at Beech House Stud. (*W.W. Rouch*)

.mmy's Pet, an outstanding sire of two-year-olds, spent his stud innings at Barleythorpe Stud. *'ona Vigors*)

Four generations at Bloomsbury Stud. Left to right: Bluebook and her 1991 Mtoto colt, her dam Pushy and her grandam Mrs Moss. (*Laurie Morton*)

The late Mrs Leonard Scott of Buttermilk Stud, the most successful 'small breeder' of her generation. (*John Slater*)

Cheveley Park Stud. One of the biggest studs in the country and one of the most picturesque. (Camilla Russell)

Tombstones of famous horses in the immaculate main yard at Childwick Bury Stud. (Jack R. Curtis)

Mr and Mrs Louis Freedman of Cliveden Stud with Shadywood and her 1987 filly, Madame Dubois. (*Gerry Cranham*)

Heatherwold Stud. Mrs Peter Longton and stud groom Ian Bailey, with Fiesta Fun (dam of Saumarez), and her Mtoto colt of 1990. (*Laurie Morton*)

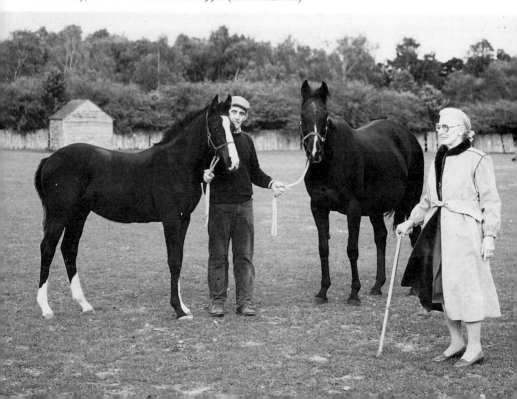

Sheikh Mohammed's Newmarket empire. From top: Dalham Hall, Hadrian, Rutland and Warren Studs. (*Laurie Morton*)

The grandeur of Highclere Castle provides a wonderful backdrop for yearlings. (*Fiona Vigors*)

Home Stud

WEST TYTHERLEY · WILTSHIRE

During the 1980s, John Coggan's Home Stud, West Tytherley, a backwater of north Hampshire about twelve miles east of Salisbury, has been responsible for Group or Grade 1 winners in three countries with Iroko (Pan American Handicap) and Luge (Laurel Futurity) in the USA, Devon Air (Rothmans' July Handicap) in South Africa, and Colorspin (Gilltown Stud Irish Oaks).

Both Iroko and Devon Air were actually bred by Home Stud Limited, whereas Luge and Colorspin were bred there from mares owned by James Wigan, whose parents own West Blagdon, and the Weinfelds' Meon Valley Stud respectively. Iroko on the other hand goes back at three generations to the Coggans' foundation mare, Millstream.

It was in November 1946 that Jack Coggan (John's father), who originally kept a handful of mares on a rented farm at Stratford-sub-Castle, acquired Home Stud. Then known as Norman Court Stud, it had been developed in the early twenties by Washington Singer on part of his 20,000-acre estate.

A son of the American sewing machine magnate, Isaac Singer, he owned Orwell, who retired to stand at King Edward's Place Stud, near Swindon. Now defunct, this stud was run for a number of years by Captain Frederick Barker whose mother was Washington Singer's step-daughter.

Jack Coggan had bought Millstream (Mieuxce – Millrock) as a two-year-old in the autumn of 1943 for £500 from her breeder, James V. Rank, together with a nomination to his stallion Epigram. Coggan was a wholesale butcher and Rank was the country's foremost flour miller. Initially they had become friends through coursing up at Druids Lodge, a remote outpost at Middle Woodford, near Stonehenge, owned by Rank and presided over by his trainer, Noel Cannon.

A half-sister to Rank's good stayer, Strathspey, Millstream never went into training. However nine of her fourteen foals won, amongst them the

St Leger third Medway (Goodwood Cup). Also classic placed was Mill-stream's daughter, Reel In (Nassau Stakes), by Rank's homebred Jock Scot, a son of Strathspey's sire, Scottish Union. It was her misfortune to be a contemporary of Meld and Ark Royal to whom she finished third in the Oaks.

Although Reel In emulated her dam with nine winning offspring, the long-term interests of the family were better served by her half-sisters, Sunol, grandam of Princely Son (Vernons' Sprint Cup) and Stamegna (Premio Dormello), and Palestream, grandam of Manado and Iroko.

Rated the top two-year-old of his generation, Manado won the Grand Criterium and the Prix de la Salamandre. Having succeeded his own sire, Captain's Gig, standing under the Airlie umbrella in Ireland, he was exported to Japan. Manado's half-brother, Iroko, won the Valdoe Stakes, Goodwood, prior to winning the Grade I Pan American Handicap, Gulfstream Park, as a five-year-old in 1987.

Between 1950 and 1970, some 240 winners of 376 races were produced from mares resident at Home Stud. A large percentage were the progeny of boarding mares, two celebrities being the James V. Rank-bred Gay Time, who was runner-up in the Derby, and the Patricia Cannon-bred Rich and Rare, winner of the Cheveley Park Stakes.

However the lion's share belonged to Phil Bull's Hollins Stud which during that period bred a stream of winners, all with names derived from mythology. Top of the class was Romulus, who was probably the top miler sired by the illustrious Ribot. In 1968, after twenty years, all the Hollins mares departed to Sezincote Stud, owned by Phil Bull's great friend William Hill, but they never enjoyed comparable success again.

Ironically the one Hollins mare to excel subsequently was Djerella. Given to Jack Coggan following a near fatal paddock accident as a yearling, she is the dam of Stilvi. This triple Group winning sprinter, who cost George Cambanis 6,200 guineas as a yearling, proved a brilliant broodmare with Tachypous, Tromos and Tyrnavos. At the 1982 Newmarket December Sales, her daughter Tenea realized 1,020,000 guineas to become the first equine millionaire at public auction in Britain.

By contrast Home Stud procured the unraced mare Tekka for a bargain 160 guineas and she made a handsome contribution to the Irish bloodstock scene by breeding not only Richmond (Anglesey Stakes, Beresford Stakes) but also Garvey Girl, who excelled as a broodmare at Killarkin Stud, Co. Meath. Mated with Habitat, she is responsible for two stars in Hot Spark and Bitty Girl.

Since the late seventies, James Wigan of London Thoroughbred Services has kept the occasional boarding mare at Home Stud. One, Last Call (whose sire, Klairon, used to stand at King Edward's Place Stud), bred Final Straw and Achieved. Own-brothers by Thatch, they won the Laurent Perrier Champagne Stakes in 1979 and 1981 respectively. Final Straw duly became a stallion at Egerton Stud and then at the neighbouring National Stud before departing to Italy. His own-brother Achieved was exported for stallion duties in the USA. This was also the destination of the previously mentioned Luge, another James Wigan-bred to bring reflected glory to the Coggans' stud.

Achieved cost Robert Sangster 162,000 guineas as a yearling. However the two top prices for yearlings from Home Stud were for colts consigned to the 1983 Highflyer Sales by Egon Weinfeld (Meon Valley Stud). They were by Habitat out of Odeon at 250,000 guineas, and by Kris from One in a Million at 220,000 guineas. The former was the smart Si Signor. Also raised for the Weinfelds was Colorspin, the Gilltown Stud Irish Oaks heroine.

Since Jack Coggan died in 1986, the stud was been leased to Home Stud Limited which is under the management of his son, John. He has been actively involved in running the stud (the impressive main yard is painted in the Coggan racing colours, chocolate and cream) since 1948, with the help of two stud grooms, Fred Rowland, the present holder of the title, and his predecessor, Alan Watts.

Juddmonte Farms

WARGRAVE-ON-THAMES · BERKSHIRE

Juddmonte Farms is the collective title of Prince Khalid Abdullah's world-wide racing and breeding empire which has its headquarters at the private stud of that name at Wargrave-on-Thames in Berkshire. The prince is a close relative of King Fahd of Saudi Arabia.

Also under the Juddmonte umbrella are two public studs in Newmarket, Banstead Manor and Eagle Lane Farm; Juddmonte Farms in Ireland, comprising Ferrans Stud, Co. Meath, and New Abbey Stud, Co. Kildare; and Juddmonte Farms in the USA, incorporating three separate Kentucky studs. Between them, they cover about 3,500 acres. The prince also owns Fairlawne, the late Peter Cazalet's famous training quarters, near Tonbridge in Kent.

The strength of Khalid Abdullah's enormous commitment to thoroughbreds was evident in 1990 when three homebred colts came within an ace of bringing off an historic Derby treble. First, Sanglamore won the Prix du Jockey Club Lancia, second, Quest for Fame won the Ever Ready Derby, and third, Deploy was runner-up in the Budweiser Irish Derby.

All three were trained at Beckhampton by first-season trainer Roger Charlton, and were ridden by Pat Eddery on whom Khalid Abdullah has first claim. Both Quest for Fame and Deploy were bred from mares based at Wargrave-on-Thames, whereas Sanglamore is a protégé of the American establishment.

Khalid Abdullah had become the first of the Arabs to own an English classic winner when Known Fact was awarded the 1980 2000 Guineas upon the disqualification of Nureyev. Known Fact was amongst the first batch of yearlings that the prince ever bought – former Newmarket trainer Humphrey Cottrill selected him as a yearling at the 1978 Keeneland July Sales for $225,000.

The now famous 'green, pink sash and cap, white sleeves' gained a first homebred success two years later at the Guineas meeting with Fine Edge. He belonged to the first crop of foals that Khalid Abdullah ever bred from just nine mares. Five of them had been bought, together with Cayton Park Stud, from Gerald Leigh, now owner of Eydon Hall Farm in north Oxfordshire.

Cayton Park, where Mrs Gerald Trimmer-Thompson stood March Past (sire of Queen's Hussar) for a while, was originally the public sector of Juddmonte Farms, while the other side, a former dairy farm belonging to the Gilbey family, was to be home of Khalid Abdullah's own mares, but this proved only a temporary arrangement.

The two properties were developed as separate entities to the highest specification by James Delahooke of Adstock Manor Stud, who was the prince's stud and racing manager from August 1979 until August 1985. Not only was he responsible for ensuring that all the building was completed within the space of nine months during 1981, but also for establishing a broodmare band second to none.

By the 1990s their number had grown to over 150 with over 230 horses in training, the lion's share being divided between Andre Fabre, Guy Harwood, Roger Charlton, John Gosden and Barry Hills. Both Jeremy Tree, Charlton's predecessor at Beckhampton, and Guy Harwood won the Prix de l'Arc de Triomphe for Abdullah, the former with Rainbow Quest and the latter with Dancing Brave.

James Delahooke bought both colts as yearlings at Fasig-Tipton's Kentucky Summer Sales, paying $950,000 for Rainbow Quest in 1982 and $200,000 for Dancing Brave in 1984. In due course their respective dams, I Will Follow and Navajo Princess, were both recruited to Juddmonte's harem, along with a host of other celebrities gathered from the four corners of the globe.

Today Philip E.H. Mitchell, former manager of Brook and Side Hill Studs, is general manager of Juddmonte Farms. He took over from Delahooke's successor, Anthony Chapman of Aston House Stud, in October 1988. It was during Chapman's tenure that Juddmonte Farms gained a valuable foothold in Newmarket. First came the acquisition of Banstead Manor Stud in the spring of 1987 and then Eagle Lane Farm, formerly the Vanian brothers' Dullingham Stud, a year later.

As from 1990 both Rainbow Quest and his close relative Warning (both grandsons of Noblesse's daughter, Where You Lead) have covered at Banstead Manor. Rainbow Quest had completed his first two seasons (1986/87) at Wargrave-on-Thames when Known Fact left for Whitsbury Manor Stud *en route* to the Kentucky division of Juddmonte Farms.

Rainbow Quest is responsible for three individual Group I winners from his first crop with Quest for Fame (Ever Ready Derby), Knight's Baroness (Kildangan Stud Irish Oaks), and Saumarez (Ciga Prix de l'Arc de Triomphe, Grand Prix de Paris Louis Vuitton). Known Fact's two top performers are Khalid Abdullah's Warning and Gerald Leigh's Markofdistinction, these two homebreds both winning the Queen Elizabeth II Stakes at the Festival of British Racing.

It was surprising that Danehill (Ladbroke Sprint Cup) did not join the home team of Banstead stallions, but instead was sold for a reputed £4 million to stand at Coolmore. The prince's second-eleven stallions are located at Eagle Lane Farm (the first stallion station in the country restricted to walking-in mares). This is where Deploy joined his owner's Vernons' Sprint Cup hero Dowsing for the 1991 season.

Khalid Abdullah's international broodmare band is more or less equally divided between England and America. The majority of UK mares foal down at Wargrave-on-Thames before being mated, those that are visiting Newmarket stallions being sent to Banstead Manor. All weaned foals are transferred to New Abbey Stud. Twenty miles away is Ferrans Stud which is used for breaking yearlings and as a temporary home for mares visiting Irish-based stallions.

Stud manager at Wargrave-on-Thames is Jim Cowe, his counterpart at Eagle Lane Farm being Alan Walker. Another key personality in the organization is Rhydian Morgan-Jones. Managing director of Eagle Lane, he is known to be Prince Khalid Abdullah's right-hand man and close confidant.

Kingwood Stud

LAMBOURN · BERKSHIRE

Kingwood Stud is the former Lambourn Stud, a name Mrs Ossie Bell took with her when she sold the property in 1966 and moved to Woolstone, near Faringdon. Today, Kingwood is a thriving boarding establishment owned by the Vigors family – the new Lambourn Stud in the Vale of the White Horse is no longer utilized for thoroughbreds.

Meanwhile that part of Kingwood owned previously by Captain Mark Smyly has been developed into an ultramodern training complex by the Shadwell Estates (Sheikh Hamdan Al Maktoum). This was built specifically for Major Dick Hern who switched his training base from West Ilsley to Lambourn for the start of the 1991 season.

Renée Bell was Captain Ossie Bell's second wife. Born in Australia in 1871, Ossie Bell moved to Lambourn after the First World War having trained previously in India and at Epsom. Based at Delamere stables and then at Stork House, he won the Derby with Felstead and the 1000 Guineas and Oaks with Rockfel.

Both Felstead and Rockfel are synonymous with the old Lambourn Stud which overlooks the village in the valley below. Ossie Bell bought the stud in 1924 in partnership with Sir Hugo Cunliffe-Owen and Captain George Drummond, although the latter soon relinquished his involvement. The first stallion was Scherzo whom Bell trained to win 12½ races.

With his Australian upbringing, Bell had a great admiration for Carbine blood. This influenced him to buy the mare Felkington, carrying to Spion Kop, at the 1924 Newmarket July Sales for 2,100 guineas on behalf of Cunliffe-Owen, his principal patron. The resulting produce, who carried three lines of Carbine, was Felstead.

Hero of the 1928 Derby in record time, Felstead did not race again, being retired to start covering at Lambourn Stud in 1930 at a fee of 300 guineas. He was still in active service when he died there in April 1946, just a few weeks before his daughter, Steady Aim, triumphed in the Oaks.

That season Felstead had been joined at stud by another horse owned and bred by Hugo Cunliffe-Owen and trained by Ossie Bell in Rockefella (Hyperion – Rockfel). Once again Bell was instrumental in his breeding. In 1934 he bought Rockliffe, whom he had once trained, privately for £3,000. The Felstead foal 'in utero' was Rockfel.

Having started her career in sellers, Rockfel won the 1000 Guineas, Oaks and Champion Stakes in 1938 to share top place on the Free Handicap with the Derby winner Bois Roussel. Sadly Rockfel died from a twisted gut in November 1941, having produced Rockefella, her one and only foal.

Rockefella, whose three victories were gained within the space of eighteen days as a three-year-old, proved a fine progenitor. Fourth on the list of leading sires in 1963, his sons include Rockavon (2000 Guineas), Linacre (Irish 2000 Guineas), Bounteous, and the own-brothers, Gay Time, Elopement and Cash and Courage.

When Ossie Bell died in 1949, his widow Renée formed the Lambourn Stud Limited with Brigadier Wyndham Torr as a fellow director. At the 1958 Newmarket Houghton Sales, the brigadier, who lived locally at Shefford Woodlands, bought the mare Chambiges for just eighty-five guineas.

Mated with Rockefella in three consecutive seasons from 1959 to 1961, Chambiges had three daughters. The first was Outcrop (Yorkshire Oaks, Park Hill Stakes), the best staying filly of her generation, while the other pair excelled in the paddocks. Rocchetta became the dam of Sharpen Up, one of the most important sires of the eighties, and Riches produced Richboy.

Two years before Outcrop was foaled, Lambourn Stud Limited was responsible for another top filly in Cynara. A 3,300-guinea yearling, she won the Queen Mary Stakes and Molecomb Stakes for Gerald Oldham and has proved one of the mainstays of his Citadel Stud as the dam of Stintino (Prix Lupin), and the grandam of Zino (2000 Guineas).

When Renée Bell moved from Lambourn to Faringdon, she took twenty-five-year-old Rockefella with her and he survived for another couple of years. Amongst his former stud companions were March Past (sire of Queen's Hussar) and Set Fair. Subsequently Mrs Bell sold Lambourn Stud to bookmaker and garage proprietor Harry Hopgood. One of the stallions he stood was Dublin Taxi, a homebred son of Sharpen Up.

Meanwhile the Arrowsmith-Browns, the owners of the renamed Kingwood Stud, installed the top French miler Klairon for an interim period. During the seventies, Kingwood Stud changed hands on three more occasions. First came Newmarket trainer, Tim Hollowell, then a Spanish consortium headed by Antonio Blasco (owner of Pharly), and finally Mr and Mrs Terence Vigors.

The Vigors arrived in 1979 from Burgage Stud, Co. Carlow, where they had stood the highly influential Sovereign Path throughout his stud innings. The parents of Jockey Club starter, Nicky Vigors, then training in Upper Lambourn, they maintained a nucleus of mares at Kingwood, offering most of the progeny as foals at the December Sales.

Since 1985 Fiona Vigors, Nicky's wife, has managed Kingwood. An expert bloodstock photographer, she is the eldest daughter of the late George Forbes, veterinary surgeon, bloodstock agent and founder of Burley Lodge Stud, originally based in Epsom. His widow Jean, continued with the stud outside Reading, her last important stallion, Derrylin, spending a couple of seasons at Kingwood before being exported to Italy – he is now in Shropshire.

Fiona Vigors, who provides much needed boarding facilities for the Lambourn area, specializes in sales preparation. In recent years she has also done well buying foals to resell as yearlings. The two star performers in this category are Gallic League and Rock City, the winners of eight Group races between them. Gallic League retired to stand at Coolmore for the 1990 season and Rock City covered his first mares at the National Stud the following year.

Kirtlington Stud

KIRTLINGTON · OXFORDSHIRE

The name Windmill Girl must be engraved upon Arthur Budgett's heart for this mare enabled the former Whatcombe trainer to own, train and breed two winners of the Derby within the space of four years – the part-owned Blakeney in 1969 and Morston in 1973, both named after Norfolk villages, as is Blakeney's sire, Hethersett.

Arthur Budgett and his elder brother, Alan, were brought up at Kirtlington Park, just north of Oxford, an estate which the family acquired in 1922 from the financier and gambler Jimmy White. Their father, Hugh Maitland Budgett, who died in 1951, was Master of the Bicester and an authority on hunting.

It was at Kirtlington that Arthur embarked upon his training career pre-war and where Alan continued to run the polo. Arthur's Park Farm, which is now owned by his elder son, James, is bordered to the north by Middleton Stoney. Here the 5th Earl of Jersey bred ten classic winners, including the Derby winners Middleton and Bay Middleton.

As there were so many studs known as Park Farm (the official breeders of Blakeney and Morston), Arthur Budgett and his wife, Bay, started trading as Kirtlington Stud Limited from 1972 onwards. They remain directors of the company along with their younger son, Christopher, who is also the stud manager.

In 1989 the adjoining Manor Farm was acquired and this is where all the bloodstock was transferred after the following year's covering season. Here 200 acres have been laid down to permanent pasture and a whole new range of stud buildings have been erected to provide accommodation for forty head of stock.

Although the original Park Farm Stud had been founded just after the war with Harry Deakin as stud groom, it was not laid out formally for breeding thoroughbreds until about 1957. One of the original mares was

Auricula. She produced two Budgett-trained winners of the Great Metropolitan Handicap at Epsom in Barnacle and Hollyhock.

No one engaged in breeding bloodstock would deny that luck is a primary ingredient. The Budgetts certainly had their share with Windmill Girl (the only mare to breed two Derby winners during the twentieth century), for they were lucky to buy her and equally lucky not to sell her!

The path to Epsom glory started at the 1961 Newmarket December Sales when a homebred filly foal offered by the late Major Lionel Holliday (a very rare commodity) failed to make her reserve, whereupon Arthur Budgett, accompanied by his brother-in-law, Major Peter Towers-Clark, then manager of the stud, agreed to purchase her for 1,000 guineas.

By Hornbeam, she was bought to resell as a yearling, but due to a superficial injury was consigned to the December rather than the October Sales where nobody was prepared to bid the reserve price of 6,000 guineas. Named Windmill Girl, she proceeded to win the Ribblesdale Stakes and was second in the Oaks and third in the Irish Guinness Oaks. Transferred from Whatcombe to Kirtlington, she had six foals (five winners), in seven years, Blakeney being the first of her offspring. Sadly the mare died out in her paddock at the age of eleven from a fractured skull.

By then Blakeney was already installed at the National Stud having remained in training as a four-year-old when runner-up at Ascot in the Gold Cup and King George VI and Queen Elizabeth Stakes. Very popular with owner-breeders, Blakeney is responsible for the classic winners, Juliette Marny, Julio Mariner, Tyrnavos and Mountain Lodge. Another daughter is Kirtlington-bred Believer, winner of the Princess Royal Stakes. Blakeney, who had failed to make his 5,000 guinea reserve as a yearling, was still covering mares at the advanced age of twenty-five in 1991.

Morston, who has had various homes since retiring to the now defunct Tedfold Stud in Sussex, was the first colt to win the Derby on only his second start since Bois Roussel in 1938. Arthur Budgett says that Morston (by Ragusa), whose career was terminated by a strained tendon, would have been much less backward had Harry Deakin not died in the year that he was foaled.

One of Morston's leading winners is More Light (Jockey Club Stakes, Gordon Stakes). He was homebred by Alan Budgett at Slade Farm on the Kirtlington Estate, as was his distinguished half-sister, Shoot a Line (Irish Guinness Oaks, Yorkshire Oaks).

Windmill Girl's two lesser known sons, Alderney (March Stakes, Goodwood) and Mendham (Handicap de Saint-Cloud), both became sires in Australia, while her only daughters, Derry Lass and Cley, were retained for the stud. The continuation of the line has revolved around Derry Lass.

Unraced due to a hip injury as a foal, Derry Lass is dam of the winning Good Lass. She in turn bred three Group/Grade winners. First came the retained half-sisters, Bonne Ile (Grade I Yellow Ribbon Invitational Handicap), one of the top fillies of her generation on turf in North America, and Hi Lass (Ciga Prix Gladiateur).

Derry Lass is by Derring-Do, sire of top sprinter Huntercombe. Both father and son were owned by Horace and Nona Renshaw and trained at Whatcombe by Arthur Budgett, homebred Huntercombe being reared at Kirtlington as a yearling. At the 1987 Highflyer Sales, the Budgetts sold Bonne Ile's own-brother (by Ile de Bourbon) for 46,000 guineas to Prince Yazid Saud. Named Ile de Nisky, he finished third in the Budweiser Irish Derby and fourth in the Ever Ready Derby. In 1990 he gained his reward for consistency in the top class by victory in the Hoover Cumberland Lodge Stakes before continuing his racing career in Saudi Arabia.

Before returning to Park Farm, Kirtlington, in 1984, the Budgett mares spent an interim period at Whatcombe, on the Oxfordshire–Berkshire border, near Wantage. This was after Arthur Budgett relinquished his training licence and before he sold the property to Robert Sangster. A change of heart then saw Sangster buy Manton with Whatcombe being sold to Paul Cole's principal patron, Prince Fahd Salman.

Lanwades Stud

NEWMARKET · SUFFOLK

The bloodstock community in Newmarket was mildly surprised, to say the least, when Colonel Nat Frieze sold his Lanwades Stud at Kentford in April 1980 to a striking, but unknown, Swedish girl still in her twenties, called Kirsten Rausing.

On the eve of that year's Newmarket December Sales, Miss Rausing took up residence at Lanwades which coincided with the arrival there of the Nijinsky horse, Niniski. Any credibility the young Swede might have had evaporated overnight as the Irish and French St Leger winner could not be regarded as a commercially viable proposition.

Within the shortest possible time her critics were eating their words. In 1983 the stud had just five yearlings with two particular colts belonging to Niniski's first crop. One, Kala Dancer (bred from a boarding mare), won the William Hill Dewhurst Stakes to be ranked the champion two-year-old of Europe. The other was Petoski whom Kirsten bred herself.

Racing for the Dowager Lady Beaverbrook, who owned Niniski and became the major shareholder in the horse with Kirsten Rausing, Petoski gained a memorable victory in the 1985 King George VI and Queen Elizabeth Diamond Stakes to earn second place behind Slip Anchor on the International Classification.

Petoski, who retired to stand at the National Stud, is out of Sushila, whom Kirsten Rausing bought for 12,000 guineas as a yearling from her breeder, Captain Tim Rogers of Airlie Stud in Ireland. Having spent three years as Tim's assistant, she regards him as one of her three mentors, along with Mrs Allan Wettermark of Vasaholm Stud and Dr Lennart Olsson, formerly chief veterinary officer of the Swedish National Stud.

A graduate in business studies from Stockholm University (her father is a professor of archaeology at Lund University), and the first lady member of the Swedish Jockey Club, Kirsten had taken charge of the family's Simon-

127

torp Stud, near Blentarp, when her grandfather decided to live in Italy.

By the time Simontorp finally closed down in the autumn of 1981 (breed-ing thoroughbreds in Sweden had become totally uneconomic), Kirsten Rausing was effecting great changes at Lanwades which was once owned by Caroline, Duchess of Montrose (1818–1894), Fred Archer's greatest admirer and the breeder of Canterbury Pilgrim.

Nat Frieze had owned the property for forty years and when he took it over during the war all the paddocks were under the plough. Soon he was standing his marvellous old sprinter, Mickey the Greek. From 1952 to 1980 there was a remarkable sequence of stallions with Pardal, his son Pardao and the latter's son, Moulton.

During the 1980s Kirsten Rausing not only transformed Lanwades Stud (150 acres: 91 boxes), but she also more than doubled her acreage with the acquisition of Rosemary Farm in the summer of 1983. Formerly arable land on the opposite side of the Bury St Edmunds–Newmarket road, this has been converted into St Simon Stud (300 acres: 46 boxes).

As well as commemorating that most famous of racehorses, St Simon Stud was so named because of its connotation with Simontorp and Simmon-stown, part of the Airlie complex. Originally the landscape at St Simon was devoid of all grass, fencing and trees. Today it is prime stud land and its formerly bleak aspect has been much enhanced by the planting of 14,000 young trees and 25,000 hedge plants.

For the 1987 covering season Niniski was joined at Lanwades by a second stallion in the French 2000 Guineas winner Nishapour, the first horse that the present Aga Khan had actually stood in Newmarket. Accommodated in the impressive new stallion quarters, both have sired classic winners, Niniski with Minster Son (Holsten Pils St Leger), and Nishapour with Mouktar (Prix du Jockey Club Lancia).

Lanwades Stud and St Simon Stud are run as totally separate entities, each with its own stud groom and staff. The former is the public half of the operation to which yearlings are transferred after the covering season, while the latter provides a home for Kirsten Rausing's own broodmare band together with boarders.

Boarding stock, both permanent and seasonal, are an important item on the agenda. A number of the most eminent studs in Ireland entrust mares visiting Newmarket stallions to Kirsten's care, amongst them Airlie, Ballymacoll, Ballymany, Citadel, Gilltown and Stackallen.

Kirsten Rausing's involvement with Airlie and with Niniski's trainer, Major Dick Hern (whom she met through Margaretta Wettermark), has proved of great benefit. Airlie, which has recruited some distinguished

West Ilsley horses for stallion duty, is now run by Captain Tim Rogers's widow, Sonia. The scenario continues as Airlie is the base of Gerald Oldham's mares (Citadel Stud), and Stackallen is owned by Sonia's mother, Mrs Elizabeth Burke.

Nat Frieze, who still lives in the main house at Lanwades, has earned the gratitude of the breeding fraternity as a trustee of the TBA's Equine Fertility Unit, now centred on Mertoun Paddocks, and naturally he was delighted when his successor at Lanwades became a council member of the association. More recently she has also become a substantial shareholder in the British Bloodstock Agency.

As someone who is involved at first hand with all the day to day problems in running a top-class public stud, Kirsten Rausing places great emphasis on combating the spread of disease and infection. Interestingly she is not an advocate of the fashionable American barn, much preferring traditional boxes placed in strategic groups. Coming from such an enlightened breeder, it is an opinion not to be dismissed lightly.

Lavington Stud

GRAFFHAM · WEST SUSSEX

Nestling at the foot of the Sussex Downs on the north side, not far from Goodwood, Lavington Stud is owned by Captain John Macdonald-Buchanan, a former senior steward of the Jockey Club, and his son, Alastair. John's brother-in-law, Major Christopher Philipson, is owner of Lofts Hall Stud, near Saffron Walden, and managing director of the British Bloodstock Agency.

John Macdonald-Buchanan's late parents, Sir Reginald and Lady Macdonald-Buchanan, owned Lavington Stud for many years together with Egerton and Lordship Studs at Newmarket. Catherine Macdonald-Buchanan had inherited Lavington when her father, Lord Woolavington, died in 1935. James Buchanan (created a peer in 1922) had started Lavington Stud when converting a dairy farm on his Sussex estate near Petworth in about 1900.

The first two stallions at Lavington were Black Sand and Santry, but the horse that is synonymous with the stud is Hurry On (Marcovil – Tout Suite). A 500-guinea yearling, who soon stood over 17 hands, he was regarded by Fred Darling as the best he ever trained. Undefeated, he ran only as a three-year-old, his six victories including the New St Leger of 1916 at Newmarket.

Hurry On, who was rated superior to the wartime Triple Crown winners, Pommern (1915), Gay Crusader (1917) and Gainsborough (1918), proved the saviour of the Matchem male line. By the time of his demise in 1936, he was responsible for the winners of seven classics. Champion sire of 1926 when Coronach won the Derby and St Leger, he got two more Derby winners in Captain Cuttle and Call Boy. However the most influential of his sons was Precipitation (Ascot Gold Cup). Foaled when Hurry On was twenty years old, he sired Airborne, Chamossaire, Premonition and Sheshoon. Hurry On was also three times leading sire of broodmares.

Captain Cuttle and Coronach provided Lord Woolavington with two homebred Derby winners within the space of four years. Resulting from the very first mare that Hurry On ever covered, Captain Cuttle retired to Lavington Stud in 1924. Four years later he was exported to Italy which coincided with his daughter, Scuttle, winning the 1000 Guineas for King George V.

That year Coronach covered his first mares at Westerlands Stud, another farm conversion on the Lavington Estate. Also successful in the Eclipse Stakes and Coronation Cup, he was exported to New Zealand in 1940 where he became the first Derby winner to stand at stud there. Coronach left behind two continental celebrities in Niccolo dell'Arca and Corrida.

The dams of both Derby winners had been bought as in-foal mares. Bellavista, dam of Captain Cuttle, cost 1,950 guineas as a sixteen-year-old at the 1915 Newmarket December Sales. Coronach's dam, Wet Kiss, was acquired privately in 1918 as a five-year-old.

Following Lord Woolavington's death, his daughter and son-in-law sold Northaw Stud, in Hertfordshire, to which the yearlings used to be sent, to Dorothy Paget, and Westerlands Stud to Florence Nagle, prior to adding an entirely new dimension to their breeding operation with the purchase of both Lordship and Egerton Studs in Newmarket.

Meanwhile their increasing broodmare band continued to be based at Lavington. Two French-bred mares of note were Brulette (Oaks), whose granddaughter Belle Sauvage is the grandam of Vaguely Noble, and Mary Tudor II (French 1000 Guineas), the dam of Owen Tudor. Both Belle Sauvage and Owen Tudor were bred by Catherine Macdonald-Buchanan, the latter becoming the key stallion at Egerton Stud.

Perhaps the most celebrated of all Lady Macdonald-Buchanan's mares was Rustom Mahal whom she bought privately from her breeder, the old Aga Khan. To a mating with Owen Tudor, she produced the brilliant grey Abernant. Considered by Sir Noel Murless to be the fastest he ever trained, Abernant achieved double victories in the July Cup, King George Stakes and Nunthorpe Stakes.

For a thirty-year period from the mid-fifties to the mid-eighties, all the Macdonald-Buchanan owned mares were based at Lordship Stud rather than at Lavington. Most of Lavington had been ploughed up during the war and it was felt that a run of bad luck with their runners in the post-war period could be a direct consequence of the reseeded paddocks.

The exodus of between thirty and forty mares to Newmarket enabled Lavington to concentrate its activities as a public establishment. Over the last three decades, stallions to have stood there include Sing Sing, Relko,

Ragstone, Castle Keep, Morston, and the present residents Formidable, Aragon and newcomer Warrshan.

Although he suffered at the hands of dopers, Sing Sing is much the most important, the son of Tudor Minstrel being a leading sire and sire of sires – his son Mummy's Pet is sire of Aragon. The latter actually completed his first two covering seasons at Egerton, but was transferred to Lavington for the 1986 season when the two Newmarket properties were sold.

Formidable has sons at stud of his own, amongst them the National Stud's Chilibang. Song's close relative Aragon is also proving a very useful sire and his progeny include the top two-year-olds Argentum and Only Yours.

In 1990 Lavington Stud had its own sensational star in In the Groove (Night Shift – Pine Ridge). Winner of three Group 1 events, the Dubai Champion Stakes, Juddmonte International Stakes and Goffs' Irish 1000 Guineas, she realized only 20,000 guineas at the October Sales where John Macdonald-Buchanan had procured her dam for 12,000 guineas in 1981. He only sold the Night Shift filly as a yearling as he felt she was too big and backward to make much impression on the flat!

Pine Ridge is one of nine mares that John and Alastair Macdonald-Buchanan share, with the occasional filly being trained either by Sir Mark Prescott, John Dunlop or Michael Stoute. The new manager at Lavington is Timothy Reed whose predecessor, Michael Ashton, MRCVS, remains a consultant. Two recent winners from boarding mares at Lavington are the late Elspeth Riley-Smith's Sergeyevich and Kenneth Higson's Karinga Bay.

Limestone Stud

GAINSBOROUGH · LINCOLNSHIRE

When the late Clifford Nicholson died in October 1972, the future of his Limestone Stud looked in jeopardy. A widower with no children, he had progressed from being a leading owner of jumpers to one of the biggest breeders for the flat, both in terms of his own broodmares and the standing of stallions at Limestone and the affiliated Tara Stud in Co. Meath.

One of the founders of the Injured Jockeys' Fund, Clifford Nicholson, who was never seen on a racecourse without his bowler hat and red carnation, was first and foremost a farmer. During the thirties and forties, when land prices were depressed, he acquired thousands of Lincolnshire acres. His maxim that no depression lasts for ever was vindicated when his 15,000 acres, many of them bought for around £10 an acre became worth £2,000 an acre.

He also had considerable farming interests in Natal, South Africa. In 1958 he took on John Rowles as a partner and in 1967 he came to England at Nicholson's request to help run his Lincolnshire acres. When Clifford Nicholson died five years later, John Rowles took over the Limestone Farming Company centred on the village of Willoughton, near Gainsborough. Today he runs the business with his sons, Graham Rowles Nicholson and Bruce Rowles. William Morgan is stud manager.

A renowned sheep and cattle breeder, Clifford Nicholson's interest in jumping had been kindled by his homebred hunter-chaser, Empire Knight, winner of a pre-war Cheltenham Foxhunters'. The horse was ridden by Alec Marsh. He was to become senior starter under Jockey Club Rules, while his former wife, Elisabeth, was to manage Limestone Stud for more than forty years.

During the fifties, Nicholson's colours, 'grey, scarlet sleeves, collar, braid and cap', which have been adopted by John Rowles, were carried by a succession of top-class jumpers, trained by Charlie Hall at Tadcaster, amongst them champion hurdler Doorknocker. Gradually switching his allegiance to the flat, he soon had a large string divided between England (including Bill Elsey, Fred Armstrong and Fulke Johnson Houghton), Ireland, France and Italy.

Over the years, Clifford Nicholson stood a multitude of stallions at Limestone. One of the first was Portlaw, who was acquired in 1940 following the death of his owner, Sir Abe Bailey. By the time Clifford Nicholson died there were eight horses in residence, including Galivanter, Sheshoon, Right Boy and Royal Palm.

Many more came and went in the interim, amongst them Nearco's half-brothers Niccolo dell'Arca, Naucide and Torbido. Thanks to Bebe Grande, Niccolo dell'Arca was the leading sire of two-year-olds in 1952. Their dam, Nogara, also became a member of the Limestone broodmare band; she died at Tara Stud.

The one stallion with which Limestone Stud is most readily identifiable is Sheshoon (Precipitation – Noorani). A half-brother to Charlottesville, he embarked upon stud duties here in 1961 and he was twenty-three when he died in 1979. Winner of the Ascot Gold Cup, he proved one of the mainstays of the Matchem male line and was a strong influence for stamina. Many of his best progeny raced in France where Sassafras won the Prix de l'Arc de Triomphe (beating Nijinsky) and the Prix du Jockey Club. His only classic winner in England was Mon Fils, a surprise victor of the 2000 Guineas.

The leading sire in Europe in 1970, Sheshoon produced a classic winner for Limestone Stud in Pleben (Grand Prix de Paris, Prix Royal Oak). Clifford Nicholson had sold him as a foal for only 1,350 guineas less than three years before he died. Accrale (Gran Premio d'Italia, Gran Premio di Milano) was another Limestone bred. Sold as a yearling for 3,600 guineas, his maternal grandsire Umidwar used to stand at Tara Stud.

Amongst the multitude of winners owned and bred by Clifford Nicholson (one, Grasp Saint, scored at Newmarket on the very day he died) was Haymaking. Trained by Fulke Johnson Houghton, she won the 1966 Coronation Stakes and Nassau Stakes. Along with Hayrake and New Way, Haymaking was one of three relatives inherited by John Rowles. All three are descended from New Moon. Clifford Nicholson had bought this half-sister to Hyperion as an unraced two-year-old from Lord Derby for 3,000 guineas at Newmarket in September 1942.

New Moon is the sixth dam of Limestone's most recent Group scorer, On Tiptoes (1990 Queen Mary Stakes). Bought in for 7,000 guineas at the Highflyer Sales (she was offered without a wind certificate), On Tiptoes returned to Willoughton to be trained by Jim Leigh. Her dam, Pennyweight, is half-sister to Wassl. Their dam Hayloft (Molecomb Stakes) is a daughter of Haymaking.

A 300,000-guinea yearling and the first horse to get Sheikh Ahmed Al Maktoum interested in racing, Wassl won the Airlie Coolmore Irish 2000 Guineas. The son of Mill Reef completed five seasons at Derrinstown Stud, Co. Kildare, before going to Japan. In 1983 Limestone sold his yearling half-sister by Troy for 500,000 guineas, a European record for a filly. Another celebrity is New Way's son, Star Way. Successful in the Chesham Stakes, Royal Ascot, and fourth in the 2000 Guineas, the son of Star Appeal became a champion sire in New Zealand.

Since Clifford Nicholson's time, the Limestone stallion roster has included Tower Walk, Sagaro, Gunner B and Nomination. Tower Walk, who died at Limestone in retirement in 1989 aged twenty-three, had commenced stud life in Ireland. He was an infinitely superior sire to Sagaro. With the unique distinction of three Ascot Gold Cup victories (1975/76/77), he was boarded for the National Stud. Gunner B sired some winners of merit, while Nomination was one of the leading first-season sires of 1990. This son of Dominion defeated Green Desert (that season's champion first-crop sire) for the OCL Richmond Stakes. The only two stallions at Limestone for 1991 were Nomination and the young Nureyev stallion Komaite, a half-brother to Avatar.

Towards the end of the last century, Limestone Stud was owned by a Mr J.C. Hill who bred Gallinule there. Unsound of his wind with a tendency to break blood vessels, he was champion sire of 1904 and 1905 and five times leading sire of broodmares. He earned immortality as the sire of Pretty Polly.

Littleton Stud

LITTLETON · HAMPSHIRE

Jeffrey Smith has the considerable distinction of breeding two Group I winners from only his second crop of 'Littleton' foals. Amazingly both were sired by the ill-fated Elegant Air. They are triple Group I scorer, Dashing Blade, winner of the 1989 William Hill Dewhurst Stakes and GPA National Stakes as well as the Gran Premio d'Italia Trofeo Saima, and Air de Rien, heroine of the 1990 Prix Saint Alary.

Whereas Air de Rien was sold for a bargain 5,000 guineas as a yearling, Dashing Blade carried his breeder's purple and light blue colours which first sprung to prominence with top sprinter Chief Singer. The latter was trained by Ron Sheather upon whose retirement Jeffrey Smith transferred his horses to Dashing Blade's handler, Ian Balding at Kingsclere.

Jeffrey Smith purchased Littleton Stud in November 1984, about the same time that Chief Singer took up residence at Side Hill Stud. The stud is situated in undulating countryside about three miles north of Winchester, a very convenient location for its owner – he lives close by at Hursley and commutes daily to his aviation business in Southampton.

Littleton Stud was owned previously by Bruce Deane of Tattersalls, and as the home of Song throughout his stallion innings it is well known to commercial breeders up and down the country. Laid out by a Mr F.W. Talbot just before the First World War, the stud was acquired by Gerald Deane, Bruce's father, to augment his adjoining estate at Littleton House.

Senior partner of Tattersalls, Gerald Deane was also stud and racing manager to the 2nd Lord Astor (1879–1952), owner-breeder of the winners of eleven classic races at his famous Cliveden Stud. A number of famous Astor horses stood at Littleton, amongst them Buchan, Craig an Eran, Rhodes Scholar, Mannamead and Hurstwood. In 1927 Buchan was champion sire by virtue of Astor's filly, Book Law.

Due to ill health, Gerald Deane was forced to relinquish his association with Lord Astor in 1937. Consequently no more of his animals graced Littleton after the Second World War. Stud groom during Gerald Deane's lifetime (he died in 1951) was Ernest James. There from the time that Buchan, the dual Eclipse Stakes hero, covered his first mares in 1921, James retired in 1964.

Only the previous year, Vilmorin, another stalwart, was put down at the age of twenty. Having commenced stud life at Stackallen Stud, Co. Meath, the King's Stand Stakes winner was duly replaced by another sprinter in Ennis (Nunthorpe Stakes), also a grandson of that great speed progenitor Gold Bridge. Ennis was then joined by his exact contemporary, Quorum, winner of the Sussex Stakes and runner-up to Crepello in the 2000 Guineas.

A son of Vilmorin and a grandson of Bulolo, Quorum is bred on identical lines to another sprinting grey in Vigo. Both were bred by Thomas Farr of Ruddington Grange in Nottinghamshire, a cousin of Bryan Farr of Worksop Manor Stud. Quorum arrived at Littleton Stud after six seasons at Balreask Stud, Co. Meath, having been sold in the interim for 10,500 guineas at the 1964 Newmarket December Sales.

Quorum, whose principal claim to fame is as the sire of triple Grand National hero Red Rum, was put down at Littleton Stud in 1971. That very season he had been joined by champion sprinter Song (Sing Sing – Intent). Occupying the box left vacant by temporary resident Floribunda, Song was an appropriate choice, his maternal grandsire being none other than Vilmorin.

Bred by Shelton Stud, as were his close relatives King of Spain and Aragon, Song excelled at Ascot winning the King's Stand Stakes, Diadem Stakes and New (now Norfolk) Stakes. It was after his second Royal Ascot victory that the colt was sold by Bryan Jenks to Jim Joel of Childwick Bury Stud, the latter selling a half share in the son of Sing Sing to Littleton.

A fine speed sire, Song spent eighteen seasons at Littleton Stud where he was put down in 1988 aged twenty-two. His longevity was a tribute to his own tough constitution. Back in the autumn of 1972 he had broken his off-fore fetlock. In 1979 he missed the entire covering season due to contracting an infection. Song's leading sons include the sires Music Maestro and Sizzling Melody. Both won the Flying Childers Stakes; so too did Song's brilliant daughter, Littleton-bred Devon Ditty.

Thanks to Devon Ditty, Song was the champion two-year-old sire of 1978. Having cost Lord McAlpine (Dobson's Stud) 7,800 guineas as a yearling, she won the William Hill Cheveley Park Stakes, Flying Childers Stakes, Cherry Hinton Stakes and Lowther Stakes. Later sold to Robert Sangster

(Swettenham Stud), she found a permanent home at Prince Khalid Abdullah's Juddmonte Farms in the USA.

Prior to transferring his breeding operation to Bishop's Down Farm on the opposite side of Winchester, Bruce Deane bred two Italian classic winners in Don Orazio (1985 Derby) and Comme l'Etoile (1986 St Leger).

Song, who shared his quarters in turn with Major Portion, Sharp Edge and Fair Season, was the only stallion at Littleton when the stud was taken over by Jeffrey Smith. Soon there were two new additions with Mashhor Dancer in 1986 and Forzando in 1987. Both encountered fertility problems and were only temporary residents – Forzando moved down to the West Country (Britton House Stud) and Mashhor Dancer was exported to Peru.

In 1989 Forzando was replaced by the American import Robellino. He had been the leading first season sire in the British Isles thanks to Faustus – he now stands at Fawley Stud, near the famous Whatcombe training stables outside Wantage.

Jeffrey Smith has a private broodmare band of around two dozen, under the supervision of stud groom Richard Martin. He has been there since 1972 having worked for many years with stud manager Audrey Westerdick (now Mrs Mac Old). Littleton Stud has just embarked upon a new era, homebred Dashing Blade having joined Robellino for the 1991 covering season.

Manor House Stud

MIDDLEHAM · NORTH YORKSHIRE

At the 1987 Newmarket December Sales, Mrs Richard Peacock paid 13,000 guineas to buy out her partner, Robert Sangster (Swettenham Stud) in a Thatching foal. Resubmitted from her Manor House Stud, Middleham, at the following year's Highflyer Sales, the colt realized 52,000 guineas to the bid of trainer Richard Hannon.

Tirol, as he was named, is one of only three winners of the English and Irish 2000 Guineas, following Right Tack in 1969 and Don't Forget Me (also trained by Richard Hannon) in 1987. The son of Thatching is also a third individual English classic winner to have been bred and raised at Manor House Stud after the Nearco brothers, Dante and Sayajirao. Tirol now stands alongside Don't Forget Me at Coolmore.

When Lennie Peacock's husband, Dick, died in 1984, it marked the end of 100 years' occupation of the historic Manor House stables by the Peacocks. Dick had succeeded his father, Matthew, in 1951, and he in turn had succeeded his father, Dobson, in 1935. Matthew's brother, Harry, also trained at Middleham (Spigot Lodge) before moving to Richmond.

Both Dante and Sayajirao, respective winners of the 1945 Derby and 1947 St Leger, were bred officially by Friar Ings Stud, the title by which Sir Eric Ohlson's handful of mares kept at Manor House Stud were known. A shipping magnate from Hull, he had a farm at Catterick called Friar Ings.

Eric Ohlson had acquired Dante 'in utero' when paying 3,500 guineas for the mare Rosy Legend at the 1941 December Sales from the late Lord Furness. Trained by Matthew Peacock, Dante, who had failed to make his reserve as a yearling, became the first northern trained winner of the Derby (albeit a substitute affair at Newmarket) since Pretender in 1869 – the feat has yet to be repeated.

Within a few months of Dante's great triumph, his own-brother Sayajirao was purchased on behalf of the Maharajah of Baroda for 28,000 guineas. This remained a record price for a yearling until superseded twenty-one years later by a Charlottesville colt which realized 31,000 guineas.

Plagued by moon blindness, Dante spent the duration of his stud life in Yorkshire at Theakston Stud. He is sire of the classic winners Darius (2000 Guineas), sire of Derring-Do, and Carrozza (Oaks). Sayajirao, who also won the Irish Derby, spent his entire stud innings at his owner's Baroda Stud, Co. Kildare. His progeny include Indiana (St Leger), Gladness (Ascot Gold Cup), and Lynchris (Irish Oaks, Irish St Leger).

One of the outstanding winners out of a Dante mare is Tudor Melody whom Dick Peacock bought and trained for Fred Ellison. A chemical manufacturer from Birkenshaw, near Bradford, Ellison kept his breeding stock at Manor House Stud. His foundation mares were Path of Peace and Sylvia's Grove. Both were purchased as mares during the war, the former from Lord Glaneley's executors and the latter from Sledmere.

Path of Peace's daughter Colombelle did well for Fred Ellison, breeding two winners of the Seaton Delaval Stakes in Dornoch and Lindsay. The latter won the Cheveley Park Stakes and was the top-rated filly on the Free Handicap which was headed by Tudor Melody, both trained by Dick Peacock.

Colombelle continues to do well at Manor House Stud through another of her daughters, Arrangement. She is the dam of Bold Arrangement, who finished second in the 1986 Kentucky Derby (trained in Newmarket by Clive Brittain) and is the grandam of Galitzin (Guardian Classic Trial Stakes). To Galitzin's sire Hotfoot, Lennie Peacock also bred Hotbee (Molecomb Stakes), who at 100-1 is the longest priced winner ever of a Group race!

Another of Path of Peace's daughters, Mountain Path, is dam of Theakston-bred Sovereign Path, as well as Grischuna. The latter became one of the mainstays of Gerald Oldham's Citadel Stud and is grandam of Sagaro, hero of three consecutive Ascot Gold Cups, a unique achievement.

Sylvia's Grove produced another top juvenile for Fred Ellison in Precast (Gimcrack Stakes). Colombelle's half-sister Queen's Fable also did well for the late Duke of Roxburghe, her son Sweet Story (Yorkshire Cup) becoming a stallion at his Floors Stud.

The mare responsible for breeding Tirol is Alpine Niece (Great Nephew – Fragrant Morn), whose sire and dam were both bred by the late Jim Philipps (Dalham Hall Stud). Lennie Peacock bought her privately for £1,000 from the Upper Lambourn stable of her brother-in-law, Major Peter Nelson. Alpine Niece died *en route* to Ireland to revisit Thatching in 1990, but Manor House does have two unraced half-sisters in Nice Point and Classic Design.

Earlier the Peacocks had been responsible for Marisela who finished runner-up in the 1972 1000 Guineas to Waterloo. Culled from Manor House Stud, Marisela's half-sister Golden City is the grandam of a very smart sprinter in Indian Ridge.

The Peacocks have had plenty of boarding mares over the years and when Cecil Moores of Littlewoods Football Pools retired from breeding Aberdeen Angus cattle he asked Dick and Lenny to buy and keep him a few mares. One Tudor Romp (by Tudor Melody) bred Whitstead (Great Voltigeur Stakes). Cecil Moores called his breeding operation Mayfield Stud after his Liverpool home.

Lenny Peacock has been involved in running Manor House Stud since the early fifties. There have only been three stud grooms during that time, the present one, Alan Hogg, having been there since 1968. Apart from having the right mares, Lennie Peacock considers that three essential ingredients for any stud are a good staff, good limestone land and good water, and they have all three up at Middleham which can now boast an impressive new yearling yard.

Although Manor House Stud has been involved with some substantial prices at the yearling sales, Lennie Peacock hit the jackpot at Sothebys rather than Tattersalls. In December 1986 a gold and sapphire reliquary pendant dating back to the fifteenth century, which had been discovered on one of her tenanted farms, realised £1.2 million at public auction in London!

Meon Valley Stud

BISHOP'S WALTHAM · HAMPSHIRE

In 1979, Helena Springfield Ltd won the 1000 Guineas with One in a Million. Seven years later the distinctive black colours with white spots triumphed with homebred Colorspin in the Gilltown Stud Irish Oaks. In the interim Bella Colora, a half-sister to Colorspin, was third in a virtual three-way dead-heat for the fillies' classic at Newmarket.

Not only was One in a Million the first company-owned winner of an English classic but she also belonged to the first crop of runners to represent Egon and Elizabeth Weinfeld under the Helena Springfield label – and unbelievably Bella Colora came from only the second crop of foals that they bred themselves.

Understandably when the Weinfelds were looking for a suitable advertising slogan for their Meon Valley Stud in which they are partners with their grown-up children, Mark and Helena, they chose 'Cradle of the Classic Thoroughbred'. Since the war many newcomers have aspired to owning and breeding classic winners, but very few have succeeded.

The foundations of Meon Valley Stud were laid in Tattersalls' Park Paddocks during the autumn of 1977 when four yearling fillies were bought with the help of Richard Galpin of the Newmarket Bloodstock Agency. Two of them, One in a Million (18,500 guineas) and Odeon (38,000 guineas) were at the Houghton Sales (now Highflyer Sales), while Reprocolor (25,000 guineas) was at the December Sales.

All four remained in Newmarket to be trained, One in a Million and Odeon by Henry Cecil, and Reprocolor by Michael Stoute. Between them this trio made twenty-seven racecourse appearances at two and three years, and they finished in the frame in all but two of them (both Group I), a breathtaking record of consistency. Nine of the ten victories and ten of the fifteen places were in stakes races.

Rated 125 by Timeform at three years, One in a Million justified favouritism in the 1000 Guineas, Coronation Stakes and Ladbroke Nell Gwyn Stakes; Odeon won the Galtres Stakes, York, and was Group placed eight times; and Reprocolor won the Lingfield Oaks Trial Stakes and Lancashire Oaks and was fourth in the Oaks. What aspiring breeder would not have been delighted with any one of these fillies, never mind three?

Initially they commenced their stud careers as boarders, since the Weinfelds did not possess their own stud at the time. However the following year Egon and Elizabeth found the ideal property south of Winchester. This was Dean Farm at Bishop's Waltham, on the fringes of the Meon Valley, once utilized by Bill Wightman and overlooking his gallops.

Acquired from Lord Penrhyn in the autumn of 1980, Dean Farm met all the Weinfelds' priorities. Firstly it was virgin land so far as horses were concerned, and secondly it had a sufficient acreage to enable Mark Weinfeld to farm independently. In due course the 100 acres in the immediate vicinity of the house were converted into an idyllic private stud.

Egon Weinfeld is a perfectionist and always seeks expert advice. Consequently all the amenities at Meon Valley are of the highest standard. No detail has been overlooked so far as the creation of the paddocks and buildings are concerned, but the number one priority was the seeding down of all the pasture on what was predominantly arable downland on chalk.

Meon Valley first became operational in the spring of 1982, most of the mares taking up permanent residence following that season's coverings. The Weinfelds were in business as commercial breeders supplying yearlings to the Newmarket sales, but initially they had a preponderance of females, so they retained more animals than they sold.

Once the produce of the stud came on stream, Michael Stoute has been their principal trainer. He has handled three exceptional homebred fillies in the half-sisters Bella Colora and Colorspin, followed by Milligram. A Group winner in England (Waterford Candelabra Stakes) and France (Prix de l'Opera), Bella Colora was beaten two short heads by Oh So Sharp and Al Bahathri for the 1000 Guineas. At the 1988 Highflyer Sales, Sheikh Mohammed bought Bella Colora's Sadler's Wells colt (Stagecraft) for 520,000 guineas, a record for Meon Valley Stud.

The year after producing Bella Colora, Reprocolor foaled Colorspin. One of a vintage collection of fillies trained at Beech Hurst stables, she won the Gilltown Stud Irish Oaks in commanding fashion and was a major contributor to her dam gaining the TBA's Broodmare of the Year award.

There was great expectancy regarding the appearance of Reprocolor's Mill Reef colt at the 1986 Highflyer Sales, but the Weinfelds then withdrew him, having decided to race him themselves. Named Classic Connection, he injured himself as a juvenile on his only start and was eventually exported for stallion duties in Italy.

However the Weinfelds did have a top-class performer by Mill Reef in Milligram, One in a Million's foal of 1984. Runner-up in the General Accident 1000 Guineas (to Miesque) and Goffs' Irish 1000 Guineas (to Forest Flower), she then won the Queen Elizabeth II Stakes at the inaugural Festival of British Racing, Coronation Stakes and Waterford Crystal Mile. Based in the USA since retiring to stud, Milligram produced her first foal in 1989 – a colt by Alleged. Since then she has had fillies by Alysheba and Nureyev prior to visiting Dayjur in 1991.

One of the key figures on any stud, public or private, is the stud groom, and Meon Valley's for the first nine years was Tony Hopes. Previously he had occupied that position for nineteen years at the Riley-Smiths' Brewhurst Stud, now disbanded, in Sussex.

To have produced fillies of the calibre of Bella Colora, Colorspin and Milligram, in so short a space of time, is a singular achievement. By the law of averages, the Weinfelds should soon be making their mark with some comparable colts. One for whom there are high expectations is Opera House (Sadler's Wells – Colorspin). A first foal, Opera House, who represents the formidable Sheikh Mohammed–Michael Stoute combination, was one time ante-post favourite for the 1991 Ever Ready Derby.

Minster Stud

BARNSLEY · GLOUCESTERSHIRE

Champion jockeys Steve Donoghue and Lester Piggott feature as the respective breeders of 1919 Ascot Gold Cup hero By Jingo and 1973 Derby runner-up Cavo Doro, but five times champion Willie Carson became the only jockey to breed (and ride) the winner of an English classic when Minster Son triumphed in the 1988 Holsten Pils St Leger.

Minster Son, who was saddled by Neil Graham, the temporary licence holder at West Ilsley while Major Dick Hern was recovering from a serious operation, was a 36,000-guinea yearling purchase by the Dowager Lady Beaverbrook at the 1986 Newmarket October Sales. She named the Niniski colt after Willie Carson's stud at Barnsley, near Cirencester, in Gloucestershire.

When he purchased the property from Mrs Joane Wood in the spring of 1980 it was known as Ampney Stud. For a time, Joane Wood, who died six years later, stood three modest stallions there simultaneously, Wynkell being one of two sons of inaugural Washington DC International winner Wilwyn. To the same sire she also bred Ampney Princess (Diadem Stakes), whose son Ampney Prince stood at her stud in the Cotswolds.

The first Group winner bred by Willie Carson (actually a partnership venture) was Sovereign Rose whom he partnered to win the 1980 Diadem Stakes for Dick Hern. The Sharpen Up filly was reared at Thomas Warner's Red House Stud at Exning, on the outskirts of Newmarket, where her dam Sovereign Flower was boarded. Unfortunately she died foaling, so Sovereign Rose was reared on a bottle.

Prior to Dick Hern, Willie Carson was stable jockey to Bernard van Cutsem for whom he rode Sharpen Up to win the Middle Park Stakes. The colt was homebred by Mimi van Cutsem at her husband's Northmore Stud Farm, also at Exning. In fact it was Bernard van Cutsem who originally suggested that Willie Carson should involve himself in bloodstock breeding.

Willie Carson's very first mare, Hay-Hay, was responsible for getting him off the mark as a breeder with Willie Sing. By the Red House resident Mansingh, he won a seller at Nottingham in October 1978. Hay-Hay was a great favourite. Still going strong in her twenties, she joined Willie Carson's parents-in-law up in Cheshire to breed jumpers.

An enormous amount of work was necessary to convert the original Ampney Stud from a dilapidated public stud into a modern commercial yearling unit. Fencing and building soon transformed the property which was renamed Minster Stud, the former Glebe Farm being owned by the Church. Adjoining land has since been added and the stud is now just under 100 acres.

It was a considerable bonus to inherit stud groom Jim Smith. Such is his wealth of experience that Willie Carson has no worries about leaving the day-to-day running in his hands – all the mares are foaled at home whenever possible as a matter of routine. Willie and his wife moved to Minster House in December 1982, by which time their handful of mares had arrived from John George, near Stroud, amongst them Honey Bridge.

It was Rhydian Morgan-Jones, then associated with the British Bloodstock Agency, who had secured Honey Bridge for 10,000 guineas as a three-year-old out of Henry Cecil's stable at the 1978 Newmarket December Sales. By Crepello, from the family of that good Italian horse Stateff, she had scored as a juvenile for her breeder, Sir John Hornung of High Hurst Manor Stud.

Although she has not proved the most regular of breeders, Honey Bridge has excelled to matings with Niniski, one of many leading winners ridden by Willie Carson for the former Dick Hern–Lady Beaverbrook combination. The first of these unions produced Gianchi. Ridden by his breeder to be placed in the Derby Italiano, Gianchi died at stud in Ireland before his first crop ran (and won) during 1990. Four years earlier Willie Carson completed the Derby Italiano Lancia and Gran Premio di Milano double on John Dunlop's Tommy Way. Reared at Minster Stud out of the boarding mare Tilia, he was actually consigned to the Milan yearling sales only to fail the conformation scrutineers!

The second of those Niniski matings was responsible for Minster Son whom Willie Carson describes as a real character. One of his idiosyncrasies was to stop dead in his tracks and only condescend to move when it suited him. However this did not prevent him from excelling as a three-year-old, his St Leger victory being prefaced by wins in the Newmarket Stakes, NM Financial Predominate Stakes and Gordon Stakes.

That season Minster Son's only reversal came in the Ever Ready Derby.

e ultramodern foaling unit at Gainsborough Stud. (*Gerry Cranham*)

scombe Stud. A wintry scene in the thatched main yard. (*Lesley I. Sampson*)

Kirtlington Stud's illustrious mare, Windmill Girl, whilst in training at Whatcombe. (*R. Anscomb*)

Juddmonte Farms. The impressive foaling unit, similar in style to Gainsborough Stud. (*Gerry Cranham*)

...niski, classic winner and ...ssic sire, at Lanwades ...d. (*Tim Hannan/TCA*)

...on Valley Stud's three ...ndation mares. Left to ...ht: One in a Million, ...procolor and Odeon. (*...uart Newsham*)

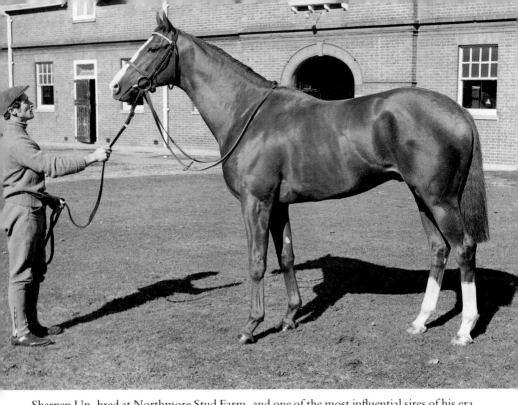

Sharpen Up, bred at Northmore Stud Farm, and one of the most influential sires of his era.
(*W.W. Rouch*)

The National Stud's stallion unit which attracts visitors from all over the world. (*Gerry Cranham*)

Yearlings parading in front of the fine Georgian house, Overbury Court. (*Fiona Vigors*)

Sandringham Stud. Leading sire Shirley Heights with Persimmon's statue in the background. (*Gerry Cranham*)

The luxurious new stallion barn at Nunne
Stud, part of the Shadwell complex. (*Ger
Cranham*)

Lord Derby's Hyperion, six times champion
sire, and a stalwart of Stanley House and
Woodlands Studs. (*W. W. Rouch*)

Contented mares enjoy the solitude of
leafy Stetchworth Park Stud. (*Fiona
Vigors*)

well Hill. Bred by Bob McCreery, gh Top is sire of five European classic nners, including Top Ville. (*Colorlabs ernational*)

Kris, an outstanding contemporary sire, at Thornton Stud. (*Laurie Morton*)

est Blagdon has a ique reputation for ding foals at the wmarket December es. (*Peter Greenland/ CA*)

Whitsbury Manor Stud, home of the young stallions, Midyan, Cadeaux Genereux and Distant Relative. (*Pascal Bouclier*)

LEFT An historic commercial stud, Worksop Manor celebrated its centenary in 1990. (*Fiona Vigors*)

BELOW Mrs Roger Hue-Williams of Woolton House Stud with the luckless Rock Roi. (*Central Press*)

BOTTOM A champion sprinter, Cadeaux Genereux (seen in training), was bred at Woodminton Farm. (*John Crofts*)

Ridden by his breeder in preference to two other fancied stable companions, he ricked his back in running. Although the son of Niniski remained in training as a four-year-old, he never ran again and was retired to stand at the late Lady Durham's Longholes Stud at Newmarket.

Shortly after the St Leger, Lady Beaverbrook bought Minster Son's yearling half-brother privately (although he was in the Newmarket October Sales catalogue) and he scored for her as Myhamet. His sire Gorytus was another Dick Hern star and Willie Carson was responsible for breeding his very first winner, Precious Platinum. She was one of three of Sovereign Rose's progeny to be trained at West Ilsley, the others being Hauwmal and Zeeko.

The top price that Minster Stud has obtained for a yearling at public auction is the 165,000 guineas paid by Sheikh Mohammed for the Habitat filly, Model Village, at the 1988 Highflyer Sales. One of four purchases made at that year's December Sales (thereby doubling his broodmare band at a single stroke) was Model Bride. Two years later her half-sister Modena made headlines as the dam of Elmaamul (Coral-Eclipse Stakes, Phoenix Champion Stakes), bred by Willie's good friend Rhydian Morgan-Jones.

There is no denying the influence of West Ilsley at Minster Stud. According to Willie Carson it is of great benefit to have ridden the animals in question, particularly with regard to temperament. One day soon he is going to have to forfeit that advantage.

Moyns Park Stud

BIRDBROOK · ESSEX

From 1964 to 1984 Mr and Mrs John F.C.Bryce bred the winners of over 350 races at their picturesque Moyns Park Stud. Throughout that time the stud was managed by Captain Bobby Dolbey who then became manager of Sheikh Hamdan Al Maktoum's Shadwell Stud. One of the Shadwell broodmare band is none other than Dish Dash – she became Ivor Bryce's last notable winner in the 1982 Ribblesdale Stakes.

Ivor Bryce died in 1985 whereupon the Moyns Park Estate was inherited by the brothers George, Marquess of Milford Haven, and Ivar, Lord Mountbatten, their mother being the former Janet Bryce, Ivor's cousin. Since then, George Milford Haven, whose father-in-law, George Walker, was chief executive of the Brent Walker leisure group (owners of bookmakers William Hill and Mecca), has become the outright owner of the property.

Moyns Park, which is situated at Birdbrook, fifteen miles to the south of Newmarket just over the Suffolk county boundary into Essex, is dominated by a magnificent Elizabethan mansion. This moated house was built four centuries ago by a local landowner, Sir Thomas Gent, not long before receiving his knighthood in 1586. The estate came into the Bryce family towards the end of the last century.

An American, Mrs Ivor Bryce was well known in racing circles on both sides of the Atlantic. In her home country she raced as Mill River Stable and also owned Black Hole Hollow Farm, one of few studs in the small New England state of Vermont. Two horses which she raced there were Chop Chop, who was destined to become a very influential broodmare sire, and top race mare Miss Grillo, the grandam of Meadow Court.

Sam Armstrong and his son, Robert, trained most of the Bryce runners at home, but initially, like so many of her compatriots, Josephine Bryce had horses with Sir Cecil Boyd-Rochfort. The first to carry her colours of red, orange triangle and cap, were the contemporaries Big Dipper and

North Carolina, the former being the champion two-year-old of 1950. It was in 1959 that Ivor and Jo Bryce started the stud at their Moyns Park home where the thatched roofs to the stabling, painted in a red and white colour scheme, were an undoubted feature. The following year it became operational with eight mares. One of two that had previously been boarded elsewhere was Maliki. Her son Afghanistan (1957) had scored seven times for Jo Bryce before becoming a sire in New Zealand.

The very first crop of Moyns Park foals included two fine colts in Con Brio (Ribot − Petronella) and Birdbrook (Mossborough − Game Bird). The former won the Brighton Derby Trial while the latter scored sixteen victories altogether having been sold cheaply as a three-year-old − the subsequent policy of the stud was to sell all colts as foals.

Both horses made their names as sires. Con Brio sired Cawston's Clown, the champion juvenile filly of 1970, before departing to Argentina. Birdbrook, who stood at the late Lord McAlpine's Dobson's Stud, Henley-on-Thames, sired the champion Italian miler Brook and Girl Friend.

Of even greater significance from that 1961 crop of foals was another son of Ribot in Prince Royal II whose dam was boarded there for American Charles Wacker III. Prince Royal placed the stud on the international bloodstock map by defeating Santa Claus for the 1964 Prix de l'Arc de Triomphe.

Animals bred by Moyns Park Stud have gained their share of successes in France, notably with Rose Laurel (Prix Eugene Adam, Prix Daru, Criterium de Maisons-Laffitte) and his half-sister, Rambling Rose (Prix du Petit Couvert). Bally Game, a grandson of one of the original foundation mares, Game Bird, was runner-up in the Poule d'Essai des Poulains.

A couple more mares to have at least two good sons to their credit are Rave Notice, dam of Riot Act and Laurentian Hills, and Lovely Lady, dam of the own-brothers Patron Saint and St Columbus, the winners of eighteen races between them. St Columbus has made his own contribution to jump breeding as the sire of Maori Venture (1987 Grand National) and the maternal grandsire of Norton's Coin (1990 Cheltenham Gold Cup). Funny Man is another jumping sire bred by the stud. One of Jo Bryce's best bargains was Shoolerville. A $10,000 yearling at Saratoga, he won the Temple Stakes before retiring to Lockinge Stud.

In no time at all Moyns Park Stud had established a solid reputation as one of Tattersalls' leading foal vendors, just like Lady Wyfold's Sarsden House Stud from whom the Bryces procured Nymphet (Nearula − Circassia) as a foal in 1958 for 4,000 guineas. Her daughter, Loose Cover, became the best known of all the stud's mares.

Responsible for a new world record time for a mile recorded at Brighton,

149

Loose Cover had as her first foal the Exbury filly Canterbury Tale – she established a new world record for a foal at public auction when realizing 37,000 guineas at the 1968 Newmarket December Sales. Purchased on behalf of Paul Mellon, Canterbury Tale was the first of her dam's three black-type winners followed by Smoggy (also in the USA) and Dish Dash.

One of comparatively few filly foals to have been sold by Moyns Park Stud in its annual foal consignment is Triple First (High Top – Field Mouse), whose grandam, Meadow Song, had been procured halfway through her stud innings. A 7,800-guinea foal, Triple First won the Nassau Stakes, Sun Chariot Stakes and Musidora Stakes and was fourth in the Oaks. That season she was sold for 118,000 guineas to Hesmonds Stud for whom she proved an exceptional broodmare. Jo Bryce's colours were also carried into third place in the Oaks by Tender Annie (Ribblesdale Stakes), a yearling purchase from the National Stud.

In recent years the future of Moyns Park Stud has hung in the balance. For an interim period the stud was leased to Graham Beck. The leading breeder in South Africa, who now owns Gainesway Farm, one of the great stallion stations in Kentucky, he operated there as Guiting Stud having originally bought the stud of that name in Gloucestershire. For the moment, at least, there are more polo ponies at Moyns Park than thoroughbreds.

The National Stud

NEWMARKET · SUFFOLK

Mill Reef is the most famous of the many great horses to have stood at the National Stud, which has its origins in Ireland rather than England. In 1916 the British Government accepted the generous offer of Colonel Hall-Walker (later Lord Wavertree) of his entire breeding stock subject to buying at its own valuation his stud at Tully, Co. Kildare, and training stable, Russley Park, near Baydon, in Wiltshire.

William Hall-Walker's unorthodox method of determining his matings with the aid of a horoscope yielded surprising dividends, highlighted by Cherry Lass (1000 Guineas, Oaks), Minoru (Derby), who was leased to King Edward VII, and Prince Palatine (Ascot Gold Cup, twice). The stud had only been in existence since 1900 so the forty-three mares offered to the nation constituted some of the most prized bloodlines in the Stud Book.

The new National Stud under its first two directors, Sir Henry Greer and Noble Johnson, flourished. Three colts produced between the wars exercised a worldwide influence. First and foremost came Blandford, three times champion sire with four Derby winners to his credit in Trigo, Blenheim, Windsor Lad and Bahram. Challenger became a champion sire in the USA, and Stardust sired Star Kingdom (later Star King), who founded a male dynasty in Australasia.

Following the classic successes of The Panther (2000 Guineas) and Royal Lancer (St Leger), the National Stud had the winners of four of the five substitute classics run at Newmarket during 1942 with Big Game (2000 Guineas) and Sun Chariot (1000 Guineas, Oaks, St Leger). Both celebrities carried the colours of King George VI. Hitherto animals leased from the National Stud carried Lord Lonsdale's colours, the new arrangement being at the instigation of Peter Burrell.

Director of the National Stud for 34 years (1937–1971), Peter Burrell,

CBE, had the onerous task of transferring the operation from Ireland to England. In 1943 the Irish Government laid claim to Tully (now the Irish National Stud), whereupon Peter Burrell was able to negotiate the purchase of Compton Stud, near Gillingham, in Dorset, from the executors of Lord Furness.

In due course Gillingham's 400 acres (now Sandley Stud) were augmented by 600 leased acres at West Grinstead Stud in West Sussex. While Big Game, who became an outstanding broodmare sire, and Elopement held court at Gillingham, West Grinstead provided a home for such as Jock Scot, Tenerani, Pindari and Never Say Die.

Meantime the National Stud added to its classic roll of honour, with Chamossaire triumphing in the St Leger and Carrozza winning the Oaks for the Queen. Her Majesty subsequently leased another top performer in Hopeful Venture.

In 1963 responsibility for the National Stud switched from the Ministry of Agriculture, Fisheries and Food, to the Horserace Betting Levy Board. It also decided to concentrate on standing stallions. Consequently the prized broodmare band was dispersed at the following year's Newmarket December Sales. As neither Gillingham nor West Grinstead were suitable for further expansion, a new purpose-built stud was masterminded by Peter Burrell on 500 Newmarket acres held on a 999-year lease from the Jockey Club. Situated adjacent to the July Course, it incorporates the old Heath Stud which provides access at Stetchworth Toll where the London and Cambridge roads to Newmarket converge.

The Queen officially opened the new National Stud on 17 April 1967, by which time Never Say Die, champion sire of 1962, and Tudor Melody were already installed. One of the finest stallion stations in Europe, the stud is a testimonial to Peter Burrell's vision and enterprise. Hygiene was high on his list of priorities and to facilitate controlling any outbreak of disease or infection, the ten barns for visiting mares are all strategically placed well apart.

Never Say Die was the first of five Derby winners to have stood at the National Stud, his successors being Mill Reef, Grundy, Royal Palace and Blakeney. Homebred by Paul Mellon, the great Mill Reef is responsible for the 1978 and 1987 Derby winners, Shirley Heights and Reference Point – in each of those two seasons he was champion sire.

Other famous stallions to have covered at this impressive establishment are Stupendous, Tudor Melody, Hopeful Venture, Habat, Star Appeal, Moorestyle, Final Straw, Natroun and Rousillon, along with the present occupants Blakeney (now in his dotage), Chilibang, Jalmood and Petoski,

and 1991 newcomers Be My Chief and Rock City. The National Hunt
sires Town and Country and Weld are boarded out.

The National Stud purchased a quarter interest in Be My Chief as a
two-year-old when he was the unbeaten winner of the Lanson Champagne
Vintage Stakes, Imry Solario Stakes and Racing Post Trophy. He was
homebred in America by Peter Burrell. He retired as director of the National
Stud in the summer of 1971; his two successors were Lieutenant-Colonel
Douglas Gray and Michael Bramwell.

In accordance with the recommendations of the Sparrow Committee
of Enquiry into the future of the National Stud, a new board took over
from the Levy Board in 1986. This has been chaired in turn by Christopher
Collins, Sir John Sparrow himself (he is now chairman of the Levy Board),
and Nicholas Jones – managing director of Lazard Brothers, he took charge
on 1 April 1991. The remaining directors are David Gibson of Barleythorpe
Stud, former trainer Bruce Hobbs, bloodstock writer Peter Willett, and
Sir Philip Payne-Gallwey of the British Bloodstock Agency. Since Michael
Bramwell's departure, the new role of manager has been filled by his erst-
while assistant, Miles Littlewort.

Nowadays the National Stud opens its doors to the paying public and
has generally widened the scope of its activities. A comprehensive training
course for students takes place for the duration of the breeding season.
During the December Sales, when Newmarket plays host to visitors from
all over the world, there is a stallion show held in conjunction with the
British Bloodstock Agency, as well as a specialist trade fair for all sections
of the thoroughbred industry.

New England Stud

NEWMARKET · SUFFOLK

Travelling along the Newmarket by-pass towards the east coast, the first indication of the vast number of studs on the periphery of the town are the tall trees hiding the paddocks of New England Stud on the right-hand side. During and after the last war, the property was owned by James Vose Rank, whose father founded the great flour milling business which still trades as Ranks Hovis McDougall.

A substantial patron of racing under both Rules, James Rank had a private training establishment at Druids Lodge, high on the Wiltshire Downs not far from Stonehenge, presided over by Noel Cannon. Rank had purchased the remote Druids Lodge in 1934 which coincided with his first notable winner, Annihilation, in Epsom's Great Metropolitan Stakes.

Annihilation was by Obliterate. He was probably the best colt bred by Sir Robert (Buchanan) Jardine whose son, Sir John, had sold New England Stud to James Rank in 1939. One of the founder members of Jardine Mathieson, the famous Scottish trading company based in the Far East, Robert Jardine won the 1920 1000 Guineas with homebred Cinna. Her son Beau Pere became an outstanding sire in Australasia.

Baroness la Fleche, dam of Cinna, was bred by Sir Tatton Sykes at Sledmere. So too was Scottish Union who was probably the top colt to race for James Rank. A 3,000-guinea yearling, he triumphed in the 1938 St Leger having finished runner-up in the 2000 Guineas and Derby. Over a period of time, Rank did well with Sledmere stock, another being Orthodox.

Amongst the leading three-year-olds of his generation, Orthodox was one of six Sledmere colts scheduled for the 1939 Doncaster sales – when these were cancelled, Jimmy Rank bought the sextet privately. It was during the war that the Rank colours gained their only classic success with a homebred runner, Why Hurry, capturing the New Oaks of 1943.

James Rank used to say that he had three sporting ambitions, to win the Derby, the Grand National and the Waterloo Cup. Prior to Scottish Union finishing second in the Derby, his Cooleen had occupied the same position at Liverpool in 1937, and Joker's Resort had been second at Altcar in 1935. Of the numerous good chasers he owned, the best was Prince Regent, hero of the 1946 Cheltenham Gold Cup.

When James Rank died in January 1952, he owned no less than seven stallions. Scottish Union, Hyperbole and Vigorous were at New England Stud, Orthodox, Epigram and Jock Scot also stood in Newmarket, and King Legend was based outside Reading. Apart from Scottish Union and Epigram, all featured at the Rank dispersal that July when eighty-three lots aggregated 172,560 guineas.

At 8,900 guineas, the top-priced mare was homebred Daring Miss whose dam Venturesome had been acquired from Sledmere. Only the previous month her son Gay Time had finished runner-up in the Derby for Mrs Rank – by the terms of her husband's will, she was able to choose six animals to keep for herself. Daring Miss's then yearling was Elopement and she was carrying Cash and Courage.

Gay Time, Elopement and Cash and Courage were all colts by Rockefella. After the Derby, Gay Time was bought by the National Stud, but as he proved temperamental, he was soon banished to Japan. Later the National Stud acquired and stood his own-brother Elopement, winner of the Hard-wicke Stakes for Sir Victor Sassoon.

Towards the close of 1952 New England Stud was acquired by the present Lord Derby's younger brother, Richard Stanley, who installed Commander N.J.W. Barttelot as manager. One of the first stallions under the new regime was Migoli (Prix de l'Arc de Triomphe) and he was joined by Premonition. Of far greater significance was the arrival of Lord Derby's Mossborough.

Bred by the 17th Earl (who died when the colt was a yearling) and raced by the 18th and present Earl, Mossborough (Nearco – All Moonshine) was a far better sire than he was a racehorse, but then he had the right pedigree – his dam is a three-parts sister to Hyperion.

Initially retired to Longholes Stud, Newmarket, Mossborough was sold by Lord Derby to a partnership comprising Richard Stanley, Captain Philip Dunne and Bernard van Cutsem. After four seasons at Longholes, he came to New England for the 1956 season and remained there until his demise in 1971, aged twenty-four.

Mossborough was champion sire of 1958 by virtue of Ballymoss (Prix de l'Arc de Triomphe, King George VI and Queen Elizabeth Stakes, St Leger, Eclipse Stakes, Coronation Cup), who in turn was champion sire of 1967. Outstanding amongst Mossborough's fillies is Noblesse (Oaks); he is also broodmare sire of Exbury (Prix de l'Arc de Triomphe). To Mossborough, Richard Stanley bred Beaufront (Lingfield Oaks Trial Stakes).

The Stanleys each bred a Group 1 winner, Richard with African Sky (Prix de la Foret), who became an Irish National Stud stallion, and his wife, Susan, with Waterloo (1972 1000 Guineas), whom she sold later to Mrs Peter Burrell. Both animals have strong Stanley House connections. African Sky's grandam was bred by Lord Derby and Hyperion is Waterloo's maternal grandsire.

Since Mossborough, New England stallions have comprised Silly Season, Pieces of Eight, Hittite Glory, Hot Grove, Bustomi, Precocious and the present incumbent Celestial Storm. The latter had his first crop of runners in 1991. Silly Season was homebred by Paul Mellon. He used to keep a few mares at New England (his UK mares are now with Emma Balding at Kingsclere), and his good horse Glint of Gold was bred there.

When Richard Stanley died in 1983, the stud became the property of his nephew, Peter Stanley, whose brother Edward is heir to the present Lord Derby. Peter manages the stud himself having taken over from Henry Plumptre who used to run Egerton Stud and Moyns Park Stud too before returning to Australia – it was in New Zealand that the 1991 Seagram Grand National hero, Seagram, was sired by New England-bred Balak.

Northmore Stud Farm

NEWMARKET · SUFFOLK

From 1940 to 1991, Northmore Stud Farm was owned by the van Cutsem family. During that period this establishment at Exning, on the outskirts of Newmarket, produced two particular celebrities in Sharpen Up, one of the most influential stallions of his generation, and Celtic Cone. The stud is now owned by Peter Trivass, a newcomer to racing and breeding.

Both Sharpen Up and Celtic Cone were trained by Bernard van Cutsem. Upon his death in 1975, the stud was inherited by his two sons, Hugh and Geoffrey, the former soon becoming the outright owner. At that juncture the *modus operandi* switched from breeding to race, to breeding to sell, in conjunction with a significant boarding involvement.

Northmore Stud Farm had belonged to Major James Borland Walker of Johnnie Walker whisky renown. A member of the Jockey Club, he was a moderately successful owner-breeder during the thirties. From his mare, La Chance, he bred Bouldnor (Ascot Stakes) and Chancery (Richmond Stakes). He also acquired Shalfleet 'in utero' with whom he won the Portland Handicap at Doncaster in 1935 and 1936.

Most of James Walker's horses were trained by Harvey Leader, and on moving stables he named his new yard Shalfleet. Here under Leader's tutelage, van Cutsem learnt the rudiments of training as a young man, having bought Beechwood House (long since demolished) at Exning upon coming down from Cambridge.

Back in Newmarket after wartime service with the Life Guards, Bernard van Cutsem purchased Graham Place (the premises are now occupied by Gavin Pritchard-Gordon), where Jack Leach trained for him. When Leach retired in 1957, van Cutsem took out a licence himself. Then in 1964 he moved to Stanley House having leased this historic establishment from Lord Derby.

Van Cutsem's most popular horse was the great Park Top. He had bought her as a yearling for only 500 guineas for the Duke of Devonshire as she was, by Kalydon, one of the first good animals bred at Northmore. Kalydon's stud career was divided between Willie Stephenson's Tudor Stud in Hertfordshire, and Side Hill Stud, Newmarket, of which van Cutsem was part owner for a number of years.

As an owner-trainer-breeder, Bernard van Cutsem utilized stallions of the 'Derby' breed extensively, but his two most significant foundation mares were closely related individuals of Lord Rosebery's breeding. Acquired as fillies in training, they were the minor winners Wood Fire and Coal Board. Granddaughters of Straitlace (Oaks), their dams were own-sisters by Blue Peter.

Wood Fire bred eight winners. They included Fircone, whose sire Mossborough was owned in partnership by van Cutsem and the late Richard Stanley of New England Stud. Fircone is dam of Celtic Cone (Yorkshire Cup), who became one of England's premier jumping sires at Cobhall Court Stud in Herefordshire.

Ironically the most successful branch of the family has been developed in the USA through Fircone's half-sister, Beaver Street. Once sold for a world broodmare record of $300,000, Beaver Street bred Native Street (Kentucky Oaks), dam of Royal and Regal (Florida Derby), and grandam of Dowsing (Vernons' Sprint Cup), who now stands at Eagle Lane Farm.

Coal Board went one better than Wood Fire with nine winning offspring. She did particularly well to matings with Kalydon and Mossborough. One of the best winners bred by Hugh van Cutsem is Miner's Lamp (Oettingen-Rennen), whose dam is Coal Face (Kalydon – Coal Board). Beyond the confines of Northmore, Coal Board's descendants include champion hurdler Lanzarote.

The top winner that Bernard van Cutsem bred to Kalydon is Ksar. Belonging to the same female family as Park Top, he won six Group races, in England, France and Italy. Fourth in the Derby to Morston, he became a sire in Australia.

All these Northmore winners pale into insignificance when compared to Sharpen Up (Atan – Rocchetta), who was bred, foaled and raised at Northmore for Bernard's third wife, Mimi, she having acquired the dam as a yearling from Lambourn Stud for 2,900 guineas. The nomination to Atan cost just 100 guineas. Doubtless Mimi only utilized his services as her parents, Jimmy and Alice Mills, had raced Atan themselves in the USA.

Undefeated in five juvenile starts culminating with the Middle Park Stakes, Sharpen Up retired to Side Hill Stud where he remained for eight seasons until departing to Gainesway Farm in Kentucky; he was pensioned off in 1989. With the own-brothers, Kris and Diesis, he has proved an outstanding sire of sires. Additional sons of Sharpen Up include Sharpo, Trempolino and Sanglamore, all Group 1 winners in France.

Hugh van Cutsem developed Northmore into one of Newmarket's best known commercial studs. Boarding mares and young stock became increasingly important with many patrons from home and abroad. One of these foreign clients was Walther Jacobs of Gestut Fahrhof. His top winners foaled at Northmore include the half-brothers Lagunas (Deutsches Derby) and Lirung (Prix du Haras de Fresnay-le-Buffard Jacques le Marois).

Another classic winner is Circus Plume (1984 Gold Seal Oaks). She was consigned from Northmore as a foal on behalf of her breeder, Mrs Camilla Drake (then based in Hong Kong), when realizing 98,000 guineas. Reared at Crichel Stud in Dorset, owned by Lieutenant-Commander Toby Marten (owner of Dead Certain), Circus Plume is a daughter of the Bernard van Cutsem-trained High Top.

Not only did Hugh van Cutsem increase the acreage of Northmore Stud Farm by leasing adjacent land and generally improving the facilities, but in 1985 he also bought part of an estate in Norfolk where he developed an entirely new breeding complex. This is Hilborough Stud, near Thetford, where the emphasis has always been on laying out mares and young stock for the duration of the winter. It was here that Hugh van Cutsem transferred his breeding enterprise when Northmore Stud Farm changed hands in February 1991.

Overbury Stud

OVERBURY · GLOUCESTERSHIRE

The King George VI and Queen Elizabeth (Diamond) Stakes was first run in 1951, the year of the Festival of Britain. Since then it has become established as the most important all-aged event in the British racing calendar. No renewal of this championship contest at Ascot in July has proved more memorable than when Grundy prevailed over Bustino in 1975 in a new course record time for one and a half miles.

That occasion is generally regarded as one of the great races of the century, a view that has persisted with the passing of the years. While congratulations were bestowed upon the owner (Dr Carlo Vittadini), trainer (Peter Walwyn), and jockey (Pat Eddery), there were celebrations too at Overbury Stud where this striking chestnut with a flaxen mane and tail was bred.

At that time Overbury was owned jointly by Edward (Ruby) Holland-Martin and his nephew, Tim Holland-Martin, and managed by the latter, a highly proficient amateur rider who was still competing under Rules in his fifties. Tim had taken over the running of the stud following the death of Ruby's brother, Thurstan, in 1968. The family, whose ancestors founded Martins Bank, have lived at Overbury since the early 1700s and they built the lovely Georgian house that is the centrepiece of the estate.

Overbury's postal address is near Tewkesbury in Gloucestershire, but most of the estate is in Worcestershire, at the extremity of the Cotswolds and that wonderfully fertile region known as the Evesham Vale. Forming part of a 5,000-acre estate in an area designated as being of outstanding natural beauty, the stud nestles beneath the southern slopes of Bredon Hill, immortalized by the pen of A.E. Houseman.

One of the most successful commercial yearling studs in the country over the last two decades, Overbury had its beginnings pre-war when Ruby Holland-Martin and his younger brother, Thurstan, bred hunters there.

It was during the war that Thurstan acquired two fillies, Farthing Damages and Lundy Parrot. To them the great success of Overbury is owed.

In 1940 Thurstan bought a couple of yearling fillies from a neighbour, Mrs V. Yorke of Forthampton, who was giving up breeding. The pair of them cost 120 guineas. One was Farthing Damages (Fair Trial – Futility). Destined to breed seven winners, she is dam of Whistler and third dam of Mummy's Pet, both very fast performers who did well as sires.

Winner of the Coventry Stakes, Royal Ascot, and a brilliant two-year-old, Whistler failed to score the ensuing season when troubled by breaking blood vessels. He spent the duration of his stud life (1955–69) at Cloghran Stud, Co. Dublin, where he died in 1975. His stallion sons include Mountain Call, Sound Track, Gentle Art, Tin Whistle, Sammy Davis and Whistling Wind.

Another sire of sires, Mummy's Pet was likewise based at the same location throughout his life as a stallion. At Barleythorpe Stud from 1972 to 1986, he was an outstanding sire of two-year-olds, heading that particular tabulation on two occasions. The son of Sing Sing was a smart sprinter himself, winning the Norfolk Stakes (now Flying Childers Stakes) at two, and the Temple Stakes at three.

Mummy's Pet was one of seven winners out of Money for Nothing, two more being Parsimony (July Cup, Cork and Orrery Stakes), dam of Scarcely Blessed (King George Stakes), and Arch Sculptor, who did well as a sire in Australia. Money for Nothing's granddaughter, Posada, also won the Cork and Orrery Stakes.

Grundy likewise stems from a sprinting family, his third dam being the second foundation mare, Lundy Parrot (Flamingo – Waterval). She proved an even bigger bargain than Farthing Damages having cost just thirty-five guineas as an unraced three-year-old from Lord Glanely's Exning Studs in December 1941. As dam of ten winners, she also improved on Farthing Damages's record numerically, albeit none of her offspring was in the Whistler class.

Like Grundy, Tower Walk is a great-grandson of Lundy Parrot, and he emulated Whistler by winning the Norfolk Stakes. Kept to sprinting after finishing runner-up in the 2000 Guineas, he proceeded to win the Prix de l'Abbaye de Longchamp, Nunthorpe Stakes and Palace House Stakes. A very useful sire, he died at Limestone Stud in 1989.

Six years earlier, Grundy (Great Nephew – Word from Lundy) departed to Japan following eight seasons at the National Stud. An 11,000-guinea yearling purchase by agent Keith Freeman, he was the leader of his generation at two and three years, winning the Derby, King George VI and

Queen Elizabeth Diamond Stakes, Irish 2000 Guineas and Irish Sweeps Derby. Unfortunately he was less successful at stud, although his progeny include Bireme (Oaks), one of his first crop, and Little Wolf (Ascot Gold Cup).

Whereas the Lundy Parrot family no longer exists at Overbury, the line stemming from Farthing Damages continues to flourish. In 1988 six yearlings were consigned to the Highflyer Sales and no less than five of them were descendants of this particular foundation mare.

The biggest money spinner has proved to be Parsimony. In 1978 her colt by Grundy (Sand Hawk) realized 264,000 guineas, which constituted a new European record for a thoroughbred at public auction. Three years later at the same venue, Parsimony's Mill Reef colt (Reefer Madness) sold for 460,000 guineas. Since that time Overbury has survived the one nightmare that breeders fear above all else – an outbreak of virus abortion. One of the most worrying aspects of this particular occurrence was that if it could happen at Overbury, a strictly private stud and one of the best appointed establishments in the country, it could happen anywhere.

Jack Nicholls played a major role at Overbury as stud groom from 1944 to 1967, the year after Tower Walk was foaled and the year before the arrival of Mummy's Pet. The present stud groom, Stuart Hall, succeeded Peter Diamond (who now runs a boarding establishment on part of the Tavistocks' Woburn Estate) in the early eighties. Like the majority of Overbury's stud staff, he was born and bred there.

Pinfold Stud

MARKET DRAYTON · SHROPSHIRE

Pinfold Stud has made a major contribution to bloodstock breeding through Petingo. He was champion sire of 1979 by virtue of Derby winner Troy, and another son, Pitcairn, was champion sire the following year when Ela-Mana-Mou emulated Troy in winning the King George VI and Queen Elizabeth Diamond Stakes. Troy was homebred by Sir Michael Sobell at his Ballymacoll Stud in Ireland; Ela-Mana-Mou raced for his grandson, Simon Weinstock.

Owned and managed by Alister Hall, Pinfold Stud is at Hales, a few miles east of Market Drayton on the Shropshire–Staffordshire border, where the Battle of Blore Heath was fought in 1495. Although 600 feet above sea level, the paddocks are well sheltered by substantial thorn hedges, with three sides of the stud being surrounded by even higher ground.

The stud extends to 300 acres of heavy loam with its own supply of calcium-rich spring water. It was originally known as Lloyd Stud when started as an adjunct to the original Pinfold Stud, at Marthall, near Knutsford, in Cheshire. Here Nicholas Hall, Alister's father, then chairman of the family-owned engineering business in Shrewsbury, created his successful breeding operation on what had been just a farm.

Nicholas Hall acquired his first two mares at the 1956 Newmarket December Sales. The first, Myrrha, bred Tournella, who carried his wife's colours to victory in the Falmouth Stakes before being sold to the USA. The second, Mistress Grace, is dam of Prince Supreme (Prix du Muguet). Beyond the confines of Pinfold, she became the grandam of Yelda (Cheshire Oaks), and No Mercy (Prix de Meautry).

Cassydora and Baby Doll were two important mares bought at the December Sales two years later. The former was carrying Cassarate. Sold as a foal, this Abernant filly was to triumph in the King's Stand Stakes for Vincent O'Brien. It was for the same trainer that Pieces of Eight (Relic

– Baby Doll) won the 1966 Eclipse Stakes and Champion Stakes. After standing in the USA, Pieces of Eight had an interim period in Newmarket before departing to Italy.

Petingo (Petition – Alcazar), who was conceived when his sire was twenty years of age, proved an even bigger star than Pieces of Eight. Representing a family that was synonymous with Kildangan Stud, his dam Alcazar, a winner at three years, and half-sister to Ambergris (Irish Oaks), had been bought for 8,000 guineas as an in-foal mare at the 1961 December Sales.

Petingo, a 7,800-guinea yearling purchase by Captain Marcos Lemos of Ashley Heath Stud, was the top-rated juvenile of his generation when unbeaten in three starts, including the Middle Park Stakes and Gimcrack Stakes. Runner-up to Sir Ivor in the 2000 Guineas, he then proved an outstanding miler with victories in the Sussex Stakes and St James's Palace Stakes.

Syndicated for £200,000, Petingo did brilliantly at Simmonstown Stud, Co. Kildare, part of the late Captain Tim Rogers's complex in Ireland. Sadly he suffered a fatal heart attack after completing only seven full covering seasons in February 1976. Alas his champion son Troy died at Highclere Stud after only three seasons. In that short space of time he accredited Ballymacoll Stud (where he was bred) with Gilltown Stud Irish Oaks heroine, Helen Street.

In 1971 Nicholas Hall decided to sell the original Pinfold Stud (a model establishment), whereupon he transferred the name and the stock to his Lloyd Stud. Amongst the very first batch of foals to arrive there was Royal Manacle. Sold privately as a yearling, he stayed remarkably well for a son of Manacle. Successful in the Thirsk Classic Trial, he was second in the William Hill Middle Park Stakes and St James's Palace Stakes and fourth in the 2000 Guineas.

Within a short space of time, Alister Hall, who had been brought up at Hales Hall on the estate, took over Pinfold Stud when his father decided to retire to Jersey. The new regime had two good colts from the 1974 crop with Limone and French Pageant. The former won the Chesham Stakes, Royal Ascot, and Ladbroke Craven Stakes, and the latter became a Group 1 winner in Mexico.

A member of the great American Gallorette family, Limone had a smart half-brother in Crested Grebe. He won the valuable Northern Dancer Handicap at the 1979 Epsom Derby meeting. Crested Grebe was a foal of 1975 when Robert Kitching, the present stud groom at Pinfold, took up that appointment and he has been responsible for foaling the majority of mares since that time.

The two best winners produced by Pinfold Stud during the eighties are probably the Group scorers Lemhill and Duca di Busted. Lemhill's victories include the Lanes End John Porter EBF Stakes while the most prestigious of Duca di Busted's eleven victories in Italy came in the Gran Premio Citta di Napoli.

That pair were noted for their durability and so too is Lemhill's year junior half-brother, Luna Bid. Having failed to attract a single bid as a yearling at the 1984 Newmarket Highflyer Sales, this son of Auction Ring was retained to carry Alister Hall's navy blue and emerald green colours, and he has proved an admirable sprint handicapper for Michael Blanshard's Upper Lambourn stable.

Their dam Moonscape, who was responsible for filly foals by Bellypha and Night Shift in 1989 and 1990 respectively, has proved the mainstay of Pinfold Stud just recently. She is half-sister to two Pinfold-breds who finished fourth in the Derby in Great Wall (King Edward VII Stakes) and Moon Mountain. Their dam Trip to the Moon was bought from Barton Stud, carrying Zamia (Prix des Foals, Deauville, Prix des Reves d'Or, Vichy), just before Petingo's dam in December 1961. His family is currently represented at Pinfold by Racemosa whose half-sister, Grecian Charter, is now pensioned off. The latter used to be one of three grey mares there by Runnymede, a son of Petingo's sire Petition.

Pinfold Stud has an enviable record of achievement. However Alister Hall was far from optimistic about the viability of breeding bloodstock at his level long before the present recession became manifest. He says that he cannot continue to subsidize the operation indefinitely, but with eight well-bred mares, who is to say that the stud will not emerge with another star during the nineties?

Plantation Stud

NEWMARKET · SUFFOLK

In the wake of Kris, Diesis, Slip Anchor and Paean, all homebred champions in different categories, it seems inconceivable that the all-apricot colours of their owner-breeder, Lord Howard de Walden, were previously considered to be singularly unlucky.

The marked change of fortune dates back to December 1967 when the three times senior steward of the Jockey Club, then a patron of Sir Noel Murless's stable, completed a package deal with Lady Sassoon for her Thornton Stud, resident stallion Hard Sauce, four in-foal mares and three fillies.

In due course the bulk of the Sassoon bloodstock was sold to Louis Freedman of Cliveden Stud, but by then two choice lots had already gone to Lord Howard de Walden. The solitary foal turned out to be Parmelia, the best staying filly of her generation, while one of the mares was Soft Angels, destined to become the grandam of Kris and Diesis.

Thornton Stud, near Thirsk in north Yorkshire, became an adjunct to its owner's Plantation Stud at Newmarket, and Templeton Stud at his Berkshire home, Avington Manor, near Hungerford. Since New Year's day 1973, Leslie Harrison has doubled up as Lord Howard's stud and racing manager.

Previously manager of the Hue-Williams' Woolton House Stud, Leslie Harrison took over at Plantation from Lieutenant-Colonel Adrian Scrope to whom he had once been a student. As stud manager to the 17th Earl of Derby, Bunty Scrope had a long association with Plantation Stud which Lord Howard de Walden purchased from Lord Derby in July 1958 – he had also owned Thornton Stud for a time.

Lord Howard inherited his distinctive colours from his father, the 8th baron, apricot having been Augustus John's choice as the colour that would contrast best with a green background. His most noted winner was Zinfandel

(Ascot Gold Cup), whom he acquired, together with Snailwell Stud, upon the death of Colonel Harry McCalmont in 1902.

Before buying Plantation, the present Lord Howard de Walden boarded his stock at Cheveley Park Stud. In 1948 he had acquired Sanlinea as a yearling and Silvery Moon in foal and they became his two original foundation mares. Each was associated with a top-class colt, Sanlinea as dam of Amerigo (Coventry Stakes), and Silvery Moon as grandam of Oncidium (Coronation Cup). Amerigo never recaptured his juvenile form here, only to do so in the USA, winning the San Juan Capistrano Handicap, Santa Anita, while Oncidium was a disappointing second favourite in the Derby prior to rewriting the record books as a sire in the Antipodes.

Lord Howard de Walden sold Silvery Moon's daughter, Argentina (dam of Falkland), to Captain Marcos Lemos, carrying the smart Averof. However Oncidium's dam, Malcolmia (fourth dam of Bellypha), set in motion a unique winning sequence from mother to daughter in the Ribblesdale Stakes thanks to Ostrya, Catalpa and Strigida. Parmelia also won this Royal Ascot feature.

It was only natural that Henry Cecil should continue as Lord Howard's principal trainer when Noel Murless retired (in the early days Jack Waugh had been in charge), and he handled the Group 1 scorers Kris (Sussex Stakes), Diesis (William Hill Dewhurst Stakes, William Hill Middle Park Stakes), Slip Anchor (Ever Ready Derby), Paean (Ascot Gold Cup), and Shavian (St James's Palace Stakes).

But for losing Soft Angel's first two (filly) foals, Lord Howard would have sold their half-sister, Doubly Sure, without whom there would have been no Kris and no Diesis. Mated with a cheap, local stallion in Sharpen Up (but not without due consideration, emphasizes Leslie Harrison), Doubly Sure produced Kris as her first foal. Fortunately no one listened to Henry Cecil's advice to sell him as a youngster and he became champion European miler of 1979 and 1980! At the age of twenty, Doubly Sure produced her thirteenth and final foal, a Danzig filly, in Kentucky in February 1991. Sadly, the mare, who was due for retirement, died only a few hours later.

The greatest celebrity to retire to stud north of the Trent since Dante, Kris has excelled at Thornton Stud. Champion sire of 1985 thanks to Triple Crown heroine Oh So Sharp (a member of his first crop), he was also leading British-based sire in each of the next two years. As it would not be expedient to stand two such own-brothers in England, a majority interest in Diesis was sold to Dr and Mrs John Chandler of Mill Ridge Farm in Kentucky. He too has made a big impact with such as Diminuendo and Elmaamul.

Lord Howard de Walden's solitary classic winner is Slip Anchor (Shirley Heights – Sayonara). He owes his existence to Leslie Harrison's belief that it might prove advantageous to mate a stallion of the refined Nasrullah male line with a tough German mare, Sayonara being acquired privately from the famous Gestut Schlenderhan. Unfortunately Slip Anchor failed to enhance his record as a four-year-old before covering his first mares at Plantation Stud in 1987.

While Slip Anchor was recording his initial winners in 1990, Lord Howard de Walden's colours were being carried to great effect by Shavian (Kris – Mixed Applause). That season he won the St James's Palace Stakes and Beefeater Gin Celebration Mile prior to becoming a syndicated stallion at Brook Stud. He is Lord Howard's first Group winner by Kris.

Shavian is also half-brother to Paean who provided his owner-breeder with yet another Group I victory at Royal Ascot in the 1987 Gold Cup. The son of Bustino was promptly sold to Ireland as a potential sire of jumpers, a sphere in which the all-apricot colours made their mark with champion hurdler Lanzarote. Another Plantation-bred in service as a National Hunt sire is Weld (Doncaster Cup, Jockey Club Cup), whom the National Stud purchased in 1990 to stand in Shropshire.

Lord Howard de Walden breeds to race rather than races to breed. Although he is given to saying that he cannot compete with the Arabs, he has actually managed to do so with conspicuous success. However there is no denying that the old English school of owner-breeder is an endangered species.

The Royal Studs

SANDRINGHAM · NORFOLK

With Highclere (1000 Guineas), Pall Mall (2000 Guineas), and Dunfermline (Oaks, St Leger), Her Majesty the Queen is owner-breeder of the winners of four of the five English classics. Only the Derby eludes her. Ironically the Queen sold Height of Fashion, dam of the 1989 Blue Riband hero Nashwan, to his owner-breeder, Sheikh Hamdan Al Maktoum of Shadwell Stud.

The Royal Studs have been in existence longer than the thoroughbred itself, having been founded by King Henry VIII at Hampton Court. Successive monarchs bred horses there, but none with greater success than Queen Victoria. She used to sell all the produce as yearlings, amongst them Sainfoin (Derby), Memoir (Oaks, St Leger), and La Fleche (1000 Guineas, Oaks, St Leger).

Even more consequential were the achievements of George II's son, William, Duke of Cumberland. At his stud in Windsor Great Park, 'The Butcher of Culloden' bred Eclipse and Herod, the two most brilliant racehorses and sires during the second half of the eighteenth century.

The present Royal Studs under manager Michael Oswald, comprise Sandringham and Wolferton, which are three miles apart, near King's Lynn in Norfolk, and Polhampton Lodge on the Hampshire–Berkshire border, near Kingsclere. It was in the 1880s that the Prince of Wales (later King Edward VII) decided to have a stud on his recently acquired Sandringham Estate.

The Prince of Wales owned an exceptional broodmare in Perdita II. Mated with St Simon, she produced the own-brothers Florizel II, Persimmon and Diamond Jubilee, all of whom stood at Sandringham. Persimmon, whose life-size statue presides over the forecourt to Sandringham, won the 1896 Derby and St Leger. Diamond Jubilee went one better by winning the Triple Crown four years later.

Both King George V and King George VI achieved a solitary homebred classic success in the 1000 Guineas, the former with Scuttle (1928), and the latter with Hypericum (1946). It is Hypericum's dam, Feola (Friar Marcus – Aloe), who has proved the cornerstone of the Royal Studs down to the present time. Acquired as a yearling for 3,000 guineas in 1934 by Brigadier Mouse Tomkinson, her sire had actually been bred by George V.

Placed in the 1000 Guineas and Oaks, Feola had three very influential daughters in Hypericum, Angelola and Above Board. Angelola bred Aureole (King George VI and Queen Elizabeth Stakes, Coronation Cup), who was runner-up for the Queen in her Coronation year for the Derby. Based at Wolferton Stud, he was champion sire in 1960 and 1961. The son of Hyperion is also grandsire of Vaguely Noble, another dual champion sire.

Above Board (Yorkshire Oaks) had two stallion sons in Doutelle and Above Suspicion. Two more half-sisters, Knight's Daughter and Starling II, exercised a worldwide influence through their respective sons, Round Table in the USA, and Sideral in Argentina.

The Queen maintains a broodmare band of about twenty of which approximately a third are descendants of Hypericum. In 1974 her granddaughter Highclere (Queen's Hussar – Highlight), became the first ever winner of the 1000 Guineas and Prix de Diane (French Oaks). It is Highclere's daughter Height of Fashion by the Wolferton resident Bustino, who was sold to Hamdan Al Maktoum for a reputed seven-figure sum.

Her Majesty's first homebred classic winner was Pall Mall in the 1958 2000 Guineas. Manager Captain Charles Moore had acquired the dam Malapert as a three-year-old for just 100 guineas because she was in-bred to that paragon of speed The Tetrarch. Moore and Sir Cecil Boyd-Rochfort, who trained the Queen's horses for so long, admired The Tetrarch as much as they despised Phalaris, a handicapper who was destined to become the grandsire of Nearco.

Nineteen years after Pall Mall's victory at Newmarket, the Queen celebrated her Silver Jubilee year with Dunfermline gaining fairy tale wins in the Oaks and St Leger. The Queen had selected her grandam Stroma entirely on her own judgment at the Doncaster yearling sales of 1956 for 1,150 guineas. To a mating with Doutelle, Stroma produced Canisbay (Eclipse Stakes). Both horses stood at the Royal Studs. They span the era when the present stud groom at Sandringham, Jimmy Scallan, worked alongside his father whom he succeeded.

Unfortunately Dunfermline (Royal Palace – Strathcona) had a disappointing stud record having proved difficult to get in foal – like Highclere she was trained by Major Dick Hern at West Ilsley. Yet another top racemare who never fulfilled expectations in the paddocks was Yorkshire Oaks heroine, Almeria.

Breeding fortunes tend to run in cycles. Whereas the Royal Studs did well in the fifties and seventies, they were much less successful in the sixties and eighties, albeit at least one 'black type' winner emerged from every crop of foals from 1971 to 1987.

During the last decade the public side of the operation has come into its own by virtue of the syndicated stallions Bustino, who retired to Wolferton in 1976, and Shirley Heights – he covered his first mares at Sandringham three years later. For the 1991 season, Bustino was joined by the previous year's King George VI and Queen Elizabeth Diamond Stakes hero Belmez.

Bustino (Busted – Ship Yard), whose dam is by Doutelle, has proved an eminently successful sire, and thanks to champion Nashwan he was leading broodmare sire of 1989. While Bustino won the St Leger and Coronation Cup, Shirley Heights (Mill Reef – Hardiemma) won the English and Irish Derbys. Quickly established as a classic sire, he has two Derby-winning offspring in Slip Anchor (Epsom) and Darshaan (Chantilly).

Viewed in retrospect it was a mistake to sell Height of Fashion, but there are indications of a revival in royal fortunes through the mare Pas de Deux. The Queen's new number one trainer, Lord Huntingdon, Dick Hern's successor at West Ilsley, saddled Pas de Deux's son Unknown Quantity to win the 1989 Grade I Arlington Handicap in Chicago, together with his half-sister, Starlet, winner of a Group 2 race in Germany in 1990. A gelding, Unknown Quantity (now deceased) was the Queen's very first homebred winner in the USA.

Rutland Stud

NEWMARKET · SUFFOLK

One can only speculate as to what the late Edgar Cooper Bland would have thought of the Arab domination of British bloodstock in general and the acquisition of his Rutland Stud by Sheikh Mohammed in particular. Cooper Bland died at the age of ninety-one in April 1984 and the Sheikh purchased his stud at Saxon Street, outside Newmarket, that November.

A lifelong friend and admirer of Sir Alfred Munnings and one of the old school, Cooper Bland was always forthright and to the point. However he may well have had his tongue in cheek when expressing the view that William Wilberforce was guilty of a marked disservice to the community!

Rutland Stud is synonymous with two horses in Bois Roussel, champion sire of 1949 and a leading broodmare sire, and Bustino, who headed the broodmare sires' list exactly forty years later. Coincidentally both have ties with Shadwell Stud, now owned by Sheikh Mohammed's brother, Sheikh Hamdan Al Maktoum.

Having completed seven covering seasons (1940–1946) at Rutland Stud, Bois Roussel was transferred to Melton Paddocks, the public half of Sir John Musker's Shadwell Stud. This is now part of Hamdan Al Maktoum's considerable domain in Norfolk and the star Shadwell mare is none other than Bustino's daughter, Height of Fashion, dam of Nashwan.

Stationed in Newmarket during the First World War, Edgar Cooper Bland became friendly with Alfred Sadler, then training at Freemason Lodge. Sadler also owned Hall Stud at Burrough Green and Cooper Bland became so fascinated with breeding that in 1921 he bought 300 acres around the hamlet of Saxon Street, converting about one third into Rutland Stud.

Not long before, the Jockey Club had acquired the property following Colonel Harry McCalmont's death, this being yet another part of his ubiquitous Cheveley Estate. McCalmont had bought the estate in 1892 from the

5th Duke of Rutland whose family came to Cheveley early in the nineteenth century.

Quality rather than quantity was always Cooper Bland's hallmark. Over the years he established a very select band of mares. It was strictly a commercial operation directed towards Tattersalls' yearling sales where he was a regular vendor for over half a century with breeders ever anxious to acquire any filly on offer.

The one mare with whom Rutland Stud will always be associated is Rosetta (Kantar – Rose Red). Purchased for 700 guineas at the 1935 Newmarket December Sales from her breeder, Lord Derby, this half-sister to Aurora was carrying the 2000 Guineas third, Fairstone. He proved the best of her sons, but her five daughters (all with the prefix or suffix stone), all excelled in the paddocks.

One of the most important from Edgar Cooper Bland's point of view was Fairstone's own-sister, Paving Stone, whose daughter Ship Yard is dam of Bustino. Sold as a yearling for 21,000 guineas to the Dowager Lady Beaverbrook, he triumphed in the St Leger and Coronation Cup and only succumbed to Grundy after an epic duel for the King George VI and Queen Elizabeth Stakes.

The son of Busted was syndicated for £600,000 by the British Bloodstock Agency to stand at the Queen's Wolferton Stud where he replaced dual champion sire Aureole. An appropriate acquisition by the Royal Studs (his maternal grandsire Doutelle stood at Sandringham), Bustino bred three smart sons for Lady Beaverbrook in the homebred pair Easter Sun and Bustomi, as well as Terimon. He finished second to Nashwan in the 1989 Ever Ready Derby at 500-1.

In due course Cooper Bland acquired other of Rosetta's relations, paying just thirty guineas for Heavenly Wind as a yearling from Banstead Manor Stud in 1938. Her first foal was the New Oaks runner-up Monsoon, two of whose daughters made history at the James Dewar dispersal in 1954. Festoon (1000 Guineas) realized 36,000 guineas, the highest price ever paid for a filly in or out of training, and her half-sister Refreshed fetched 30,000 guineas, a record price for a broodmare. The respective purchasers were Anthony and Gerald Askew, nephews of the late James V. Rank. Another of Monsoon's descendants is the Gazeley Stud stalwart Hotfoot.

Over the years fillies bred by Rutland Stud have exercised a worldwide influence. One leading commercial breeder to benefit from Cooper Bland's expertise was his old friend Marcus Wickham-Boynton of the famous Burton Agnes Stud in Yorkshire. Amongst a handful of fillies acquired from Rutland Stud was Sipsey Bridge from whom Wickham-Boynton bred Derring-Do.

Sipsey Bridge was something of a rarity for Rutland Stud in so far as she was not a member of the Marchetta (granddam of Rosetta) family. Her dam Claudette was bred by another great Yorkshire breeder in the late Major Lionel Holliday being a representative of his illustrious Lost Soul family.

During his long innings as a commercial breeder, Edgar Cooper Bland was never averse to boarding mares for friends, amongst them Peter Beatty (uncle of Jeremy Tree) and Bobby Watson. Peter Beatty prevailed upon Cooper Bland to stand his 1937 Derby hero, Bois Roussel, much against the latter's better judgement – but Edgar managed to persuade Peter to pay for half the cost of building the stallion accommodation! The last boarder at Rutland Stud was Lady Hothfield's Belle of All. Winner of the 1951 1000 Guineas, she spent the duration of her stud life there where she died in 1971.

The house at Rutland Stud is now the home of Robert Acton, general manager of Sheikh Mohammed's enormous racing and breeding operation centred on Dalham Hall Stud. One of the benefits in purchasing Rutland Stud, apart from its proximity to Dalham Hall, was that 200 of the 300 acres were arable, a rare bonus in an exclusively breeding orientated locality. Instead of cornfields, these hitherto horse-free acres are now pristine paddocks and there is stabling for 200 of Sheikh Mohammed's own mares. Needless to say this is the largest private broodmare band in the country.

Sandley Stud

GILLINGHAM · DORSET

The fact that Simon Wingfield Digby's Sandley Stud at Gillingham in Dorset is the largest and best appointed stud in the West Country is owed to Peter Burrell. He developed the property as the National Stud from wartime, when the enterprise was uprooted from Ireland, to the mid-sixties when it moved to its present purpose-built premises at Newmarket.

The National Stud produced numerous top winners at Gillingham, the majority sold as yearlings. A handful were leased for the duration of their racing careers to the Queen (mostly fillies retained for the paddocks), amongst them the 1957 Oaks heroine, Carrozza.

Two names synonymous with the National Stud of that era are Big Game and Sun Chariot, who between them accounted for four of the five substitute classics during 1942. That pair spent their active stud life at Gillingham, their burial place there being marked by inscribed headstones. Big Game, who was twice champion broodmare sire, used to stand alongside Elopement.

Also buried there is Amphion (1886). The first noted stallion at Gillingham, he sired Sundridge, champion sire and champion broodmare sire. For Jack Joel of Childwick Bury Stud, Sundridge sired Sunstar (2000 Guineas, Derby) and Jest (1000 Guineas, Oaks), dam of Humorist (Derby). He also established an important male line in the USA.

In Amphion's day Sandley was known as Compton Stud which used to issue much coveted silver medals to deserving breeders. However by the time that Peter Burrell negotiated the purchase of the property from the executors of Lord Furness, who died in 1940, it was called Gilltown Stud. That name was derived from Furness's stud in Kildare from which he transferred his breeding stock due to the economic climate in Ireland during the 1930s.

Marmaduke Furness, whose family fortune came from shipping and shipbuilding in the north-east, was a regular yearling vendor at Tattersalls' old Glasgow Paddocks at Doncaster. From the final draft of homebreds came Kingsway, winner of the 1943 (New) 2000 Guineas.

By the time the National Stud moved to Newmarket, the Gillingham premises had grown from 190 to over 400 acres, all on broken limestone rock. It was fortuitous for Simon Wingfield Digby that the property came on the market at the very time that he was anxious to expand his own breeding operation centred on Sherborne Castle.

Originally from Warwickshire, the Digby family took up residence at the castle (built for Sir Walter Raleigh) in 1617 when they became one of the biggest land-owners in Dorset. It was Simon Wingfield Digby's great, great-uncle who founded the Blackmore Vale Hunt, a really fashionable country between the wars under the mastership of his father, Freddie.

Simon Wingfield Digby, who was Conservative Member of Parliament for West Dorset for thirty-two years, had kept a handful of mares at his Sherborne Stud. However the land was not suited ideally to rearing thoroughbreds, besides which it would have been uneconomical to modernize the old-fashioned hunter stabling.

Simon's entrée into bloodstock breeding was through Wiltshire owner-breeder Lord Margadale of Fonthill Stud. He was a patron of Noel Cannon's Druids Lodge stable, as was James Dewar at whose executors' sale in 1954 Wingfield Digby acquired Feria as a two-year-old. Winner of the Fred Darling Stakes and third in the 1000 Guineas to Meld on her first two starts for her new owner, she failed as a broodmare.

The best winner that Simon bred at Sherborne was the retained Ballywit (Old Newton Cup). He was purchased 'in utero' when his dam Witness was sold at the 1961 Newmarket December Sales for 10,500 guineas, the third highest price of the week for a mare.

Feria and Witness were two of the five mares transferred from Sherborne to Sandley in the spring of 1965. That summer Meadow Court won the King George VI and Queen Elizabeth Stakes and Irish Sweeps Derby. The next year he retired to stand at Sandley alongside top sprinter Floribunda, who was also trained by Paddy Prendergast in Ireland.

Neither Meadow Court nor Floribunda cut much ice as stallions before being exported to Canada and Japan respectively, but the latter produced a good mare for Sandley in Rose Copse. Mated with Sassafras, she bred the own-brothers Saros, who was second to The Minstrel in the Dewhurst Stakes, and French Sassafras, runner-up in the Hollywood Derby.

Subsequent stallions at Sandley comprised Floribunda's son Porto Bello, Crozier, Knightly Manner and Air Trooper. The latter carried Wingfield

Digby's apple green and black colours having been bought as a replacement for Flying Nelly. She was a foal purchase for 3,500 guineas from Swettenham Stud at a time when Sandley was managed by Christopher Watkins – he now runs the adjacent Blackmore Vale Stud.

The grey Flying Nelly, who died in 1988, provided her owner with his most exciting moment in racing when winning the 1974 Irish Sweeps Cambridgeshire. The foundation mare of the present stud, her five winning offspring include Neltino, who stands at The Elms Stud in Northamptonshire.

Since Air Trooper was exported to Sweden in 1986, Simon Wingfield Digby has kept about half a dozen mares of his own, the progeny being consigned to the yearling sales. That year's crop of six foals all scored. They include three good staying handicappers in Further Flight (Tote Ebor), Retouch (Ascot Stakes) and Travelling Light (Ladbroke Chester Cup). The first pair are homebred grandsons of Flying Nelly.

The viability of Sandley Stud rests upon being part of an extensive agricultural estate with additional revenue generated by boarding mares, notably those owned by Prince Fahd Salman (Newgate Stud). His outstanding 'Sandley' produce is Knight's Baroness, heroine of the 1990 Kildangan Stud Irish Oaks.

Sandwich Stud

NEWMARKET · SUFFOLK

The most extensive stud development outside Arab ownership in and around Newmarket is the 750-acre complex at Dullingham Ley where William Gredley has built an extension to his Stetchworth Park Stud. However the most aesthetically pleasing building in this category is probably David and Patricia Thompsons' new yearling facility at Sandwich Stud.

The Thompsons acquired Sandwich Stud as an addition to their Cheveley Park Stud which lies on the other side of the Ashley road out of Newmarket. Opposite Sandwich is the Oppenheimers' Hascombe Stud. Sandwich has strong classic connections. Here Noorani, dam of Charlottesville (French Derby), was bred and Blakeney (Derby) was sired by Hethersett.

Noorani was a foal at foot with her dam, Empire Glory, when both were bought in 1950 from Wilfred Harvey in a package deal for Sandwich Stud by the late Aga Khan and his son, Prince Aly Khan. Noorani's first two progeny proved to be the distinguished half-brothers Charlottesville and Sheshoon. Hero of the 1960 Ascot Gold Cup, Sheshoon did well as a sire at Limestone Stud.

In the year that Wilfred Harvey sold Sandwich Stud, his colours were carried to victory in the Ascot Gold Cup by Supertello. A yearling acquisition from Herbert Blagrave of Harwood Stud (now Gainsborough Stud), Super-tello retired to stand at Sandwich in 1952. Troubled by infertility, he died in 1957 at Cranagh Castle Stud, Co. Tipperary, then owned by Ted Corbett, father of bloodstock agent John Corbett.

The Aga Khan sold Sandwich Stud right away to the late Robert Boucher. A hop farmer and fruit grower from Sittingbourne in Kent, Bob Boucher was the owner-breeder of Wilwyn, inaugural winner of the 1952 Washington DC International at Laurel Park. Successful in twenty races at home, Wilwyn stood at the now non-existent Phantom House Stud, Newmarket, before export to South Africa. One of his progeny was Tenacity (Yorkshire

Oaks), a key mare homebred by the Riley-Smiths of Brewhurst Stud.

Two more top winners for Bob Boucher were homebred Realm, twice successful in the July Cup, and 1000 Guineas heroine Fleet, a yearling acquisition. However Realm was bred by his owner in Kent where he had established Norton Court Stud upon selling Sandwich Stud in 1958 to the late Major Lionel Holliday.

One of the great owner-breeders of his generation, Lionel Holliday named all his horses with the same first letter as the sire and, being a great admirer of Nearco, he had a great number beginning with the letter N. A dye manufacturer from Huddersfield in his native Yorkshire, he lived at Copgrove Hall (now owned by Guy Reed of Warpath renown), his breeding operation being centred on Cleaboy Stud in Ireland.

He also owned Lagrange stables in Newmarket. It was here that Major Dick Hern embarked upon his training career, he being Lionel Holliday's private trainer from 1958 to 1962. During his final season, he prepared Hethersett to win the St Leger. This was due compensation as the colt had been brought down in the Derby for which he started favourite.

Hethersett (Hugh Lupus – Bride Elect) was syndicated by the British Bloodstock Agency at £3,000 a share to stand at Sandwich Stud for the 1964 season. He joined Champion Stakes hero Narrator, another of Holliday's homebreds tracing to his illustrious foundation mare, Lost Soul. Unfortunately Hethersett died in August 1966 upon the completion of only three covering seasons. His intermediate crop of foals included the 1969 Derby hero, Blakeney. Trained, bred and part owned by Arthur Budgett (Kirtlington Stud), Blakeney has enjoyed an honourable career at the National Stud. He was still in service in 1991 at the advanced age of 25.

The outstanding horse bred by Lionel Holliday was Vaguely Noble, but he was foaled in the year that the major died, 1965. Two years later Brook Holliday, his son, sold Vaguely Noble at the Newmarket December Sales for a record 136,000 guineas prior to his great victory in the Prix de l'Arc de Triomphe. Meanwhile Cleaboy Stud was retained with Sandwich Stud being utilized principally as a public stud.

Other resident stallions there included I Say, Salvo and Relko. Both I Say (Coronation Cup) and Salvo (Grosser Preis von Baden) started stud life at Sandwich, but were failures. Conversely Relko, who had stood at Lavington Stud, made his mark without ever becoming fashionable. His sons include the Cleaboy-bred Relkino.

Gradually Brook Holliday reduced his father's considerable broodmare band. At the same time he switched the emphasis from breeding to race, to breeding to sell. Then in February 1978 he sold Cleaboy Stud, whereupon he transferred his own nucleus of mares to Sandwich Stud under the management of Michael Russell (now involved with Warren Park Stud, formerly Ashley Heath and Warren Hill Studs). His father Dr William Russell bred Rheingold.

The progeny of Brook Holliday's mares foaled and reared at Sandwich Stud were still officially attributed to Cleaboy Farms Company. Most notable of the winners bred there at this time is Embla (1985 Tattersalls' Cheveley Park Stakes), who was sold as a yearling to Charles St George.

Having never shown the same degree of interest in racing and breeding as his father, Brook Holliday finally sold Sandwich Stud to the Thompsons in the autumn of 1986. At about this time he also sold a dozen mares to the Aga Khan, retaining just three which he boarded with his sister, Mrs Diana Gillam, at her Tarbrook Stud in Yorkshire. This trio included his homebred Oaks third, Britannia's Rule.

Sandwich Stud has undergone a complete reorganization and restoration since then, under the direction of Cheveley Park Stud's new managing director, Chris Richardson, who formerly had charge of Stavros Niarchos's Spring Oak Farm in Kentucky. Sandwich now houses the cream of the Thompsons' broodmares as well as their yearlings. A feature of the property is the new yearling yard which first became operational in the spring of 1990.

Shadwell Stud

THETFORD · NORFOLK

Having purchased the 5,000-acre Shadwell Estate from Sir John and Lady Musker in November 1984, Sheikh Hamdan Al Maktoum subsequently bought 1,000 adjoining arable acres from Jeremy Lowndes. Of that total, 800 are utilized for stud purposes, 500 at the new Nunnery complex, and 150 acres apiece at Melton Paddocks and Snarehill Stud.

Sheikh Hamdan also has Derrinstown and Ballygoran Studs at Maynooth in Co. Kildare, with a combined acreage of 1,000, together with the fine Shadwell Farm in Lexington, Kentucky, where the new stallion complex is named Nashwan Stud. However, it is worth recording that before the First World War, the Shadwell Estate extended to 12,000 acres. Melton Paddocks consisted of eight separate studs, five of which had stallions.

John Musker, Sir John's grandfather, had bought Shadwell Park, which is situated between Thetford and Diss in Norfolk, in 1898. Founder of the Home and Colonial Stores, he retired with a considerable fortune whereupon he repatriated the 1885 Derby winner, Melton, from Italy. The then fourteen-year-old stallion became the lynch pin of his enormous breeding operation – in 1914 his private stud book accounted for 238 mares and fillies.

Melton's greatest influence was through his daughters, two of whom rendered yeoman service to Childwick Bury Stud. Yours bred the classic winners Your Majesty (St Leger) and Our Lassie (Oaks) for Jack Joel, while Absurdity is ancestress of virtually all the good horses bred by his son, Jim.

Absurdity was actually bred by John Musker who died in 1926. Latterly the stud was managed by his son, Harold, who became the family's trainer for a time on the estate. When he died in 1946, the enterprise was inherited by his son, Sir John (knighted in 1952). A banker by profession, it was he who sold the property to Hamdan Al Maktoum, the finance minister for the United Arab Emirates.

Since the last war, Shadwell Stud operated as two separate entities, with Melton Stud the public half, and Snarehill Stud, on the opposite side of the Thetford road, the private one. Amongst the stallions were Bois Roussel, Tehran, Tropique, Martial, Counsel, Reform and Pyjama Hunt.

Previously based at Rutland Stud, the Derby hero Bois Roussel was located at Shadwell from 1947 to 1954. A noted broodmare sire (including Petite Etoile, Cantelo and St Paddy), he was champion sire in 1949 thanks to Ridge Wood. Another St Leger winning son, Tehran, who was only a temporary resident, was champion sire in 1952 due to Tulyar.

Reform spent his entire stud life at Shadwell where he died in 1983. Successful in the Champion Stakes, Sussex Stakes and Queen Elizabeth II Stakes, he sired classic winners in successive years with Roi Lear (1973 Prix du Jockey Club) and Polygamy (1974 Oaks). Another of his daughters is the Tavistocks' celebrated broodmare Mrs Moss.

The demise of Reform coincided with the arrival of stud manager William Edmeades (now manager of Brook Stud), whose predecessors include Captain Jimmy James, Lieutenant-Colonel G.Campbell, John Day, Frank Chapman and Major John Critchley-Salmonson. Will Edmeades was succeeded by the present manager, Captain Bobby Dolbey, who used to preside over Moyns Park Stud.

Three mares in particular contributed to Sir John Musker's role as a breeder: Stone of Fortune with Fastnet Rock and Fortuity; Sun Helmet with Woodburn and Sanlinea; and Stella Polaris. A 2,000-guinea foal, Stella Polaris was placed in the Oaks and Irish Oaks and is the dam of Discorea (Irish Oaks), and the grandam of Reform's son, Anguillo (Gran Criterium). He also bred Jock Witney's fine broodmare Peace.

Of course the scale of Shadwell Estate's bloodstock under Sheikh Hamdan Al Maktoum is altogether different. Nunnery Stud, which name has been resurrected from one of the long-since-forgotten studs there, has been purpose built with no expense spared to provide accommodation for six stallions. The buildings have marked similarities with Robert Clay's Three Chimneys Farm in Kentucky.

So far as the Sheikh's own European based mares are concerned, they are kept at either Melton Paddocks (formerly the public half of Shadwell) or at Derrinstown Stud in Ireland where there is also accommodation for three stallions. All weaned foals are sent to Derrinstown. Yearlings (including those bought at the sales) go to Beech House Stud in September prior to entering training in November. Snarehill is used for resting and rehabilitation.

The first stallion to take up residence at Melton Paddocks in its present ownership was Green Desert in 1987. This champion sprinter, who raced for Maktoum Al Maktoum, remained there for a couple of seasons prior to becoming the first inmate of the Nunnery. Green Desert was the leading first season sire of 1990 in which year he covered alongside the half-brothers Nashwan and Unfuwain.

Both horses were homebred, Nashwan carrying Hamdan Al Maktoum's familiar royal blue and white colours to victory in the General Accident 2000 Guineas, Ever Ready Derby, Coral-Eclipse Stakes and King George VI and Queen Elizabeth Diamond Stakes, all in the same season, a unique achievement which earned him Horse of the Year honours. So the Maktoum family finally succeeded in winning the world's most famous race. Just to put the icing on the cake, the son of Blushing Groom was homebred, his dam Height of Fashion having been purchased privately from the Queen for a figure variously reported as £1.4 million to £1.8 million. Evidently the revenue financed Her Majesty's purchase of the West Ilsley training establishment.

Inevitably Height of Fashion is the queen of Hamdan Al Maktoum's over 100-strong broodmare band, but there is a magnificent supporting cast with young broodmares of the calibre of Salsabil, the outstanding filly of 1990, Midway Lady and Al Bahathri, the winners of six European classics between them.

Shelton Stud

When Ann Hine and her late husband, John, moved from Lincoln Lodge Stud, near Reigate, to Albourne, close to Hickstead, in June 1964, they brought with them their foundation mare, Under Canvas (twenty-one), together with her daughter, Intent (twelve). As Under Canvas is a name which might just be misconstrued for a stud, they decided to call the former dairy farm Shelton, after her dam.

The Hines started breeding thoroughbreds as a hobby in rather a casual way. At the 1956 Newmarket December Sales, John Hine met Keith Freeman in the bar and agreed to give the Norwich-based bloodstock agent a twenty-five guinea profit on a mare that he had bought for 100 guineas earlier in the week. That mare was Under Canvas. At the time she was carrying Spaniard's Close, whom the Hines sold as a foal for 100 guineas. In due course Spaniard's Close won the 1963 Royal Hunt Cup.

Results that Wednesday of Royal Ascot were highly encouraging for John and Ann Hine as, prior to the Hunt Cup, The Creditor had won the Jersey Stakes. By another marvellous stroke of good fortune, they had bought her dam, The Accused, for 2,100 guineas at the 1961 December Sales. She was seventeen years of age when taking up residence at Shelton Stud.

Thanks to Under Canvas and The Accused, Shelton Stud has become one of the country's leading commercial studs specializing in the production of yearlings for the Newmarket October and Highflyer Sales. The one great sadness is that John Hine, a great enthusiast and bon viveur, died at the tragically early age of fifty-two in April 1972.

Fortunately Ann Hine was determined to persevere with the stud, and since July 1974 Jennifer Bunting, MRCVS, has been a partner in the business. Formerly in practice in Epsom, Jenny had been a veterinary colleague there of bloodstock agent George Forbes (father of Fiona Vigors of Kingwood

Stud), who played a significant role in the Shelton Stud success story.

With Spaniard's Close and his elder half-brother, Rexequus (Cambridge-shire) doing so well, the Hines determined to buy one of Under Canvas's daughters. Through George Forbes, they succeeded in repatriating Intent from Trinidad. To a mating with Sing Sing, Intent, the winner of two sellers as a juvenile, produced Song.

A 6,200-guinea yearling, Song proved a top two-year-old and a champion sprinter. With victories in the King's Stand Stakes, Diadem Stakes and New Stakes (now Norfolk Stakes), he proved something of an Ascot special-ist.

The horse spent the duration of his stud career at Littleton Stud (where his maternal grandsire Vilmorin stood), and he was put down there at the age of twenty-two in 1988. A really prolific sire of fast animals, his progeny include three winners of the Flying Childers Stakes in Music Maestro, Sizzling Melody, and Devon Ditty, the champion two-year-old sprint filly of her generation. Two more stallion sons are the close relatives Jester and Fayruz.

In due course two granddaughters of Under Canvas were obtained for Shelton Stud and each made a major contribution. First came Sovereign Sails, who was to breed King of Spain (Mill Reef Stakes), then came Ica, dam of Aragon (Prix de la Jonchere). Ica, who is half-sister to Song, cost 50,000 guineas from Daniel Wildenstein (Dayton Ltd), who had bred her whilst their dam Intent was leased to him.

For a period Song (Littleton Stud), King of Spain (Lockinge Stud) and Aragon (Egerton Stud/Lavington Stud) stood simultaneously in England. All three are very closely related as, apart from being descendants of Under Canvas, all belong to the Tudor Minstrel male line.

Under Canvas was thirty-two when she was put down in 1975, which coincided with the arrival of a new Shelton star in Swiss Maid. She too came about by buying back into an existing family – that of The Accused. In this instance it involved purchasing not only the dam (Hornton Grange), who had been sold as a yearling, but also the grandam (Grove Hall). At just 300 guineas, Grove Hall was another fine bargain and, like Intent, both her wins were in selling races.

Ann Hine remembers Swiss Maid as a very plain yearling, but a tremen-dous walker. However, her sale price of 6,000 guineas represented little more than the cost of a nomination to her sire, Welsh Pageant.

Two years later, Swiss Maid returned to Park Paddocks. Having just won the Champion Stakes and Sun Chariot Stakes, she was bought by her trainer, Paul Kelleway, for 325,000 guineas, which constituted a new

European record for a thoroughbred at public auction. It also more than doubled the previous December Sales record of 154,000 guineas paid for Mrs McArdy in 1977. Subsequently she realized 290,000 guineas at the next December Sales and $120,000 at the Bunker Hunt dispersal at Keeneland in 1988.

Song was a champion sire of two-year-olds and Dominion is a sire who has been accorded that distinction twice. This son of Derring-Do, who replaced his own sire at Aston Park Stud, was bred and raised at Shelton Stud on behalf of the late Colonel Percy Wright, whose widow, Susan (now Lady Dunphy), continues to board her mares there.

Two more breeders who have good reason to be grateful to the Hines are David and Sally Hicks of Buckhurst Stud in Kent. Responsible for Argentum (by Aragon) and Superpower, they only became involved in bloodstock breeding as the Hines were virtual neighbours at the time – in the past the two families have owned various mares in partnership.

Ann Hine and Jenny Bunting are closely involved in the day-to-day running of the stud so any success is all the sweeter. Every so often a good sale compensates for the disappointments. In 1988 they obtained 150,000 guineas for an own-brother to Aragon – and just to think his third dam, Under Canvas, was recruited to Shelton Stud for 150 guineas!

Side Hill Stud

NEWMARKET · SUFFOLK

Owned by Lord Hartington, who embarked upon a four-year term as senior steward of the Jockey Club in the summer of 1989, Side Hill Stud, Newmarket, is home for two top stallions in Chief Singer and Salse. The stud manager is Lord Carnarvon's son-in-law, bloodstock agent John Warren.

Since inheriting Side Hill from his father, the Duke of Devonshire, in 1979, Lord Hartington has greatly improved the facilities. By the close of 1985 an extensive building programme had seen the completion of the Cavendish Yard which incorporates an American-style barn with accommodation for thirty foaling mares and a modern foaling unit all under the one roof.

There are two other principal yards. Park Top commemorates Andrew Devonshire's wonderful race-mare who was bred at Buttermilk Stud – her sire Kalydon was bred by Bernard van Cutsem. For part of 1990, the Heath Yard was utilized by Mary James of Cotswold Stud as a base for her large yearling-sales consignment. This was only a temporary arrangement for the following season she was back operating from Gloucestershire.

Bernard van Cutsem, who trained Kalydon and Park Top, ran Northmore Stud Farm in conjunction with Side Hill Stud. It was at Northmore that his wife Mimi bred the great Sharpen Up. His shares were priced at just £3,750 apiece when he retired to Side Hill for the 1973 season.

Side Hill, which is situated between Newmarket Heath and the Ashley road opposite Beech House Stud, first became a public stud in 1929 when Major Dermot McCalmont (breeder of The Tetrarch) sold the property to the 17th Earl of Derby. There he stood Phalaris, twice champion sire (his grandson Nearco was to be located at Beech House), Phalaris's son, Caerleon, and Bobsleigh, maternal grandsire of Kalydon – his fifth dam was the great Stanley House matron Serenissima.

In 1930 both Serenissima and her daughter Selene produced such small colt foals that it was decided to have them weaned at Side Hill, normal practice being for weaned foals to be sent to Lord Derby's home at Knowsley in Lancashire. Selene's colt foal was none other than Hyperion. Turned out on a part of the stud which is still called the Shepherd's House, he was barely fifteen hands when going into training with George Lambton.

When Lord Derby died in 1948, the resident Side Hill stallion Bobsleigh became the joint property of his grandson, Richard Stanley, and Bernard van Cutsem (who subsequently trained the Derby horses at Stanley House). They, together with Lord Ilchester, also became joint owners of Side Hill Stud.

As a result of buying New England Stud to stand Mossborough (Nearco ex All Moonshine, ex Selene), Richard Stanley's share in Side Hill was acquired by the Duke of Devonshire, he and van Cutsem becoming the sole owners upon Lord Ilchester's death in 1959. During that time Kalydon stood alongside another van Cutsem-trained horse in Mandamus.

Bernard van Cutsem himself died in 1975 whereupon his interest in Side Hill passed to his sons, Hugh and Geoffrey. Three years later their share was acquired by Lord Hartington – he became the outright owner when his father decided to forego his involvement in the stud the following year. At this time Major Christopher Philipson of the BBA was acting as manager.

Meanwhile Sharpen Up (whose sire Atan stood at a fee of just 100 guineas) was proving the most successful inmate of Side Hill since the great Phalaris before the war. Within twelve months of becoming the leading British-based sire for 1979, he was sold to stand at Gainesway Farm in Kentucky where he was to remain in active service until he was twenty years of age.

Sharpen Up's export to the USA coincided with the retirement of his outstanding son Kris to Thornton Stud in north Yorkshire owned by his breeder, Lord Howard de Walden. He bred not only Kris, who was a champion miler, but also his own-brother, Diesis. Both horses were bred at Plantation Stud.

Like Side Hill, Plantation is a former Derby property, as indeed is Thornton. Both Kris and Diesis became very influential stallions, the latter being sold to stand at Mill Ridge Farm in Kentucky. Kris was the champion sire of 1985.

Following Sharpen Up's departure, rumour was rife that he was to be replaced at Side Hill by his son Sharpo, winner of three consecutive runnings of the William Hill Sprint Championship as well as the Prix de l'Abbaye de Longchamp. The then stud manager, Philip E.H. Mitchell, recalls that

a deputation went to see him at Beckhampton only to report that his conformation was not commensurate with his ability.

Ironically Sharpo took up residence instead at Lord Derby's Woodlands
Stud where he has proved a considerable success. His first crop included
the smart Risk Me – he now stands at David Sullivan's Elsenham Stud,
the former Dorothy Paget establishment in Hertfordshire.

In due course Sharpen Up was replaced at Side Hill Stud by Alias Smith
who had completed one covering season at Montpelier Farm in Virginia.
In 1985 this half-brother to Auction Ring was joined by Dunbeath. Before
long both American-breds were banished to studs in the north of England,
Alias Smith to Northumberland and Dunbeath to Yorkshire.

Whitstead and Noalcoholic were two more temporary residents at Side
Hill during this period, but more important is Chief Singer. Raced by
Jeffrey Smith of Littleton Stud, owner-breeder of Dashing Blade, this com-
manding black horse who measures 16.3 hands, proved a champion miler
(Swettenham Stud Sussex Stakes) and champion sprinter (Norcros July Cup).
His syndication for stud valued him at £4.8 million. In 1989 Salse replaced
Bellypha as Chief Singer's principal stud companion. Salse won five Group
races over seven furlongs, including the Prix de la Foret.

Lord Hartington is a great advocate of good public relations. There was
a time when his annual drinks' party at Side Hill Stud on the Sunday
of the December Sales was one of the social highlights of the Newmarket
season – alas it is no longer!

Sledmere Stud

DRIFFIELD · NORTH HUMBERSIDE

The sale of Petsy at the 1988 Newmarket December Sales marked the end of an era for she was the last mare owned by the present Sir Tatton Sykes of historic Sledmere Stud in Yorkshire. She bears the name of his aunt whose husband, Adrian Scrope, managed Sledmere from 1928 until 1942. After the war the stud was run by Tatton's father, Sir Richard Sykes, who died in 1978.

With its beautiful Georgian house and park landscaped by Capability Brown, Sledmere is set in the Yorkshire Wolds, near Driffield, a magnificent panorama of woodland and open country. This has been the domain of the Sykes family for more than two centuries. Once the most eminent commercial yearling stud in the country, it has been managed by David Cecil of Cliff Stud since January 1988.

Sledmere has been a nursery for thoroughbreds since the beginning of the nineteenth century when the first Sir Tatton Sykes (1772-1863), the 4th baronet (the title was granted by William Pitt for services to agriculture) owned more than 100 mares. The man after whom the 1846 2000 Guineas winner was named, he bred one classic winner himself in Grey Momus (1838 2000 Guineas).

When the 4th baronet died there was an enormous dispersal sale with 313 lots aggregating 24,171 guineas. Amongst the foals was Lecturer who was destined to win the Ascot Gold Cup. His son and heir, also Sir Tatton Sykes (1826-1913), was much more successful as a breeder. His classic tally comprised two Derby winners in Doncaster (1873) and Spearmint (1906), as well as Mimi (1891 1000 Guineas, Oaks) and Disraeli (1898 2000 Guineas).

As the tail-male ancestor of Phalaris, Doncaster has earned immortality. He is also the grandsire of Triple Crown hero Ormonde (by Bend Or) whose dam Lily Agnes was bred by the Sledmere stud groom out of Polly Agnes, a mare given to him by the second Sir Tatton Sykes! Spearmint's greatest gift to posterity was as the sire of Plucky Liege, dam of Bois Roussel, Sir Gallahad III and Bull Dog.

Other Sledmere celebrities of this vintage include John O'Gaunt, sire of Swynford, Hapsburg (Eclipse Stakes), and Lemonora (Grand Prix de Paris). John O'Gaunt was out of that great race mare La Fleche who was acquired for a staggering 12,600 guineas in 1896 on Sir Tatton's behalf. He was so flabbergasted by the price that he refused to accept her at first. Consequently she remained in a railway horse-box at Sledmere station for two weeks before actually taking up residence at the stud.

From 1892 until 1928, the stud was managed by Henry Cholmondeley, a nephew of the 5th baronet. At that time the estate extended to 25,000 acres and was fourteen miles across at the widest point. Year in, year out, the Sledmere yearlings dominated Tattersalls' Doncaster sales in the old Glasgow Paddocks. During Cholmondeley's term of office, 481 yearlings aggregated 840,202 guineas, an average of 1,746 guineas.

Lady Juror, Teresina, Mumtaz Mahal and Straitlace were four exceptional fillies sold from 1920 to 1922. The Son-in-Law fillies, Lady Juror and Strait-lace (Oaks), became great broodmares. The former bred Fair Trial and is grandam of Tudor Minstrel, the two best horses bred by the Dewars at their Homestall Stud. Both Mumtaz Mahal (half-sister to Lady Juror), and Teresina became celebrated Aga Khan foundation mares.

Known as the flying filly, Mumtaz Mahal is one of the great foundation mares of the twentieth century. Responsible for such Aga Khan celebrities as Mahmoud, Migoli, Petite Etoile, Nasrullah and Shergar, she is also ancestress of Royal Charger and Abernant.

Latterly Henry Cholmondeley acquired the mare Trustful, and her progeny include the St Leger winner Scottish Union, this Doncaster classic being won subsequently by another Sledmere-bred in Ridge Wood. Completing the classic roll of honour is the Oaks heroine Chatelaine – incidentally Craganour, who finished first in the 1913 Derby only to be disqualified, was reared at Sledmere having been bought as a foal with his dam.

Unfortunately for Adrian Scrope, who was responsible for buying Lady of the Snows, Queen Christina and Meadow Rhu, who together with Trustful proved the key mares in Sledmere's post-war success, he became manager at an inopportune moment. Indeed had the proceeds from the 1932 sale of yearlings been on a par with the previous three years, the stud would have been disbanded. At that time it was costing 1,000 guineas to put a yearling in the ring, yet Chatelaine (Oaks) and Coroado (July Cup) realized only 500 guineas and 390 guineas respectively.

By the close of the 1950s, Sledmere Stud had forfeited its status as Yorkshire's leading nursery to Burton Agnes. However that decade did produce two leading colts in Court Harwell and Pardao. Court Harwell achieved the distinction of being champion sire of 1965 (by virtue of Meadow Court), and champion sire in Argentina. Pardao replaced his own sire Pardal at Lanwades Stud where he was replaced in turn by his son Moulton. The latter was bred by the Mollers' White Lodge Stud, as was Pardao's brilliant daughter Sovereign.

Of course fillies emanating from Sledmere have exercised a worldwide influence. One of the most famous celebrities of all has been that great matriarch Lost Soul, who became the cornerstone of the late Major Lionel Holliday's famed Cleaboy Stud in Ireland. Another distinguished mare whose influence persists down to the present time is Chambord, dam of Caro. Chambord is half-sister to another Sledmere star in Krakatao.

During the 1960s the late Sir Richard Sykes reduced his broodmare band to about a dozen, those retained to carry the 'orange, purple sleeves and cap' being trained by Mick Bartholomew in France. At that stage there was a strong boarding element with mares owned by the late Charles Engelhard (Cragwood Estates) and bookmaker Jack Swift (Mount Rosa Stud), amongst others.

In 1988 David Cecil of Cliff Stud took over the management of Sledmere for Sir Tatton Sykes and two years later it became operational as a public stud. For the 1991 season, there were three young stallions with Insan, Superpower and Waki River.

Snailwell Stud

NEWMARKET · SUFFOLK

Situated on the same side of the Snailwell road, north of Newmarket, are two striking life-size bronzes by the famous equine sculptor John Skeaping. Opposite the entrance to Stanley House is the figure of Lord Derby's Hyperion. Further on towards the by-pass is Chamossaire's statue at Snailwell Stud which is synonymous with the Stanhope Joel family.

The late Stanhope Joel, who died in 1976 leaving the stud to his wife and three daughters, Solna Thomson Jones, Dana Brudenell-Bruce (now the outright owner) and Thalia Jones, bought Snailwell Stud from Lionel Montagu in 1946 to stand Chamossaire – he had carried Joel's colours to victory the preceding year in the substitute St Leger at York.

Snailwell Stud, which adjoins the present Lord Howard de Walden's Plantation Stud and was actually founded by the latter's father, is the final resting place of Chamossaire (a plaque in the main yard marks his burial place alongside Busted), who died in 1964 aged twenty-two. That year, in the wake of an otherwise unremarkable stud life, he became champion sire with Santa Claus landing the Derby and Irish Sweeps Derby double.

Bred by the National Stud, Chamossaire had been bought for Stanhope Joel as a yearling for 2,700 guineas by Walter Earl, whose son Anthony was to manage Snailwell from 1946 to 1983. Paddy and Dana Brudenell-Bruce, whose new home is on the stud (Busted House), used to live on the other side of Newmarket at Moulton Paddocks. Here Walter Earl was private trainer to her grandfather, Solly Joel, and more recently her aunt, Eileen Rogerson, kept her broodmares.

Solly Joel was the younger brother of Jack Joel (father of Jim Joel) of the famed Childwick Bury Stud, the family fortune being derived from the South African diamond fields around Kimberley. Best known of Solly Joel's runners were Pommern, winner of a substitute Triple Crown in

1915, and Polyphontes, twice successful in the Eclipse Stakes. Both horses stood at his Maiden Erlegh Stud Farm outside Reading.

Just as Solly was less successful on the Turf than his brother Jack, so Stanhope did less well than his cousin Jim. When Stanhope Joel's private trainer, Dick Perryman, retired, his substantial string of horses was divided between Humphrey Cottrill in Newmarket, Peter Easterby in Yorkshire and Brud Fetherstonhaugh in Ireland.

Soon Sir Noel Murless, whose Warren Place yard was next door to Moulton Paddocks, was recruited. He trained two outstanding individuals bred by the Snailwell Stud Company, as it became known, in Busted, who carried Stanhope's green and pink stripes, and Lupe – she ran in his wife's pink and green checks.

In 1967 Noel Murless trained two Joel stars in Busted (four), who had just arrived from Ireland as it was thought he would have better opportunities in England, and Royal Palace (three). The pair of them only worked together once, but that was sufficient to show that Busted had enormous ability. That season he triumphed in the King George VI and Queen Elizabeth Stakes and Eclipse Stakes and was voted Horse of the Year.

By the time of Busted's death, aged twenty-five in March 1988 (just two days after the demise of his illustrious Woodlands Stud neighbour High Top), he was regarded as the most influential sire and sire of sires located in the United Kingdom. One of the last British owned champions to go to stud in private ownership, he featured in the top half dozen sires for seven consecutive seasons from 1973 to 1979.

His outstanding stallion son has been the Wolferton Stud resident Bustino (St Leger, Coronation Cup), who is himself a champion broodmare sire. However, his racecourse achievements have been superseded by the 1988 champion Mtoto (King George VI and Queen Elizabeth Stakes, Coral-Eclipse Stakes, twice). Conceived when Busted was nineteen years of age, Mtoto stands at Aston Upthorpe Stud.

During the Joel era, three classic winners have been bred and conceived at Snailwell: Your Highness (Irish Derby), by Chamossaire, Lupe (Oaks), by Primera, and Opale (Irish St Leger), by Busted.

Lupe contributed to a marvellous Epsom Derby meeting for Snailwell Stud in 1970 as Caliban won the Coronation Cup, a race that the filly won the ensuing season. At that time Stanhope Joel lived in Bermuda and he sold Lupe to Daniel Wildenstein on account of taxation. The best of her progeny is probably Louveterie, runner-up in the 1989 French Oaks.

Prior to the Noel Murless period, Stanhope Joel had horses with another Newmarket trainer in Humphrey Cottrill. He had the frustration of seeing

St Pauli Girl finish runner-up for his patron in the 1000 Guineas (to Fleet) and the Oaks (to Pia).

During his first two seasons at stud, Busted stood alongside Primera whom Charles St George had sold to Stanhope Joel in training. In addition to Lupe, Primera sired two other top fillies trained at Warren Place, Aunt Edith and Attica Meli. Also purchased in training with a view to standing at Snailwell was the sprinter Matador who likewise wound up in Japan. Eileen Rogerson's Athens Wood (St Leger) was another temporary resident *en route* to Russia.

Back in 1959 Snailwell Stud had sold the future Oaks heroine Noblesse 'in utero'. A decade later the stud was responsible for a couple more smart fillies in Circus Ring (Lowther Stakes), who failed to train on as a three-year-old, and Clare Island (Princess Elizabeth Stakes), a half-sister to Caliban. Circus Ring is dam of a smart filly herself in Lady Shipley.

Over the years the Stanhope Joel family has also been very much involved with National Hunt racing. Dana (who is a member of the Jockey Club) and her sister Solna won the 1979 Cheltenham Gold Cup with Alverton; their aunt Eileen Rogerson owned Salmon Spray (1966 Champion Hurdle), while her husband, John, owned Pas Seul (1960 Cheltenham Gold Cup); and in 1981 Nicholas Embiricos, who is married to Dana's cousin, Valda, won the Grand National with Aldaniti.

Someries Stud

The racing world was shocked to learn that Nicholas Phillips had been found dead at his home, Luton Hoo, in Bedfordshire, on 1 March 1991. Together with his mother, Mrs Harold Phillips, and his aunt, Mrs David Butter, Nicky had sold all but ten acres of their famous Someries Stud, situated between Newmarket's Duchess Drive and Woodditton Road, only the previous December to Sheikh Mohammed.

It had been the family's intention to continue trading as Someries Stud with the broodmare band of around fifteen centred on their Blackhall Stud, Co. Kildare, where all the youngsters have always been reared over the years. The animals which Nicky owned himself were labelled Somerhall Bloodstock, a name compounded from the two studs.

Nicky Phillips, who had only taken over as chairman of the Jockey Club Estates on 1 January, was a grandson of Sir Harold and Lady Zia Wernher. Sir Harold will always be remembered for owning that great stayer Brown Jack, and Lady Zia as the owner of homebred Meld. Winner of the 1000 Guineas, Oaks and St Leger in 1955, she not only bred the Derby winner Charlottown, but also the unraced Mellay, twice champion sire in New Zealand.

Only nine fillies have triumphed in the fillies' Triple Crown, and Meld is one of only five to have done so during the twentieth century. The others are Sceptre in 1902, Pretty Polly in 1904, Sun Chariot, winner of substitute events in 1942, and Oh So Sharp in 1985.

Meld is a great-granddaughter of the Wernhers' foundation mare, Double Life (Bachelor's Double – Saint Joan), whom their trainer, Sir Cecil Boyd-Rochfort, bought for them as a yearling at Newmarket in 1927 for 600 guineas. An insignificant-looking washy chesnut with a plain head, she never measured more than 15.3 hands in training. Boyd-Rochfort was attracted to her as Bachelor's Double was making his name as a broodmare sire, but she was decidedly useful in her own right. Successful twice as a juvenile, she won her last four starts the ensuing season, culminating with a Cambridgeshire victory carrying 7st 12lbs.

In the main yard at Someries Stud, named by the Wernhers after their London house and painted in their yellow and green racing colours, is a gravestone on which are annotated Double Life's achievements. However as she was purchased ten years before the stud itself, she went originally as a boarder to Middleton Park Stud, Co. Westmeath, owned by Cecil Boyd-Rochfort's brother, Arthur.

It was whilst she was there that Double Life produced Precipitation (by Hurry On). The Ascot Gold Cup hero retired to Someries Stud in 1938, the Wernhers having bought Someries the previous year from Sir Alec Black. Sire of three St Leger winners in Chamossaire, Airborne (Derby) and Premonition, he also got Why Hurry (New Oaks). Although Chamossaire was champion sire in his dotage with Santa Claus, his most influential son proved to be Sheshoon.

One of the saviours of the Matchem male line, which is invariably on the verge of extinction, Precipitation was duly joined at Someries Stud by his half-brother, Persian Gulf. Winner of the Coronation Cup, but raced exclusively at Newmarket due to the war, Persian Gulf's turf innings was terminated by a cracked cannon bone. The son of Bahram sired Parthia (Derby), Zabara (1000 Guineas), Zarathustra (Ascot Gold Cup), and Tamerlane.

With Supreme Court (by Persian Gulf or Precipitation), winning the inaugural King George VI and Queen Elizabeth (Festival of Britain) Stakes, Someries Stud has bred two winners of this Ascot spectacular in Aggressor in 1960, the conqueror of Petite Etoile, and Kalaglow in 1982. Whereas Sir Harold Wernher purchased the former 'in utero', the latter goes back through five generations to Double Life.

Additional winners originating with Double Life for the Wernhers include Casanova, Judicate, Daily Double, Double Eclipse and Duplation. Another shrewd purchase in 1946 was Miss Pecksniff, the grandam of Dickens, and the third dam of Harmony Hall.

Following the death of Lady Zia Wernher in 1977 (her husband had died four years earlier), Someries switched to commercial yearling production. In 1979 Kalaglow was sold for 11,500 guineas at the Newmarket October Sales. The grey son of Kalamoun was attributed with the wrong dam until he was a four-year-old when he won the Coral-Eclipse Stakes and King George VI and Queen Elizabeth Diamond Stakes. He was then syndicated for £5 million to stand at Brook Stud.

Charlottown (Charlottesville – Meld), who was trained by Gordon Smyth as Cecil Boyd-Rochfort was not favourably impressed with him as a yearling, won the Derby but failed to make much of an impact in nine covering seasons at Someries. The first winner of the Blue Riband to stand in Australia, he broke a leg there three years later. Meld survived him, she being put down at Blackhall Stud aged thirty-four in September 1983.

One of the stalwarts of Someries Stud was the old stud groom John Carew. Employed there for over half a century (1937-1978), he died in 1981. It was in June 1974 that John Waugh took over as manager following the death of Major Geoffrey Hull. Also manager to Lord Derby at Woodlands Stud and to Sir Robin McAlpine at Wyck Hall, John continues to live in the house at Someries. After Charlottown, he has had responsibility for the stallions Vitiges, Bay Express, Adonijah and Local Suitor – the last was boarded there for Sheikh Mohammed's Darley Stud Management.

Since the Wernher era, Someries' winners descending from Double Life have included the half-brothers King's Island (Grade 1 Sunset Handicap), and Bengal Fire (Royal Lodge Stakes), Tants (Lingfield Oaks Trial Stakes), Formulate (Hoover Fillies' Mile), and her daughter, Game Plan. Winner of the 1990 Sea World Pretty Polly Stakes, Game Plan was second in the Gold Seal Oaks. She is a great, great, great, great-granddaughter of Double Life.

By far the most distinguished of the late Nicky Phillips's own mares is Roussalka. Bred like her brilliant half-sister, Oh So Sharp, at neighbouring Dalham Hall Stud, she won the Nassau Stakes twice and is dam of the useful Gayane.

Stanley House and Woodlands Studs

NEWMARKET · SUFFOLK

It is ironic that the outstanding horse bred by the present Lord Derby is the gelded Teleprompter (1985 Budweiser Arlington Million), who is thus deprived of the opportunity of maintaining the traditions of the once great Stanley House Stud. John Derby is a grandson of the 17th Earl, the most important breeder of the twentieth century, from whom he inherited the title and the famous colours, 'black, white cap', in 1948.

The 17th Earl assisted his father, the 16th Earl, in resurrecting the Knowsley Stud at the family's Merseyside home outside Liverpool, and in founding the Stanley House Stud and Stables (including Woodlands Stud) in Newmarket. In due course this was expanded to include both Plantation and Side Hill Studs in Newmarket and Thornton Stud in Yorkshire.

Today Lord Derby's stud operation is restricted to Stanley House (the stables were sold to Sheikh Mohammed and are occupied by John Gosden) and neighbouring Woodlands Studs. The two studs are run as one, although the stallions (Sharpo and Pharly) are based at Woodlands, under the management of John Waugh who also oversees the Someries bloodstock and Wyck Hall Studs. John's predecessors were Walter Alston, Jack Paine and Adrian Scrope.

To Adrian Scrope, who also managed Sledmere for the Sykes family and Plantation for Lord Howard de Walden, is owed the credit for obtaining Teleprompter's great-grandam, Gradisca, for John Derby on an exchange basis with Elizabeth Couturie of Haras du Mesnil. Incidentally Teleprompter's half-sister Rosia Bay (by the Woodlands resident High Top) became a celebrity at Lord Carnarvon's Highclere Stud.

Apart from Teleprompter, the two best performers to race for John Derby have been Alycidon (1945) and Swallow Tail (1946), both of them bred by his grandfather. A fine stayer, Alycidon won the Ascot Gold Cup, Goodwood Cup and Doncaster Cup in 1949, when Swallow Tail was beaten two heads for the Derby. None too fertile, Alycidon was champion sire in 1955 when his daughter Meld won the fillies' Triple Crown. He also exerted a profound influence as the maternal grandsire of Petingo.

Alycidon was the sixth and last homebred 'Derby' stallion to become champion sire during the present century, which serves to illustrate the stature of this bloodstock dynasty at its zenith. The remainder consist of Hyperion (1940, 1941, 1942, 1945, 1946, 1954), Fairway (1936, 1939, 1943, 1944), Phalaris (1925, 1928), Swynford (1923), and Pharos (1931).

Alycidon's retirement to Woodlands in 1950 coincided with a last season there for Walter Griffiths as stud groom to the present Lord Derby. His successors have been Michael Ryan, Jack Relihan and Patrick Cronin. Walter's father, John, had been stud groom to both the 16th and 17th Earls – it was the former's great-grandfather, the 12th Earl, after whom the Derby (first run in 1780) is named.

Stanley House and Woodlands Studs are situated in the elbow between the Snailwell and Bury roads. This was the site of the Duchess of Montrose's Sefton Stud (named after her husband's 1878 Derby winner) which the 16th Lord Derby bought following her death in 1894. John Griffiths had been the Duchess's stud groom and, at her executors' sale, Lord Derby bought Canterbury Pilgrim, then a yearling.

Canterbury Pilgrim won the Oaks and bred Chaucer and Swynford. Chaucer made his name as a broodmare sire and none proved of greater moment than Selene, dam of Hyperion. The 17th Lord Derby owned and bred fifteen winners of nineteen classics (he also raced Swynford who was bred by his father). Sandwiched between Sansovino (1924) and Watling Street (1942), Hyperion (1933) was one of three Derby winners. When he was a yearling, trainer George Lambton told Lord Derby that Hyperion was the most perfectly conformed little horse that he had ever seen and that he would undoubtedly win the Pony Derby at Northolt Park!

Hyperion's record as six-times champion sire has only been bettered by St Simon, Stockwell and Hermit. A particular benefactor to the Royal Studs with Aureole (twice champion sire) and Hypericum, not to mention Owen Tudor, his sons spread the gospel, notably with Alibhai, Khaled and Heliopolis in the USA and Aristophanes (sire of Forli) in Argentina. Queen of the fillies was wartime Triple Crown heroine Sun Chariot. She was a product of the National Stud as was Swynford's mighty son, Blandford, who became champion sire three times.

It was from Colonel Hall-Walker (later Lord Wavertree), to whom we are indebted for the National Stud, that the 17th Lord Derby procured Hyperion's third dam, Gondolette, at the 1912 Newmarket December Sales for 1,550 guineas. That May he paid 1,300 guineas for another omnipotent foundation mare in Anchora from George Edwardes of Ballykisteen Stud.

To matings with Phalaris at Woodlands, Anchora's daughter, Scapa Flow, produced three stars in Pharos, Fairway and Fair Isle. Shunned by some breeders because he was only a handicapper, Phalaris was twice champion sire and his son Pharos was also champion sire. As the sire of Nearco (grand-sire of Northern Dancer), Pharos has assumed enormous importance in the male line down to the present time.

Just as 'Derby' stallions have exercised a worldwide reputation, so too have 'Derby' mares. The list is endless, but two names with which to conjure are Marchetta (1907, by Marco – Hettie Sorrel) and Schiaparelli (1935, by Shiavoni – Aileen). Their combined influence has been absolutely staggering to say the least – significantly Lord Derby still owns representatives of both tap-roots.

At present the star Stanley House mare is Ouija, dam of Teleprompter, whose eleven victories in England, Ireland, France and the USA accumulated prize money of £775,000. It is gratifying to note that Ouija carries plenty of 'Derby' blood on the distaff side. Furthermore she was sired by Silly Season at New England Stud. Then owned by John Derby's brother, Richard Stanley, it is now owned by their nephew, Peter, whose elder brother, Edward, is Lord Derby's heir.

Stetchworth Park Stud

NEWMARKET · SUFFOLK

In 1989 William Gredley's homebred Call to Arms nearly caused a major sensation when beaten a neck for the Three Chimneys Dewhurst Stakes. At the time his sire, North Briton, was the teaser at the owner-breeder's Stetchworth Park Stud which lies on the periphery of Newmarket.

Bill Gredley, chairman of a property company and patron of Clive Brittain's local stable, acquired Stetchworth Park Stud from Lieutenant-Colonel and Mrs Douglas Gray in 1983. Since then he has stood two horses there, both of whom carried his distinctive yellow and black colours to victory having been bought as three-year-olds at the Newmarket Autumn Sales.

North Briton (Northfields – Juliette Marny), who failed to score for his owner-breeder, James Morrison of Fonthill Stud, cost 6,000 guineas in 1982. Three years later Hadeer was purchased from Sheikh Maktoum Al Maktoum for 13,000 guineas. The Sheikh had originally paid $190,000 for Hadeer (General Assembly – Glinting) as a yearling, West Blagdon having sold him as a foal for 70,000 guineas.

Originally known as Ellesmere Stud, Stetchworth Park Stud was founded by the third Earl of Ellesmere in the 1880s. His grandson, the present Duke of Sutherland, still owns a sizeable acreage around Newmarket, including the land on which the TBA's new Equine Fertility Unit is located. This is named Mertoun Paddocks after the Duke's home in Roxburghshire.

Stetchworth Park, which is bounded to the north by the Devil's Dyke, an historic landmark dividing the Rowley and July Courses on the other side of the Stetchworth Toll roundabout, is one of the most picturesque studs in the vicinity of Newmarket. Many of the paddocks are in a parkland setting, beautifully sheltered by a profusion of mature trees and hedges.

Buried in the park is the mighty Hampton whose tail adorns the stud office. A selling-plater who became one of the great stayers of his time, Hampton was bought as a five-year-old by the third Lord Ellesmere in

1877. Champion sire of 1887, Hampton got three Derby winners in Merry Hampton, Ladas and Ayrshire, but more important for the Ellesmere Stud resident was Bay Ronald from whom the Son-in-Law and Hyperion male lines descend.

The Stetchworth Park Estate was duly inherited by the fourth Lord Ellesmere (1872-1944), who was both senior steward of the Jockey Club and president of the MCC. He also owned two brilliant but ill-fated fillies by Tetratema. The first was Tiffin (1926). Unbeaten in eight starts and one of the fastest fillies ever, she died of peritonitis at Stetchworth Park in March 1931, just after producing her first foal. Then came Four Course (1928). Winner of the 1000 Guineas, she died tragically from tetanus in her first stud season.

Pick of Ellesmere's homebreds was probably Lemnarchus. An Ascot specialist, he won the King's Stand Stakes (beating Portlaw), Fern Hill Stakes and Coventry Stakes. Another good colt of his breeding was Trespasser, successful in three Imperial Cups. Both retired to stand in Newmarket, Lemnarchus at Aislabie (now Collin Stud), and Trespasser at Meddler Stud.

In 1983 the fifth Lord Ellesmere succeeded a distant cousin as Duke of Sutherland by which time he had leased Stetchworth Park Stud to Douglas and Joan Gray. As Douglas was then managing Hadrian Stud for Sir David Wills, his wife was largely responsible for Stetchworth on a day-to-day basis. The establishment specialized in boarders, with special emphasis on sales preparation. Amongst the international clientele was the Italian concern, BBC Farms, on whose behalf a Ribot colt foal (Riboral) was sold for a record 22,000 guineas in 1967.

Three top winners bred during this period were the Duke of Sutherland's Activator (Dee Stakes) – nowadays John Egerton, 6th Duke of Sutherland, keeps a few mares (Dryburgh Stud) at his St Boswells home – Mr L.L. Lawrence's homebred Soderini (Hardwicke Stakes), and Sinthesis (Premio Regina Elena). The latter was the best winner bred by Douglas and Joan Gray.

Having bought Stetchworth Park Stud as sitting tenants, the Grays then sold the property to Bill Gredley. Soon the 100 acres there were greatly augmented by an additional 750 acres close by at Dullingham Ley. Originally three separate blocks of farmland and woodland, this has been developed as a stud and spelling station with seven American-style barns and a variety of gallops.

Each establishment has its own separate role. Stetchworth Park is utilized by the two stallions, Hadeer and North Briton, as well as providing a home for Bill Gredley's own yearlings, the majority of which go to the specialist sales. Dullingham Ley is the base not only for Bill Gredley's own mares (at one time he had as many as sixty-five) but also for all visiting mares.

The overall responsibility for Stetchworth and Dullingham Ley rests with Nigel Wright, who was once with Bob McCreery at Moreton Paddox in Warwickshire. His predecessors as manager at Stetchworth have been BBC commentator Julian Wilson, whose own bloodstock interests are labelled Seymour Bloodstock, and Alan Mason, previously manager at Bourchiers Hall Stud.

Bill Gredley did extremely well with Hadeer. Only rarely does a horse improve out of all recognition upon moving from one top trainer to another, but Hadeer was the exception. Switched from Michael Stoute to Clive Brittain, Hadeer won three Group races as a four-year-old, the Trusthouse Forte Hungerford Stakes, Kiveton Park Stakes and Federation Brewery Beeswing Stakes.

In purchasing Hadeer, whose first crop of runners appeared in 1991, Bill Gredley was spending just a fraction of the 400,000 guineas which he had received exactly four weeks earlier for a Troy filly at the Highflyer Sales. Named Port Helene, she proved a very useful performer for Sheikh Mohammed.

Two more stallions with which Bill Gredley has been involved are Wolver Heights, who had an interim period at Meddler Stud before departing to Poland, and champion sprinter Handsome Sailor – he retired to Emral Stud in north Wales in 1990.

Stowell Hill

TEMPLECOMBE · SOMERSET

Bob McCreery is the breeder of two classic winners, High Top (1972 2000 Guineas) and Old Vic (1989 Budweiser Irish Derby, Prix du Jockey Club Lancia). The former was bred at his Moreton Paddox Stud in Warwickshire, and the latter at Stowell Hill in Somerset.

A leading figure in the bloodstock world and twice champion amateur rider under National Hunt Rules during the 1950s, he owes his exalted status as a commercial breeder to his original foundation mare, Camenae (Vimy – Madrilene), the dam of High Top and grandam of Old Vic.

It was in 1963 that Bob McCreery bought Moreton Paddox at Moreton Morrell, upon the recommendation of former trainer Syd Mercer, with the intention of converting the property into a stud. Three years later he bought Camenae privately for 1,500 guineas at the Newmarket December Sales from fellow amateur jockey, Dennis Ward.

McCreery was attracted to Camenae, a modest winner at four years, on two counts. Firstly she was by Vimy, whom he was convinced would make a broodmare sire, and secondly she was a granddaughter of Marmite – she was third dam of Hollister who had scored eight flat victories for Bob and his wife, Jeanette.

Camenae, whose name had been spelt Camanae (*sic*) in the catalogue, an error perpetuated by Weatherbys for some time, was destined to produce three important offspring to Derring-Do. First came High Top, who was conceived during the last of Derring-Do's three seasons at Cheveley Park, followed by Cockade and Camden Town, both sired at Aston Park, Derring-Do's home for the remainder of his days. In due course he was replaced there by his son Dominion whom McCreery was instrumental in repatriating from the USA.

The very first yearling consigned by Bob McCreery to the Houghton Sales where he was sold privately for 9,000 guineas, High Top was a Group

1 scorer at two (Observer Gold Cup) and three years (2000 Guineas). This fine miler was syndicated to stand at Woodlands Stud where he died in March 1988, aged nineteen. By that time he was responsible for five European classic winners with Top Ville, Cut Above, My Top, Circus Plume and Colorspin – Top Ville has become an influential sire in his own right. He is also a champion broodmare sire, three of his daughters being Eldoret, Rosia Bay and Pine Ridge.

High Top's own-brother Camden Town (Jersey Stakes) has also had his share of success as a sire based in Ireland, but his achievements have been overshadowed by their own-sister Cockade.

Only a small winner at three years, Cockade demonstrated her broodmare potential with the 1983 Irish Guinness Oaks third, Green Lucia (by Green dancer), prior to foaling Old Vic. One of Sadler's Wells's first crop, Old Vic fully justified the 230,000 guineas he cost Sheikh Mohammed as a yearling by winning the Irish and French Derbys by an aggregate of elevenlengths.

On the International Classification, Old Vic was joint top rated (with Zilzal), 3lbs ahead of Nashwan whom he had never met. Due to the firm ground which prevailed all through the summer of 1990, Henry Cecil had the greatest difficulty in getting his dual classic winner fit, but he put up a brilliant display when just beaten by his owner's stable companion Belmez in the King George VI and Queen Elizabeth Diamond Stakes. Sadly tendon trouble precluded a grand finale in the Ciga Prix de l'Arc de Triomphe and he was retired to Dalham Hall Stud.

The final crop of yearlings raised at Moreton Paddox included Electric. Winner of four Group races, including the Great Voltigeur Stakes, he completed six covering seasons at Whitsbury Manor Stud before becoming a National Hunt sire under the Coolmore flag in Ireland. But for a virus, his half-brother, Les Arcs (Gerry Feilden Stakes), would have been another good middle-distance performer.

Nineteen-eighty was a watershed for Bob McCreery. In February, Camenae (nineteen) was put down, and in October his entire breeding operation was moved down to the family home, Stowell Hill, outside Templecombe, on the Somerset–Dorset border. This followed the sale of Moreton Paddox to Venezuelan petrochemicals magnate Dr José Sahagun. Initially Bob McCreery was far from convinced that Stowell Hill (noted for growing prize rhododendrons) would be suitable for breeding top-quality bloodstock. However, after extensive soil analyses, he began transforming two farms into separate stud entities, the one for mares and foals, the other for yearlings.

There was certainly a vintage collection of colt foals at Stowell Hill in 1987 with four black-type winners. A half-brother to Old Vic, Splash of Colour (Royal Whip Stakes), who had cost the beleaguered Classic Thoroughbreds IR230,000 guineas as a yearling, and General Accident 2000 Guineas third, Anshan (Ladbroke European Free Handicap), were bred by Stowell Hill. Anvari (Derrinstown Stud Derby Trial Stakes) and Theatrical Charmer (Newmarket Stakes), were reared there.

Theatrical Charmer was actually bred by Bloodstock Breeders PLC of which McCreery was managing director. A breeding enterprise under the government's business expansion scheme, it obtained 470,000 guineas for a Shareef Dancer foal at the 1985 Newmarket December Sales, a record for a colt of that age at public auction in the British Isles. So far the top price for a Stowell Hill yearling is the 500,000 guineas which Sheikh Mohammed paid for Old Vic's Green Desert half-brother (Muthhil) at the 1989 Highflyer Sales.

Bob McCreery has been involved in numerous partnerships and his colours were carried to victory in the 1986 Tote Cesarewitch by Orange Hill whom he owned jointly with her trainer, Jeremy Tree. This particular partnership was dissolved at the 1990 December Sales. Even if he had never bred a High Top or an Old Vic, Bob McCreery would still have made a handsome contribution to the bloodstock world as an administrator. A leading light of the Thoroughbred Breeders' Association, he is a former chairman and is currently serving a fourth term on the council.

Sussex Stud

WEST GRINSTEAD · WEST SUSSEX

Formerly known as West Grinstead Park Stud, Sussex Stud, near Horsham, has had four separate owners or lessees. Founded by J.P. (John Peter) Hornung, it has been occupied in turn by the National Stud, Robert Francis and Mohammed Mutawa. The Kuwaiti owner-breeder, who raced the brilliant filly sprinter Habibti, is one of the principals of the present stud owners, the Sussex Stud Ltd.

It was in 1909 that Peter Hornung bought the West Grinstead Park Estate of 3,500 acres where he started a stud four years later. Of aristocratic Hungarian descent, the Hornungs had established steel interests in Middlesbrough in the mid-nineteenth century. Later they diversified into sugar, Peter pioneering the first plantations alongside the River Zambesi in Portuguese East Africa.

Horses like 2000 Guineas third Apple Sammy (July Stakes) provided Peter Hornung with his share of success as an owner-breeder. His distinctive colours, 'white, black spots, black sleeves, red cap', also did well with yearling purchases, Copyright (Ascot Gold Vase) and Nippon (Ascot Derby) completing a memorable Royal Ascot double in 1921.

A couple of years later Papyrus was bought for £30,000 in the year of his Derby triumph from Ben Irish, a fellow Basil Jarvis patron, together with Jarvis's Green Lodge stables (now occupied by Harry Thomson Jones) in Newmarket. The son of Tracery, who had just returned from his match defeat by Zev in the States, afforded a rare opportunity of purchasing a Derby winner – all four of the other post-war winners had been retained by their owners.

Runner-up in the Eclipse Stakes as a four-year-old, Papyrus retired to stand at West Grinstead Park Stud in 1925 at a fee of 300 guineas. He was soon booked for three years in advance. Unfortunately such unbridled enthusiasm was somewhat misplaced. However Peter Hornung's Papyrus colt, Dubonnet, provided his breeder with a much coveted trophy when winning the 1939 Goodwood Cup at his favourite racecourse.

The following year Peter Hornung died (Papyrus's death at Aislabie Stud, Newmarket, was recorded in 1941), whereupon West Grinstead Park was inherited by his eldest son, Bernard. He sold the property right away to a Mr E. Cook of travel agents Thomas Cook and Son. In the first instance, Bernard, who lived close by at Ivorys, Cowfold, leased the stud back until his own model establishment had been completed.

Bernard Hornung called the home stud High Hurst Manor Stud. A patron of Sir Noel Murless's stable, he enjoyed conspicuous success as an owner-breeder, thanks largely to buying back the mares Chincona and Buckeye. His two outstanding performers were the fillies Abelia, who excelled as a juvenile and bred Casabianca, and Aunt Edith, the first of her sex to win the King George VI and Queen Elizabeth (Diamond) Stakes.

Sadly Bernard Hornung died in 1964 when Aunt Edith was an unraced two-year-old, High Hurst Manor Stud having been left jointly to his sons, John and Stephen, who traded as West Grinstead Stud Ltd. Cranberry Sauce and her daughter Sauceboat were two top fillies to race for Sir John Hornung. The latter bred two more Group winners in Kind of Hush, now a stallion in Yorkshire, and Dusty Dollar.

By 1949 West Grinstead Park was owned by Lord Glentyre who assigned a ninety-nine year lease to the Royal Veterinary College for use as a field station. Peter Burrell, then director of the National Stud, recalls that the place was in a state of limbo when the Ministry of Agriculture (then responsible for the National Stud) became the lessees.

The objective at West Grinstead was to provide the National Stud with facilities for standing more stallions for the benefit of 'smaller' breeders as there was only room for two at their Gillingham premises in Dorset. While Big Game and Elopement were based there, West Grinstead became home for Tenerani, Jock Scot, Never Say Die and Pindari. In 1968 Never Say Die became the first stallion to be installed at the National Stud's new purpose-built Newmarket establishment.

In 1972 the National Stud relinquished its interest at West Grinstead (latterly both Acropolis and Alcide stood there), whereupon Robert Francis, a new client of the British Bloodstock Agency, took over. He made a sensational, but short-lived entrée into the business by starting with three new stallions at what was now called Sussex Stud.

That syndicated trio comprised Roi Lear (Prix du Jockey Club), Sharp Edge (Irish 2000 Guineas), and Scottish Rifle (Eclipse Stakes). After just one covering season they had all found new homes, Roi Lear in his native

France at Haras du Petit Tellier, Sharp Edge at Littleton Stud, and Scottish Rifle at Lavington Stud.

At the time Sussex Stud was managed by the highly regarded and much travelled veterinary surgeon John Gray, subsequently manager of Christopher Loyd's Lockinge Stud. It was one of Gray's veterinary colleagues, Patrick Churchward, who became manager of Sussex Stud when the place was taken over, unoccupied, by Mohammed Mutawa in 1980.

The very first mare purchased was Gift Wrapped (Lingfield Oaks Trial Stakes), who cost 116,000 guineas at that year's Newmarket December Sales. Her first offspring is Reach. Successful in the Royal Lodge Stakes, this son of Kris stood at Dullingham Stud (now Eagle Lane Farm) for two seasons until exported to Japan.

Mohammed Mutawa's name first became known in racing circles through the brilliant Habibti (King's Stand Stakes, William Hill July Cup) for whom he had paid 140,000 guineas as a yearling in 1981. Unfortunately she has been contrastingly slow off the mark at stud. Mated with Shirley Heights in each of her first two seasons, she was barren in 1986 and then her foal the next year died.

Gift Wrapped and Habibti are two of a dozen mares owned by Sussex Stud Ltd which also boards animals for Dana Stud Ltd. This concern bred Kyra, the very first winner for Vincent O'Brien's Classic Thoroughbreds.

Theakston Stud

BEDALE · NORTH YORKSHIRE

As recently as 1989, Theakston Stud stood three stallions. They were Mandrake Major, who is owned outright by the stud, together with Blushing Scribe and K Battery. Blushing Scribe was exported to Australia in 1990; the previous year K Battery departed to Chesters Stud in Northumberland.

Blushing Scribe had started his stud career in Essex at the Bourchiers Hall Stud of his Hong Kong-based owner, Alex Wong. He used to keep as many as fifteen mares up at Theakston trading either as Raylex Stud Farm Company or Topspin Company.

One of the oldest established studs in the country, Theakston is situated in beautiful countryside near Bedale in North Yorkshire. The property is actually bisected by the busy A1 with the Hambleton Hills visible to the east and the Pennines to the west.

John McIntyre is the third member of his family in father-to-son sequence to have owned and managed Theakston which has a long history as a public and a commercial yearling stud. Founded by John McIntyre's grandfather of the same name in the 1890s, the stud is associated with two particular celebrities in Dante and Sovereign Path.

John's great-grandfather, Archibald, bred numerous good horses in the middle of the last century with his father-in-law, Thomas Hewett of Gibside Park, Co. Durham. In 1890 he moved to Neasham Hall Stud, near Darlington, where James Cookson bred Kettledrum and Dundee, first and second in the 1861 Derby. Three years later Archie bought Theakston Hall of 600 acres, bringing his Aberdeen Angus cattle with him – today they rank as the oldest established herd in England.

The present John McIntyre was only twenty-one when he took over the stud following the death of his father in 1968. At that time the resident stallions were Le Dieu d'Or – he was bred by the eccentric Rachel Parsons who was murdered by one of her stable staff; Rockavon, the Scottish trained winner of the 1961 2000 Guineas who deprived Theakston-bred Prince Tudor of victory; and Sweet Story, the Duke of Roxburghe's homebred who then went to his Floors Stud at Kelso.

Dante (Nearco – Rosy Legend) is the last Derby winner to have been bred and trained in Yorkshire. Reared at the Peacocks' Manor House Stud, Middleham, like his St Leger-winning own-brother, Sayajirao, he was trained by Matthew Peacock for his owner-breeder, Sir Eric Ohlson. He lived in Scarborough and had extensive shipping interests centred on Hull.

Retired to stand at Theakston in 1946, Dante remained there until his demise ten years later. Latterly he went completely blind – he had suffered eye problems in training which precluded his participation in the St Leger, much to the chagrin of Yorkshire racegoers. His highly influential son, Derring-Do, was similarly afflicted.

Due to a rift with Matthew Peacock, Eric Ohlson transferred his broodmares, which operated as Friar Ings Stud, from Manor House to Theakston. One of his numerous progeny by Dante was Asti Spumante, an influential matron whose descendants include Chilibang. Another Dante mare, Matelda, is dam of Tudor Melody. Twice champion sire of two-year-olds, Tudor Melody preceded Chilibang as a National Stud stallion.

Nineteen-fifty-six was a milestone for Theakston as Sovereign Path (Grey Sovereign – Mountain Path) was born in April and Dante died in September. Tudor Melody raced for Dick Peacock's patron, Fred Ellison, from whom Archie McIntyre (John's father) bought Mountain Path – she cost 480 guineas at the 1951 Newmarket December Sales after winning a maiden that season at Catterick.

A grey, Sovereign Path was sold by Theakston Stud as a yearling for only 700 guineas in the old Glasgow Paddocks, Doncaster. Successful in the Queen Elizabeth II Stakes and Lockinge Stakes, he became a celebrated sire of sires with Wolver Hollow being champion of 1976. Located throughout his stallion life at Burgage Stud, Co. Carlow, Sovereign Path died aged twenty-one to be replaced by his grandson, Wolverlife (by Wolver Hollow).

In England one of Sovereign Path's most successful stallion sons was Guy Reed's homebred Warpath, who was the cornerstone of his Nidd Hall Stud, an operation which subsequently moved to Copgrove Hall Stud. His progeny include Guy Reed's Derby fourth, Shotgun – his dam Brief Flight was one of a number of mares that Commander Clare Vyner used to board at Theakston.

Sovereign Path was outlived by his dam, Mountain Path, who was thirty-one years of age when buried at Theakston alongside Dante. Her daughter

Grischuna, who cost Gerald Oldham 7,000 guineas as a yearling, rendered yeoman service to his Citadel Stud, and is the grandam of his triple Ascot Gold Cup hero Sagaro.

None of the latter day stallions at Theakston has wielded the same degree of influence as either Dante or Sovereign Path. John McIntyre's own acquisitions, Saintly Song (by Aureole) and Mandrake Major (by On Your Mark) both gained prestige wins at Doncaster as two-year-olds, the former in the Champagne Stakes and the latter in the Flying Childers Stakes.

Amongst the leading winners bred by Theakston Stud in the seventies and eighties have been Darine (Prix Fille de l'Air), Berkeley Square (Cavendish Cape Handicap, Ascot), the half-brothers Kayus and Penny Forum, winners of twenty-three races between them, and Kombus, who scored fourteen times in the USA – his dam Vallée Secrete was then sold privately only to produce Mujadil, one of the leading two-year-olds of 1990.

Theakston's influence is never far away. Sometimes with a horse like Le Dieu d'Or (sire of Goldhill and maternal grandsire of Lochnager), it has been at a parochial level. Quite often a cheap yearling has achieved much wider recognition, like Hanina (820 guineas). She is dam of Mrs McArdy (1977 1000 Guineas), who was sold for a record 154,000 guineas in the year of her classic triumph, and subsequently bred Citidancer.

Thornton Stud

THORNTON-LE-STREET · NORTH YORKSHIRE

Before the advent of Kris, one of Thornton Stud's chief claims to fame was as a temporary home for Lord Derby's Hyperion. A legend in his own lifetime, Hyperion was put down at Woodlands Stud in December 1960, at the advanced age of thirty. Newmarket veterinary surgeon Fred Day administered the necessary injection and his son John now manages Thornton Stud for Lord Howard de Walden.

It is something of a coincidence that Howard de Walden's two principal studs, Plantation at Newmarket and Thornton in north Yorkshire, both used to belong to the 17th Earl of Derby. At the time of his death in 1948, he also owned studs at Knowsley Park, the family home in Lancashire, and at Newmarket with Woodlands and Side Hill.

During the war it was deemed inadvisable to keep Hyperion at Newmarket any longer than was necessary due to the danger of stray bombs intended for the profusion of air bases near the east coast, so he was dispatched to Yorkshire after the covering season. The first year, Hyperion went to Lord Bolton's Bolton Hall, and thereafter to Thornton Stud. For the last three years of the war he covered at Plantation instead of being with Fairway at Woodlands.

Situated near Thirsk, Thornton Stud is within a ten-mile radius of Cliff Stud to the east and Theakston Stud to the west. Founded in 1918 by Commander Clare Vyner, one of whose forebears owned Ormonde's great rival, Minting, the stud extends to over 430 acres with some glorious parkland, the public and private sectors being run as two separate entities.

Still in use is the magnificent stable block with its Georgian arched design. Once the site of the Vyners' Thornton-le-Street Hall, an eighteenth-century mansion long since demolished, there is a magnificent triumphal arch to the original west gate commemorating Wellington and the Napoleonic wars, as well as two small Adam lodges at another entrance.

After Lord Derby died, the number of studs under the Stanley House banner was gradually reduced. In 1955 Thornton Stud, where Alycidon, one of the great stayers of the century, and substitute Derby winner Watling Street were reared, was acquired by trainer Jack Colling, son of Yorkshire trainer Bob, and Dick Hern's predecessor at West Ilsley.

Back in the twenties, Jack Colling inherited Scaltback Stud at Newmarket, where he was then training, from his principal patron, Charles T. Garland. Just as soon as Colling had acquired Thornton he took on Paddy Lennon, previously in his employ at Scaltback, as stud groom. Paddy was at Thornton for thirty-five years until his retirement in 1989 when succeeded by his son, Patrick.

For one season Jack Colling stood the American-bred Relic at Thornton as well as having some of the National Stud yearlings that were retained to race for the Queen, but within a couple of years the property was bought by Sir Victor Sassoon. This was upon the recommendation of Sir Noel Murless, who had recently taken over the management of the Sassoon bloodstock.

Noel Murless knew this part of the country well as he had started training at Hambleton and leased Cliff Stud at Helmsley from one of his owners, Lord Feversham. The Sassoon foals used to come up from Newmarket to be reared in Yorkshire. However the pick of these weanlings went to Cliff rather than Thornton as Murless regarded the limestone land there as being more beneficial for growing bone in young stock.

Following Sir Victor Sassoon's death in 1961, his widow continued with his racing and breeding operation, but in December 1967 she sold Thornton Stud as a going concern to Lord Howard de Walden. Included in the package was the resident stallion Hard Sauce, four mares and three fillies. One of the mares was Soft Angels, destined to become the grandam of Kris, and the solitary foal was Parmelia.

Previously manager at Sir John Musker's Shadwell Stud, John Day arrived at Thornton Stud in May 1968. Exactly one year later Hard Sauce died aged twenty-one. A yearling bargain for Victor Sassoon and sire of his Derby hero Hard Ridden, who cost just 270 guineas at that age, Hard Sauce was replaced by another leading sprinter in So Blessed.

Purchased outright by Lord Howard de Walden from his racing owner, Sir David Robinson, So Blessed had also won the July Cup. Largely instrumental in getting the Verdict family elevated into the *General Stud Book*, So Blessed enjoyed a marvellous innings at Thornton until exported to Japan, the destination of so many other top sons of Princely Gift, another Sassoon flag-bearer.

After an interval of one season, So Blessed was replaced in 1981 by the homebred champion Kris (Sharpen Up – Doubly Sure). It would have been quite understandable had Dance in Time made way for Kris at Plantation Stud, but Lord Howard de Walden was not to be deflected in his resolve to stand Kris in northern territory instead of fashionable Newmarket.

Kris was a brilliant racehorse. Only defeated twice in sixteen starts over three seasons, he gained his most important victory in the Sussex Stakes. A champion miler, he has exceeded all expectations as a champion sire. Originally syndicated for £100,000 a share, his nominations were soon commanding the same figure. His progeny includes Gold Seal Oaks heroines Oh So Sharp and Unite, winners of five classics between them, as well as homebred Shavian.

So far as Lord Howard de Walden's own bloodstock is concerned, Thornton acts as a staging post between Plantation and Templeton, for it is in Yorkshire that the majority of the foals are weaned before being transferred to Berkshire for Christmas. As John Day and the Lennons, father and son, will testify, neither the Derby winner Slip Anchor nor Kris were anything special at that stage of their development.

Warren Stud

NEWMARKET · SUFFOLK

Sandwiched between Brook Stud and Banstead Manor Stud at Cheveley, Warren Stud has been owned by Sheikh Mohammed since the spring of 1989. So the great new force in British racing and breeding has almost extinguished the guttering flame of the once great Astor stud.

It was in 1930 that the 2nd Lord Astor, one of the pre-eminent owner-breeders between the wars with the winners of eleven English classics (he was also part breeder of Ambiguity), acquired Warren Stud as an appendage to Cliveden Stud from Lord Beaverbrook. He in turn had bought the stud from another great newspaper proprietor, Sir Edward Hulton.

Originally known as Warren Tower Stud, it was here that Edward Hulton enjoyed conspicuous success through his foundation mare, Silver Fowl, whose daughter Fifinella won substitute races for the Derby and Oaks in 1916. When he died in 1925, Fifinella contributed 12,000 guineas to the record-breaking dispersal which aggregated 288,380 guineas from seventy-seven lots.

In 1950 Lord Astor decided to divide his bloodstock between his two sons, William the eldest, and John the youngest. Although they operated under the collective title Astor Studs, Bill maintained his mares at Cliveden and Jakie, who became Sir John in 1978, kept his mares either at Hatley, his Bedfordshire home at Sandy, or at Warren Stud.

Jakie Astor had never anticipated sharing in such an inheritance and at the time he was in the process of establishing his own independent Hatley Stud as well as being one of three partners in Blackhall Stud, Co. Kildare. When Bill Astor, for whom Ambiguity won the 1953 Oaks, died in 1966, it was left to his younger brother to keep the Astor colours flying.

About twenty-five mares and fillies were involved in the original share-out, and the brothers tossed for first choice, taking alternate lots thereafter. As far as Jakie was concerned the most significant acquisition proved to be Indian Night. She was to breed that great stayer Trelawny as well as Tantalizer.

Culled at the 1972 December Sales, Tantalizer produced the first of Jakie Astor's two St Leger winners in Provoke. He was sold as a stallion to Russia but died shortly after arrival. At the 1980 December Sales Tantalizer's granddaughter, Vaguely, was bought by the Duke of Roxburghe (Floors Stud) for whom she bred that good horse Shady Heights.

Two Cliveden mares sold during the 1950s attained classic glory in the 1960s. They are Gambade, an own-sister to Ambiguity, who became dam of Sodium (St Leger, Irish Sweeps Derby), and Mitraille. Own-sister to that fine stayer Rally, she is the grandam of Full Dress II (1000 Guineas), a key figure at White Lodge Stud.

None of Jakie Astor's purchases proved of greater moment than Warning who cost 7,200 guineas as a yearling from Whitsbury Manor Stud. She is the dam of Escort and the grandam of Remand, both of whom won the Royal Lodge Stakes, before finishing fourth in the Derby. Warning is also dam of triple Champion Hurdle winner Persian War.

Escort became a sire in South Africa and Remand did likewise in Japan. Two more colts to become sires overseas are the half-brothers Sharp Edge (Irish 2000 Guineas, Prix Jean Prat) and Cut Above (St Leger). Their dam Cutle resulted from an exchange of mares with Jakie Astor's friend Dick Hollingsworth. Sharp Edge eventually wound up in Australia and Cut Above in Brazil.

Another mare of note was Sugar Bun. Purchased with the smart Darling Boy 'in utero', she was mated with the Astor-bred Hornbeam to produce Hornpipe. Exported to the USA, she bred Protagonist, the champion two-year-old there in 1973.

Still manager of Warren Stud, where he started in 1959 before becoming stud groom four years later, Gillon Aitken has always had a partiality for Cutle and her son Cut Above. The 1981 St Leger was a remarkable one for Warren Stud as the winner Cut Above, and the third, Bustomi, together with the latter's pacemaker, Magikin, had all shared the same paddock as yearlings.

Bustomi and Magikin were homebred by the Dowager Lady Beaverbrook. Her breeding operation is labelled Dayspring Ltd, the handful of mares, including the 560,000-guinea yearling Nemesia, being based at Crockfords Stud owned by her adviser Bob Crowhurst, MRCVS. Another Beaverbrook celebrity reared at Warren Stud is Easter Sun (Coronation Cup), while her fine sprinting gelding, Boldboy, spent his retirement here.

In the old days the policy was to foal the majority of Jakie Astor's mares at Warren Stud and to transfer them to Hatley at the close of the breeding season. In October the mares would return to Cheveley with the weaned foals being reared at Sandy until entering training as yearlings the following autumn.

At one time Jakie Astor had as many as thirty-six broodmares, but crippling taxation forced him to reduce drastically his racing and breeding activities. In 1975 he sold the West Ilsley training establishment to Lord Weinstock (Major Dick Hern remained in residence), and closed down Hatley Stud.

Warren Stud received a stay of execution only because Gillon Aitken was convinced that he could make it viable as a boarding establishment, and so it proved. Amongst the clients to utilize the stud as a base for mares visiting Newmarket-based stallions was Ballymacoll Stud Farm, the Sobell/Weinstock nursery in Ireland. It was at Warren that their champion Troy was foaled.

When Sir John Astor sold Warren Stud to Sheikh Mohammed, his own broodmare band had dwindled to just four mares. That quartet comprised Cut Loose and Cut Ahead, daughter and granddaughter of Cutle, and The Dancer, who died later from a twisted gut, and her daughter, Pretty Lucky. As Cutle has bred two classic winners and The Dancer was third in the Oaks, the Astor colours could yet improve their classic tally.

Waverton Stud

MORETON-IN-MARSH · GLOUCESTERSHIRE

Jocelyn Hambro's Waverton Stud, near Moreton-in-Marsh, is one of a handful of studs in this corner of Gloucestershire to the north of Burford. In close proximity are Cotswold Stud, founded by the late Edward Bee, Hurstwood Stud, home of a distinguished jumping sire in Idiot's Delight, and Batsford Stud, where that grand stayer Royal Gait was bred and raised.

Since 1 January 1991, Waverton and Cotswold Studs have been run in partnership under the management of Mary James. She had taken charge of Waverton in the late summer of the preceding year when the decision was taken to cease operations as a public establishment. Thus the two resident stallions, Rambo Dancer and Hubbly Bubbly, both of whom had retired to stud that season, were dispatched to Yorkshire.

Mary James had earned a considerable reputation by putting Cotswold Stud at the top of the yearling league table so far as Tattersalls' sales are concerned. However, through circumstances outside her control she had been forced to prepare her 1990 contingent from a rented yard at Side Hill Stud, but the autumn of 1991 sees her selling under her own name from both Cotswold and Waverton.

Waverton Stud used to be known as Sezincote Stud after the village where it is situated. Nearly 900 feet above sea level on typical Cotswold limestone, the stud was founded by John Hirst in 1930 upon his retirement as an electrical engineer. He enjoyed a good slice of beginner's luck as the very first mare he purchased was Glenabatrick. She cost 470 guineas at that year's Newmarket December Sales from Lord Astor, with Tiberius 'in utero'.

Having failed to make his yearling reserve, Tiberius raced for Sir Abe Bailey for whom he won the 1935 Ascot Gold Cup, defeating the odds-on French challenger, Brantome. The horse retired to stand at Terrace House, Newmarket, where he replaced his own sire, Foxlaw – he had won the

Gold Cup for Sir Abe Bailey in 1927. Tiberius was not a stud success. Following John Hirst's death in 1945, Sezincote Stud, as it was still called, was bought by William Hill, the celebrated bookmaker. His motive was not so much to extend his Whitsbury Manor Stud in Hampshire, but rather to gain a place for his yearlings at the prestigious Doncaster sales. The continuity of ownership required by Tattersalls was ensured when Hirst's nephew, Alan, became a shareholder in the new stud company.

Another shareholder was the erstwhile stud manager, Peter Parsons, one of William Hill's closest confidants. Upon his retirement he was succeeded by Norman Lonsdale, breeder of that good sprinter Compensation. The William Hill Studs (as Whitsbury and Sezincote were labelled collectively) each had about fifteen mares. The progeny excelled at the yearling sales. During the 1960s they attained the top aggregate three times at the Houghton Sales (forerunner of the Highflyer Sales) and twice at the October Sales.

Amongst the long list of distinguished Sezincote winners were the colts Mandamus, Canterbury, Biskrah and Gulf Pearl, and the fillies Cantelo, Jacinth and Bracey Bridge. Cantelo triumphed in the 1959 St Leger. Canterbury was runner-up in the St Leger, and Jacinth, the champion two-year-old of her generation, occupied the same position in the 1000 Guineas; she is grandam of Jaffa Line.

The two top colts bred by William Hill, Nimbus (2000 Guineas, Derby) and his three-parts brother Grey Sovereign, were both Whitsbury protégés. His solitary homebred classic winner Cantelo (Chanteur II – Rustic Bridge) was saddled by Captain Charles Elsey to become the first Yorkshire-trained St Leger winner since Apology in 1874. Runner-up to Petite Etoile in the Oaks, she disappointed in the paddocks.

In 1968 Sezincote gained a new dimension when William Hill's great friend and adviser Phil Bull, the Timeform supremo, sent all his Hollins mares there from the Coggans' Home Stud. Just three years later William Hill died unexpectedly. His trustees continued to operate William Hill Studs as before until the sale of the public sector at Sezincote to Jocelyn Hambro, a member of the banking family, in 1977. At that time Hot Spark had completed two covering seasons before being moved to Whitsbury *en route* to Japan.

Jocelyn Hambro, whose best winner Sammy Davis retired to stand at Derisley Wood Stud, used to own Redenham Park Stud, near Andover, and he brought his stud manager, John Wilkinson, with him to Gloucestershire. At this juncture Sezincote became Waverton Stud, Jocelyn Hambro (who built a new house there), being one half of the Mount Coote/Waverton partnership centred on Alan Lillingston's Mount Coote Stud in Ireland.

Their mare, Trial by Fire, made an incalculable contribution to National Hunt racing as the dam of champion sire Deep Run. For the Lillingston-Hambro combination, his unraced half-sister, Singe, bred the 1979 1000 Guineas winner, One in a Million, one of the star mares at the Weinfelds' Meon Valley Stud.

Unfortunately Jocelyn Hambro sold his best mare, Sledmere-bred Habituée after she had produced one classic runner-up in Acclimatise (Oaks), but before she bred another one in Dabaweyaa (1000 Guineas). Two homebred Tudor Melody mares to do well were Secret Song, dam of Royal Harmony (July Stakes), and Salsafy, dam of Baz Bombati and Macmillion. Secret Song's dam, Secret Ray, was once the prize in a competition run by the *Daily Express*.

The most recent addition to Jocelyn Hambro's band of six mares is the 1991 Keeneland January Sales purchase Hatton Gardens. Waverton has always had its share of boarders, including mares owned by Sir Reginald Sheffield (Normanby Stud). Now these have been augmented by Mary James's own clients, amongst them George Strawbridge, whose Snow Day is dam of Blue Stag, and Michael McCalmont for whom Cassina bred Top Class.

Stallions at Waverton prior to Rambo Dancer and Hubbly Bubbly comprised Vaigly Great (sire of Hallgate) and Lidhame. Both were exported, the former to Italy, and the latter to Japan. Another, Monsanto, departed to Shropshire.

West Blagdon

CRANBORNE · DORSET

Nineteen-eighty-eight was a splendid year for the mare Pelting. Three of her descendants, Careafolie, Ghariba and Gouriev, won Group races and another became the fourth member of the family to become the top-priced foal at the Newmarket December Sales. At 300,000 guineas, he was the most expensive foal sold at public auction world-wide that year.

All four animals are one generation removed from Pelting's daughter, Fighting. Ironically the Wigans sold Fighting as a foal, but subsequently acquired her daughters, Krakow and Charming Life. That pair provided West Blagdon with a memorable breeding double at Longchamp in October 1990 when Braashee (ex Krakow) dead-heated for the Prix Royal-Oak (French St Leger), and Run and Gun (ex Charming Life) won the Prix du Petit Couvert.

Their origins at West Blagdon go back more than seventy years. At Newmarket in October 1918, Dawn Wigan's father, Charles Gordon, paid 2,600 guineas for a yearling filly by Sunstar out of Glass Doll. Homebred by Jack Joel (Childwick Bury Stud), who had won three classics with the sire and dam, she was named Ocean Light – Pelting's third dam.

Dawn and Dare Wigan (he used to be racing correspondent to *Country Life* and *The Financial Times*) have lived at West Blagdon since 1953. In February 1959 Dawn's father died, whereupon she inherited West Blagdon and her sister, Thalia (Mrs Michael Gordon-Watson), inherited East Blagdon. The Blagdons are two of five farms belonging to the original Boveridge Park Estate which Charles Gordon bought in 1910 from the Thursby family.

Situated outside the village of Cranborne in Dorset and no distance from Whitsbury Manor Stud across the county boundary into Hampshire, West Blagdon is an unusually remote and unspoilt location for the south of England. Nestling in a sheltered hollow of the chalk downs, access is gained up a long track flanked by rolling arable acres.

Pelting's first three dams, Firmament, Guiding Star and Ocean Light, are by the Derby winners Windsor Lad, Papyrus and Sunstar respectively, and Charles Gordon did well with the family. His colours were carried into third place in the 2000 Guineas behind Triple Crown hero Bahram, by Sea Bequest (ex Ocean Light). However, his greatest gift to posterity proved to be Advocate (ex Guiding Star), maternal grandsire of Forli.

Dawn Wigan procured Pelting (Vilmorin – Firmament) as a yearling from her father's executors together with his racing colours, 'cherry, corn-flower blue sash and cap'. A sprinter and a grey, just like her sire, she scored twice over the minimum distance at three years, winning the Stewards' Handicap at Epsom on Derby Day in very fast time.

No one could possibly have envisaged the veritable dynasty which this grey mare established. In so doing she made West Blagdon the most consistently successful foal consignor in the country. What makes the achievement all the more remarkable is that its status was achieved with no more than three or four mares at any one time. Nowadays there are more mares as the Wigans' two sons James and Dominic are also involved.

So far the highest individual price for a foal is the 300,000 guineas paid for Adam Smith (Sadler's Wells – Krakow) in 1988. He is own-brother to Braashee (Prix Royal Oak, Kosset Yorkshire Cup, Ormonde Stakes) and half-brother to Ghariba (Juddmonte Farms Nell Gwyn Stakes), who finished fourth in the 1000 Guineas. That pair have greatly enhanced the family whose previous reputation centred on precocious two-year-olds.

Pelting's admirable record as a producer herself can be summarized in the briefest terms as twelve winners from fourteen foals in fifteen years. Two of the best were the retained pair, Splashing (Cornwallis Stakes) and Glinting. Each was responsible for an outstanding colt in 1982, the former with Bassenthwaite and the latter with Hadeer, both conceived in Ireland.

A half-brother to Glancing (Prix d'Arenberg), Bassenthwaite became the first Group 1 winner bred by the Wigans when landing the 1984 Middle Park Stakes. He was also runner-up in the Gimcrack Stakes in which Hadeer finished fourth. Hadeer came into his own as a four-year-old with three Group victories.

Both are now stallions, Bassenthwaite (by Habitat) in New Zealand and Hadeer (by General Assembly) at Newmarket – Hadeer was purchased by his owner, William Gredley, as a three-year-old for only 13,000 guineas at the Newmarket Autumn Sales (he had cost 70,000 guineas as a foal and $190,000 as a yearling) and retired to his Stetchworth Park Stud for the 1988 season.

Many West Blagdon foals have provided sound ammunition for the pinhookers (those who buy foals explicitly to resell as yearlings). Bassenthwaite himself is an example. During that brief period of time his value escalated from 85,000 guineas to 320,000 guineas. He was actually bred on a foal share with Captain Tim Rogers who stood his sire, Habitat, at Grangewilliam Stud in Ireland.

Timmy Hyde of Camas Park Stud, Co. Tipperary, also has good reason to be pleased with his acquisitions from West Blagdon. Two by his great favourite Sadler's Wells did exceptionally well. In 1988 he bought a colt out of Krakow (Adam Smith) for 300,000 guineas and sold him for 680,000 guineas. In 1989 he paid 135,000 guineas for a filly out of Glancing (Looking Brill) and she jumped in value to 450,000 guineas. This represents a staggering increase of 695,000 guineas on just two animals.

It was in March 1987 that George Collis retired as stud groom at West Blagdon. He was in fact born on the Boveridge Park Estate and the Wigans are always mindful of the enormous contribution that he made. Over the years, they have employed various trainers, notably the late Sir Noel Murless.

So far as bloodstock agents are concerned, Dawn and Dare Wigan need look no further than their eldest son, James, who runs London Thoroughbred Services. Two of his cousins are also involved in racing: Charles Gordon-Watson is a fellow bloodstock agent, and David Morley trains at Newmarket.

Whatton Manor Stud

WHATTON IN THE VALE · NOTTINGHAMSHIRE

It is a popular misconception that breeding top-quality bloodstock necessitates unlimited funds. That it is perfectly possible to operate a modern commercial yearling enterprise without an enormous financial outlay has been demonstrated by Peter Player and his wife, Catherine, at their Whatton Manor Stud in Nottinghamshire.

The Players first sprung to prominence when their homebred Prickle (Sharpen Up – Jungle Queen), trained by Henry Cecil and ridden by Lester Piggott, gained a commanding victory in the Lowther Stakes at the York festival meeting of 1983 at the expense of two star fillies in Pebbles and Desirable.

If substantial capital is not a prerequisite for breeding bloodstock, then luck most certainly is. Peter Player attributes his early success to two pieces of good fortune, buying the mare Jungle Queen from Daniel Prenn for £100 (and the promise of a case of wine if she did any good), and the acquisition of three shares in Sharpen Up at £3,000 apiece.

Peter Player is a great-grandson of John Player, who founded the famous Nottingham-based tobacco company in 1877. Ironically Peter's involvement in thoroughbreds has always gone hand in glove with the bloodstock interests of Sir David Wills, a member of the other great tobacco family centred in Bristol.

It was while managing David Wills's Hadrian Stud, Newmarket (now owned by Sheikh Mohammed), that Peter founded his own Camois Hall Stud on twenty-five acres, ten of them leased from the Duke of Sutherland. Next door was Lieutenant-Colonel and Mrs Douglas Grays' Stetchworth Park Stud. Peter's predecessor as manager at Hadrian, Gray boarded Dan Prenn's mares, Jungle Queen being one of them.

Camois Hall Stud was by no means an instant success. Indeed the first four mares owned by the Players failed, albeit one, Odessa, bred the plater

Wanweth Girl, the first winner they ever bred. She scored at Beverley in 1976.

By the time that Peter Player and his family had moved to Whatton in the Vale in 1982, they had made money by trading in stallion shares rather than in breeding horses – the three Sharpen Up shares were valued at £180,000 when the stallion was exported to the USA. The purchase of two shares in Dominion was to prove another shrewd investment.

Apart from the sum raised to buy into Sharpen Up, the Players' stud has always been self-financing. Indeed no fresh capital has been injected since its inception in 1973. Of course substantial funds were required to convert part of the 1,100 acres Whatton estate into a private stud, but Peter inherited the property from a spinster aunt.

There was also the added burden of capital transfer tax which necessitated the sale of 500 of these fertile acres on the edge of the Vale of Belvoir, in a triangle formed by Newark, Nottingham and Grantham. At present 200 of the remaining 600 acres are utilized by the stud, the lovely parkland surrounding the house being shared by a herd of Longhorn cattle and a flock of Wensleydale sheep.

By the late 1980s the Players' own broodmare band had expanded to around the twenty mark. In addition Whatton Manor provided a permanent home for a nucleus of mares owned by David Wills. They have been there since the autumn of 1983. Following the sale of Hadrian Stud to the Vanian brothers in 1981, the mares spent an interim period at St Clare Hall Stud, a farm owned by Wills near Bury St Edmunds.

If one is going to buy mares and fillies on a limited budget, it involves a mixture of priorities and compromises, but Peter and Catherine Player have always insisted upon proven female families. They have never deviated from this policy and their record of producing top winners from relatively cheap females has certainly vindicated their judgement.

The three Group winners bred by Whatton Manor Stud illustrate the point. Jungle Queen, dam of Prickle (Lowther Stakes), traces to the great Mentmore foundation mare, Paraffin; Gay Charlotte, dam of Upend (St Simon Stakes), is a granddaughter of the Ascot Gold Cup heroine Gladness; and Little Loch Broom, dam of Soft Currency (Prix de la Jonchere), belongs to the Campanula family.

Significantly Peter Player had prior knowledge of both Gay Charlotte and Little Loch Broom. Like Jungle Queen, Gay Charlotte had been a boarder at Stetchworth Park. Little Loch Broom was bought for 22,000 guineas at a major reduction of Sir David Wills's bloodstock at the 1980 Newmarket December Sales.

As commercial breeders, the Players have sold five six-figure yearlings to date. Two of them are the progeny of Little Loch Broom. In 1985 her Music Boy colt (Soft Currency) realized 120,000 guineas, a fantastic return on a stud fee of only £4,000. In 1990 Little Loch Broom's Green Desert colt (Fezzan) realized 240,000 guineas. However the highest individual price is 260,000 guineas paid for a Kris filly in 1986. Named Free Touch she met with an accident in training and never ran.

Peter Player, whose wife shares much of the work on the stud, is a member of the Jockey Club and chairman of Nottingham racecourse where he sponsors the Whatton Manor Stud Stakes. He also acts as a steward at York which he considers his favourite racecourse. Three homebred fillies have carried the grey and red colours to victory on the Knavesmire with Prickle (Lowther Stakes), Upend (Galtres Stakes) and Choire Mor. Another distinguished homebred mare is Royal Loft, winner of Goodwood's Oak Tree Stakes.

It is a fact of life with racing and breeding that disasters always involve the most valuable animals. Peter and Catherine Player (she comes from Co. Limerick) know this as well as anyone. For instance in 1986 Prickle, who was subsequently sold to Sheikh Mohammed carrying to Dancing Brave, slipped to her covering by Sadler's Wells in that horse's second season at stud. In 1990 the Players were absolutely thrilled to have a Dancing Brave filly out of Little Loch Broom, but only weeks later she died of colic out in the paddock at home.

White Lodge Stud

NEWMARKET · SUFFOLK

The late Nicky Morriss of Banstead Manor Stud had a favourite anecdote. In September 1944 he was dining at Freemason Lodge, home of the Royal trainer Sir Cecil Boyd-Rochfort, when the lady sitting next to him exclaimed, 'Some idiot paid 2,100 guineas for a Panorama filly out of an unraced mare this afternoon'.

The filly in question was Horama whom Nicky Morriss had bought on behalf of the Moller brothers, Eric and Ralph, their respective fathers having been friends in China since their boyhood. Horama was to prove just about the most successful foundation mare of the post-war era at the Mollers' White Lodge Stud.

Sadly Ralph Moller (who was always known as Budgie) died in March 1980 just a few weeks before Teenoso, the best winner ever bred by White Lodge and who represented the fifth generation of the line, was foaled. The Youth colt won the Derby and King George VI and Queen Elizabeth Diamond Stakes for Eric Moller, who had taken over the stud and the horses in training.

After Eric died in July 1988, there was considerable speculation as to what would become of the much coveted Moller bloodstock. For more than a year the status quo was maintained in the name of Eric Moller's executors. Then in the autumn of 1989 it became known that the enterprise had been taken over, virtually lock, stock and barrel, by Sheikh Mohammed.

The package deal included White Lodge Stud at Cheveley and Church Hall Farm at Woodditton, encompassing 300 acres together with the stallion Teenoso, twenty-seven mares, twenty-two yearlings, fifteen foals, and thirty horses in and out of training. About two thirds of the females belonged to the Violetta branch of the Horama family, including Braiswick. In October, on her first outing for Sheikh Mohammed, Braiswick won the Grade I E.P. Taylor Stakes at Woodbine in Canada.

229

Eric Moller had purchased White Lodge Stud and seventy adjoining acres in April 1944 when his younger brother was a prisoner of the Japanese. Born and educated in Shanghai, they made a fortune from the family shipping and insurance business established by their grandfather in 1854. For many years Eric ran the head office in Hong Kong and Budgie controlled the London headquarters in Fenchurch Street.

During the 1920s and 1930s, the Mollers rode with conspicuous success in China, both making their names as amateur jockeys. Eric, a top polo player, partnered the winner of the Shanghai Grand National. Budgie, an accomplished all-round sportsman, rode for Nicky Morriss's father who was invariably known as Manna Morriss after his 1925 Derby winner.

Bred by Newmarket trainer Geoffrey Brooke, Horama gained all four of her wins over five furlongs. For her solitary success as a two-year-old, she was ridden by Harry Wragg, who trained the Moller horses until his son Geoffrey succeeded him at Abington Place. It is from this Newmarket yard that the produce of White Lodge continues to be trained for Sheikh Mohammed.

At stud from 1947 to 1964, Horama, who died in retirement in December 1966, aged twenty-three, had six colts and eight fillies, of which nine were winners. One, Close Up, produced Moulton (Benson and Hedges Gold Cup), who proved a disappointing sire based at Lanwades Stud.

Another daughter, Urshalim, bred two outstanding fillies in Lacquer (Irish 1000 Guineas) and Sovereign. However it was their half-sister Violetta III, the Cambridgeshire dead-heater, who proved the mainstay of the family at White Lodge and beyond – she is the grandam of additional Group I winners Give Thanks, Old Country and Ashayer.

Three of Violetta's progeny are Favoletta (Irish 1000 Guineas), Furioso, runner-up in the Oaks, and Oaks fourth Laughing Girl. Furioso is dam of Teenoso, who has failed to come up to expectations as a sire at Highclere Stud, and grandam of Most Welcome (Juddmonte Lockinge Stakes), who retired to Meddler Stud for the 1990 season. Laughing Girl is dam of Braiswick. She was a last Group scorer for the Mollers' chocolate and gold braid colours in the 1989 Cheveley Park Stud Sun Chariot Stakes, a race in which they had been carried to victory before by Popkins, Cheveley Princess and Topsy.

Only the previous year White Lodge Stud had had the Derby favourite, Red Glow. He stems from Test Match, one of two Big Game mares acquired from the Astor Studs. The other is Mitraille, grandam of the Mollers' 1969 1000 Guineas heroine, Full Dress II.

Nicky Morriss's contribution to White Lodge is inestimable. Not only did he select the foundation mares but he also managed the stud until his untimely death in 1963. At present the day-to-day running of the stud is in the hands of stud groom Peter Kinsey. A Welshman, he took over the reins in 1983 following the retirement of long-standing stud groom Cecil Tilbrook – he had gone there upon being demobilized from the army in 1945.

As the stud expanded, Budgie Moller used to board stock with his brother at Bramley, near Guildford, and across the road at Banstead Manor. However, in October 1965 he bought Church Hall Farm in the neighbouring village of Woodditton which he converted into a fine stud in its own right. This was utilized for mares and foals, weaned foals and yearlings being kept at White Lodge.

Budgie Miller also used to have a nucleus of mares in Kentucky so as to utilize some of the top stallions there. However, no spectacular dividends accrued so far as the Horama family was concerned. The key in its development seems to have been the patronage of staying stallions like Ballymoss, Shantung, Pinza and Busted, all at one time Newmarket based.

Although none of them was ever regarded as ultra fashionable, they enabled an unpretentious sprinter to spawn a dynasty of star middle-distance performers, culminating with Teenoso, together with a host of talented fillies. Ironically the last Moller celebrity, Braiswick, was totally out of keeping with the rest, being by the sprinter King of Spain.

Whitsbury Manor Stud

FORDINGBRIDGE · HAMPSHIRE

The charisma of Desert Orchid (Tote Cheltenham Gold Cup) is such that Rhyme N' Reason (Seagram Grand National), his erstwhile stable companion at David Elsworth's Whitsbury Manor Stables, has never been able to compete for popularity. Just across the road is Whitsbury Manor Stud which is likewise owned by Christopher Harper.

The stables and stud at Whitsbury are part of a 1,800-acre estate comprising a farm of 1,200 acres, which is mostly arable but also has a noted herd of pedigree Friesians, 300 acres of stud (the public and private sectors being entirely separate), and 150 acres of magnificent downland gallops.

Chris Harper, who first went to Whitsbury straight from Harper Adams Agricultural College in 1963 aged twenty-one, is a nephew of the late William Hill. The doyen of bookmakers, he originally bought the estate in 1943 from the Birmingham newspaper proprietor Sir Charles Hyde, who had a private training stable there presided over by Norman Scobie.

Situated on the Hampshire–Wiltshire borders, near Fordingbridge, ten miles south of Salisbury on the northern fringes of the New Forest, Whitsbury was to be developed by William Hill into one of the foremost studs in the country. Although he proved rather wide of the mark in his choice of stallions, he was a very successful breeder of commercial yearlings.

The enterprise got off to a fairytale start as the very first yearling ever offered for sale was the 1949 2000 Guineas and Derby winner, Nimbus (Nearco – Kong). His dam had been acquired through William Hill's great friend, Timeform supremo Phil Bull, for just 710 guineas from the Charles Hyde dispersal at the 1943 Newmarket December Sales.

To a mating with Nasrullah, Kong produced Nimbus's three-parts brother, Grey Sovereign. Remembered as much for his doubtful temperament as for his ability (a characteristic he transmitted to many of his descendants), Grey Sovereign founded a worldwide male dynasty by the time of his demise in 1976 aged twenty-eight. Somewhat surprisingly Nimbus failed as a sire.

William Hill knew all about Nearco and his son, Nasrullah. He owned a substantial part of Nearco whom fellow bookmaker, Martin Benson, had imported for his Beech House Stud. In the case of Nasrullah, William Hill was under the impression that he had bought the horse until reading in his London evening paper that he had been sold to Ireland.

Nimbus was consigned to the Newmarket July Sales as his breeder could not obtain a place at Tattersalls' much more prestigious September Sales in Doncaster's old Glasgow Paddocks. He soon remedied the situation with the purchase of Sezincote (now Waverton) Stud. When Chris Harper first went to Whitsbury to supervise the farming side, Arthur Tait was stud manager – his successor, Robert Urquhart, now runs Hunsley House Stud.

William Hill had a penchant for French horses. He imported Chanteur II (who stood at Banstead Manor and Highclere Studs), Sica Boy (the first stallion to be installed at Whitsbury Manor), Taj Dewan and Gyr. All failed to come up to expectations, much to the consternation of one of Hill's principal advisers, Rex King. So too did Celtic Ash (Belmont Stakes), sire of England's premier jumping sire Celtic Cone.

Chanteur proved a beneficiary for the William Hill Studs (as the joint Whitsbury – Sezincote enterprise was known) by siring the homebred 1959 St Leger heroine, Cantelo. Cantelo and Jacinth were Sezincote products, but Whitsbury was responsible for another star filly in Be Careful (Gimcrack Stakes, Champagne Stakes).

When William Hill died at Newmarket during the 1971 Houghton Sales, Whitsbury Manor Stud had a notable stallion in Ballymoss, in whom Hill was a major shareholder. The circumstances in which Ballymoss was spirited away from Banstead Manor Stud certainly raised a few eyebrows at the time.

Two classic winners bred by Whitsbury Manor in the seventies were Red Lord (Poule d'Essai des Poulains) and Enstone Spark (1000 Guineas), the latter being by the resident Sparkler. He was also to sire Scintillate (Oaks), whose grandam is a half-sister to Be Careful. One of Sparkler's stud companions was Philip of Spain whose son, King of Spain, sired Braiswick. Two more Whitsbury stallions of this vintage were Roi Soleil and Hot Spark.

William Hill certainly had his share of disappointments with stallions. So too has Chris Harper, but in two particular instances it was not a matter of judgement. In 1986 Young Generation (ten), one of the most eminent young sires in the country, died from a twisted gut. The next year, Known

Fact, sire of Warning and Markofdistinction, made a predetermined move to the American stud of his owner, Prince Khalid Abdullah.

For the 1991 covering season, Whitsbury Manor was home to three young stallions, all of whom raced in Arab ownership. That trio comprised Prince Faisal's Midyan, a top miler, Sheikh Maktoum Al Maktoum's Cadeaux Genereux, a champion sprinter, and Wafic Said's Distant Relative, another outstanding miler. Whereas Midyan, whose first runners appeared in 1991, is a syndicated stallion, the other pair remain in their original ownership. Cadeaux Genereux is an appropriate horse for Whitsbury as he is Young Generation's best son.

Since 1989 when the stallion Electric departed to Ireland, Whitsbury Manor has also provided a permanent base for all the breeding stock owned by Canadian Galen Weston of Barrettstown Stud Farm. They were previously based at the stud of that name overlooking the Vale of Aylesbury which is now owned by champion jockey, Pat Eddery. Best known of the mares involved is Elegant Tern, dam of the ill-fated Elegant Air.

Following William Hill's death, Whitsbury was sold to the Legal and General Pension Management Fund with Chris Harper forming a new company, Whitsbury Farm and Stud Ltd. In February 1987 he achieved his objective of buying back the estate though to finance the deal he had to sell around half the prized broodmare band.

Woodditton Stud

NEWMARKET · SUFFOLK

Since July 1981, Woodditton Stud, which takes its name from the village outside Newmarket where it is situated, has been owned by Nam Seng Yong and his wife, Poh Lian Yong, from Singapore. Involved in building construction and property development, they race in Europe, Australia and the Far East. Nam Seng Yong is a steward of the Singapore Jockey Club and former chairman of the Australasian Racing Conference.

The previous owner was the great trainer Sir Noel Murless. He bought the stud from Lady Sassoon in 1970, the year before she sold her other Newmarket Stud, Beech House, to Louis Freedman. Lady Sassoon had continued with the two breeding establishments following the death of her husband, Sir Victor Sassoon, in 1961.

At one time Woodditton was owned by another local trainer, Martin Gurry (1842-1923). A successful livestock breeder, he sold the stud the year before he died to Archie Falcon, who had been a professional gambler. In 1925, Falcon sold Bungalow Stud (as it was then called), plus the stock, to Sir Victor Sassoon, before starting Brook Stud at Cheveley.

Sir Victor Sassoon, who was to become the biggest owner-breeder in the country, renamed the property Eve Stud, compounded from his initials, E.V. (Ellice Victor). His entrée into racing had been through Jimmy Crawford in India. A veterinary surgeon, whose brother Jock was a director of the British Bloodstock Agency, Crawford returned to England to train for Mathradas Goculdas, a Bombay cotton-mill owner.

When Goculdas ran into financial difficulties, Victor Sassoon took over his extensive bloodstock interests including 100 horses in India. Having inherited the baronetcy from his father in 1924, Sir Victor began purchasing bloodstock on the same lavish scale as the Aga Khan. He also continued to race in India, the Eve Bloodstock Scheme exporting mares and fillies from Europe to improve the standard of native Indian-breds.

Sir Victor Sassoon had to wait until 1937 for a first English classic success with homebred Exhibitionist in the 1000 Guineas and Oaks. That year he also won the Irish 2000 Guineas and Derby with Phideas whose half-brother Museum had won the Irish Triple Crown. Their dam, Imagery, was own-sister to Exhibitionist's sire, Solario. Phideas, who retired to Eve Stud in 1939, was to become a recurring name in future Sassoon pedigrees.

In 1952 Noel Murless agreed to advise Sir Victor Sassoon on his breeding operation. Two years later he took over management of the studs which also embraced Killeen Castle in Ireland and Thornton-le-Street in Yorkshire, and he became his principal trainer. These events coincided with a remarkable upsurge in Sassoon's racing fortunes.

Hitherto Sir Victor's success had not been commensurate with his enormous financial outlay. Now he was destined to win the Derby four times within the space of seven years, a feat that even the Aga Khan never achieved. Although Noel Murless was neither responsible for buying nor training the yearling acquisitions Pinza (1953 Derby) or Hard Ridden (1958 Derby), he was the mastermind behind both Crepello and St Paddy.

Crepello won the 1957 2000 Guineas and Derby, and St Paddy won the 1960 Derby and St Leger. Noel Murless not only trained the pair of homebreds but he also did the matings that produced them. Crepello's dam, Crepuscule (by Sassoon's French importation, Mieuxce), became the most famous of all the Eve Stud mares, as she also produced Honeylight (1000 Guineas) and Twilight Alley (Ascot Gold Cup).

The only one of these four Derby winners to stand at Eve Stud was Pinza who proceeded to win the King George VI and Queen Elizabeth Stakes as a three-year-old. Sir Gordon Richards' solitary Derby winner, Pinza spent the duration of his stallion life at Eve Stud where he was put down in 1977 at the advanced age of twenty-seven. A comparative failure at stud, his best sons are Pindari (a product of the National Stud) and Pinturischio – bred by Sassoon, he was the victim of dopers. Pinza also sired the distinguished White Lodge matron Violetta III.

Pinturischio was the first of many Warren Place recruits to stand at Eve or Woodditton Stud – the name to which it reverted when Murless ran the stud in conjunction with his Cliff Stud up in Yorkshire. He was followed by two more celebrities in Connaught (by St Paddy) and Welsh Pageant, both homebred by Jim Joel of Childwick Bury Stud. Each remained in training for four seasons, Connaught winning the Eclipse Stakes and Welsh Pageant proving a top miler. The former is maternal grandsire of champion Pebbles, and the latter sired Zino (2000 Guineas) and Swiss Maid.

Connaught and Welsh Pageant are buried in the Cherry Tree lawn at

Woodditton, as are Pinza and St Paddy's dam, Edie Kelly. Connaught was still in residence when the Yongs bought the stud from Noel Murless. He and Connaught died within two days of one another in 1987, to mark the end of an era.

Two years earlier the Yongs had two newcomers covering at Woodditton in Sayf El Arab and Superlative. Both were trained by Bill O'Gorman. His brother Dick, who is racing manager to the Yongs and a director of Woodditton Stud, had selected them as yearlings. Sayf El Arab won the King's Stand Stakes (then Group 1) while Superlative excelled as a juvenile in the Yong colours of red and yellow diamonds.

Dick O'Gorman did the Yongs another good turn when buying them Superpower from Superlative's first crop of yearlings. Winner of the Heinz 57 Phoenix Stakes, he returned to Ireland but now stands at Sledmere Stud in Yorkshire. The Yongs took on a third stallion for the 1987 season in Damister. Likewise syndicated, this son of Mr Prospector was a classic performer for Prince Khalid Abdullah for whom he finished third to Slip Anchor in the Ever Ready Derby.

At Woodditton Stud, the Yongs have shown that the Far East can make the sort of investment in bloodstock that has become so common place from the Middle East. Under Nick Angus-Smith, formerly manager at King Edward's Place Stud, Woodditton has been developed into a first-rate public establishment.

Woodminton Farm

BOWERCHALKE · WILTSHIRE

In their drawing room at Woodminton Farm, Major and Mrs Robert Kennard have a painting by Roy Miller depicting the mare L'Anguissola and her daughters, Walk By, Solar and Smarten Up, together with their 1981 foals at foot, Derby Day, Scintillo, Cutler's Corner, and Brightner. Remarkably all eight are winners.

L'Anguissola (Soderini – Posh), who died two years later, is the foundation mare of the Kennards' small, but highly successful, breeding operation. Up to 1990 they had sold seven yearling colts out of Smarten Up, amongst them the outstanding sprinter Cadeaux Genereux, and they had aggregated 925,000 guineas.

Both Robert and Helen Kennard have a horsey background. He served in an Indian cavalry regiment (the Royal Declan Horse) and rode as an amateur. After the war, he trained in Calcutta and in New South Wales. She was joint master of the Tiverton Foxhounds and is a niece of the late Oliver Watney. He lived at Cornbury Park, Charlbury, where Lord Rotherwick bred his Irish Guinness Oaks heroine Swiftfoot.

Racing and breeding run in Helen Kennard's family. Her great-grandfather, Francis Popham of Littlecote House, near Hungerford, owned and bred Wild Dayrell, the winner of the 1855 Derby.

The Kennards bought Woodminton Farm in 1978, the year after they were married. L'Anguissola was one of the handful of mares which she brought from her home at Holcombe Rogus in Devon. The widow of Cuthbert Fleetwood Hesketh, Helen had started breeding some ten years earlier and had already experienced some success.

Woodminton is part of the parish of Bowerchalke which lies in the Wiltshire Downs on the north side of the Salisbury to Blandford road. To the south is Whitsbury Manor Stud, one of the most important public studs outside Newmarket where many Woodminton foals have been born.

The farm used to be part of the enormous Pembroke Estate. In due course Bobby and Helen converted the old buildings, which had standings for twenty cart horses and a small dairy, into suitable accommodation for thoroughbreds. Originally only twenty-five of the 250 acres were pasture, but since then another 105 acres have been laid down to grass along with all the requisite fencing and shelter belts.

Helen's uncle used to have horses in training at Newmarket, first with Ted Leader and then Geoffrey Barling. When Oliver Watney, a member of the brewing family, died in 1966, his niece reregistered his colours, 'pale blue, orange stripes', and bought the filly Parradell, an own-sister to his good stayer Piaco, from the executors.

Although Parradell won the Virginia Stakes, Newcastle, she failed as a broodmare. However, Geoffrey Barling soon found an admirable replacement when securing L'Anguissola for 7,000 guineas at the 1971 Newmarket December Sales. He chose her because she was in foal to Tower Walk. The best sprinter that Barling ever trained, Tower Walk won the Prix de l'Abbaye de Longchamp.

The foal that L'Anguissola was carrying turned out to be Walk By, winner of the William Hill Portland Handicap. Walk By died from a twisted gut without making her mark in the paddocks, but she did have a couple of excellent half-sisters in Smarten Up and Solar. Likewise trained by Bill Wightman (Geoffrey Barling had retired), both finished third in the William Hill Cheveley Park Stakes.

While Solar was sold privately to Kais Al Said (at whose Charlton Down Stud she bred Desert Sun), after producing the smart Ashbrittle and Cutler's Corner, Smarten Up was retained. The Sharpen Up filly ran a dead-heat for the Temple Stakes and was runner-up in the William Hill Sprint Championship (formerly Nunthorpe Stakes).

To the end of the 1990 season, Smarten Up has been responsible for five individual winners of twenty-eight races, these being her only runners. Outstanding amongst them is champion sprinter Cadeaux Genereux, who was sired at Whitsbury Manor by Young Generation.

Sheikh Maktoum Al Maktoum paid 210,000 guineas for Cadeaux Genereux at the 1986 Highflyer Sales. According to the Sheikh's manager, Michael Goodbody of Gainsborough Stud, the name 'Generous Present' was bestowed upon the Young Generation colt as his new connections felt that the breeder and vendor had fared rather favourably with regard to price!

Cadeaux Genereux was rated the top three-year-old sprinter of his generation. He won the Van Geest Criterion Stakes (in record time) and Krug Diadem Stakes, but was then disqualified after finishing first in the Ciga

Prix de l'Abbaye de Longchamp. The following season he gained Group I victories in the Carroll Foundation July Cup (in course record time) and William Hill Sprint Championship.

The only one of the four Maktoum racing brothers not to own a public stud either in England or Ireland, Maktoum Al Maktoum decided to stand Cadeaux Genereux at Whitsbury Manor Stud where he embarked upon stallion duties at a fee of £10,000 (live foal) in 1990. It was here that Young Generation died tragically in 1986 after starting off at the now defunct Wyld Court Stud.

Smarten Up's next two offspring also made substantial prices at the High-flyer Sales. In 1987 Sheikh Mohammed paid 210,000 guineas for her Mill Reef colt (Military Fashion), and two years later the eldest brother, Maktoum Al Maktoum, spent 200,000 guineas to secure her Be My Guest colt whom he named Mathkoor.

Back at the farm, Bobby and Helen Kennard (he organizes the horses on a day-to-day basis) still have Smarten Up together with her three-parts sister in blood, Cutler's Corner, and her only daughter of racing age, La Tuerta. By Hot Spark, who used to stand at Whitsbury Manor, La Tuerta's first two foals are the retained daughters La Cabrilla and Dominio, both winners saddled by Peter Walwyn.

Woolton House Stud

WOOLTON HILL · BERKSHIRE

It was a case of 'his and hers' for Colonel and Mrs Roger Hue-Williams so far as their racing colours were concerned – he had 'white with a scarlet V', and she still has 'scarlet with a white V'. No husband and wife combination achieved more as owner-breeders of classic-type horses in the seventies, a success emanating from their Woolton House and Rathasker Studs.

Vera Hue-Williams (hence the V of the colours), whose second husband died in 1987, was married first to Thomas Lilley. Chairman of Lilley and Skinner, he started auspiciously as an owner with Radiotherapy, who was placed third in the 1946 2000 Guineas and Derby. This gave him and his Russian-born wife the incentive to start breeding on their own account.

So between them they founded Woolton House Stud at their Berkshire home at Woolton Hill, which is about four miles south-west of Newbury. No distance from Highclere, Woolton House adjoins Herbert Blagrave's old Harwood Stud (now Gainsborough Stud), while just down the road is Woodhaven Stud at East Woodhay where the Hislops bred champion Brigadier Gerard.

The Lilleys set about establishing a nucleus of mares with significant purchases at the Newmarket December Sales from 1946 to 1948. In the intermediate year they paid 8,100 guineas for Forecourt, carrying to Persian Gulf or Precipitation, from her breeder, Lieutenant-Colonel Giles Loder, she being a descendant of Eyrefield Lodge Stud's illustrious matriarch Pretty Polly.

The foal that Forecourt was carrying was Supreme Court. Trained by Evan Williams at Kingsclere, he was not entered for the classics. However, he was unbeaten as a three-year-old, gaining a memorable victory in the inaugural running of the King George VI and Queen Elizabeth Stakes, Ascot, run in Festival of Britain year which commemorated the centenary of the Great Exhibition of 1851.

Supreme Court spent all his stud innings in Newmarket, first at Banstead Manor Stud and then at Eve (now Woodditton) Stud. His best son, Pipe of Peace, became a leading sire in Australia. An influential broodmare sire, his daughters include the dams of Rheingold (Prix de l'Arc de Triomphe), Random Shot (Ascot Gold Cup), and Hopeful Venture.

Thomas Lilley died in 1959 and Vera and Roger Hue-Williams were married four years later. In the interim, Kythnos (Nearula – Capital Issue), a colt whom Thomas bred but sold as a yearling, won the Irish 2000 Guineas. By that time Woolton House Stud also had a foothold in Ireland as Rathasker Stud, Naas, Co. Kildare, had been founded in 1952 as an overflow establishment.

The most important of all the Hue-Williams's mares (and they had one of the biggest broodmare bands in England and Ireland) proved to be Bleu Azur (Crepello – Blue Prelude). Her dam, a product of the Irish National Stud, had been procured as a filly at the 1954 Newmarket December Sales for 4,600 guineas.

Bleu Azur was mated with Saint Crespin III to produce two exceptional fillies in Royal Saint (Fred Darling Stakes) and Altesse Royale. In 1971 the latter became the very first winner of the 1000 Guineas, Oaks and Irish (Guinness) Oaks. Ironically Altesse Royale proved altogether less successful in the paddocks than Royal Saint. She is the dam of Classic Example (King Edward VII stakes), who was also third in the St Leger and Irish Sweeps Derby, and grandam of Intimate Guest – she won the 1987 May Hill EBF Stakes to become the most recent Group winner bred by Woolton House Stud.

Although Altesse Royale and Rock Roi were both officially bred by Vera Hue-Williams (her own success in business was based on the Berger paint business) and owned by her late husband, the former was trained by Sir Noel Murless and the latter by Peter Walwyn. Over the years Jack Cunnington Jnr at Chantilly also trained a number of good winners, amongst them Valuta (Prix Kergorlay, Prix Maurice de Nieuil).

To Rock Roi (Mourne – Secret Session) is owed the doubtful distinction of twice finishing first in the Ascot Gold Cup only to be disqualified on both occasions – first due to a prohibited substance discovered in a post-race blood test and then for causing interference to the runner-up. An exceptional stayer, he also won the French equivalent of the Prix du Cadran before being exported for stallion duties in Australia.

Perhaps the greatest single achievement for the powerful Woolton House and Rathasker Studs came in the 1974 Irish Sweeps Derby in which the homebred colts English Prince and Imperial Prince finished first and second respectively. Also runner-up in the Derby (to Snow Knight), Imperial Prince, a Sir Ivor half-brother to Altesse Royale, became champion first season sire in Australia for 1979-80.

English Prince (Petingo – English Miss), whose dam had been acquired privately from American Winston Guest, also carried Vera Hue-Williams's colours to victory in the King Edward VII Stakes before retiring to Ballylinch Stud, Co. Kilkenny. Exported to Japan in 1980, where he died three years later, English Prince left behind an outstanding filly in Sun Princess (Oaks, St Leger), dam of Prince of Dance.

Woolton House and Rathasker Studs were run in close conjunction, the sizeable broodmare band being more or less equally divided between England and Ireland. As the majority were foaled at home, their location was determined by whether they were visiting English- or Irish-based stallions. Foals were invariably transferred from one stud to another so that they could benefit from a change of environment.

Since Rathasker was sold to Patrick Burns as a home for his stallion Red Sunset, Woolton House has maintained just a handful of mares under Robert Forbes, who combines the duties of stud groom and manager. Broodmares in his charge include the homebred trio As You Desire Me, her daughter Intimate Guest, and Seraphima, who won the Ladbroke Nell Gwyn Stakes and was placed in the 1000 Guineas and Oaks.

Worksop Manor Stud

WORKSOP · NOTTINGHAMSHIRE

In 1990 Worksop Manor Stud in Nottinghamshire celebrated its centenary. Yearling vendors at Tattersalls' sales throughout the present century, the stud was founded by Sir John Robinson (1839–1929) and has remained in his family ever since – he was succeeded by his great-nephew, Captain John Farr, whose younger son Bryan is the present owner and manager.

On the outer precincts of Worksop, between Nottingham and Doncaster, Worksop Manor is situated on the northern fringes of Sherwood Forest. For a couple of miles the 1,650-acre estate marches with Welbeck where the Duke of Portland's celebrated St Simon spent his entire stud career. Because of the many great country houses thereabouts, the locality is often referred to as the Dukeries.

John Robinson, an entrepreneur, who founded the Home Brewery at Daybrook, was knighted in 1905 as a distinguished local benefactor. The business remained a family concern until merging with the giant Scottish and Newcastle Breweries in 1986. To this day, the Worksop Manor Stakes is run at Leicester and the Home Ales Gold Tankard is staged at Nottingham.

Most breeders of Sir John Robinson's era bred to race, but he determined to operate on a commercial basis from the outset, selling all the produce as yearlings at the Doncaster September Sales. His lots became the feature of Wednesday morning's session in the old Glasgow Paddocks. Over a period of more than thirty years he sold 339 yearlings for a grand total of 278,520 guineas.

In 1917 Worksop Manor Stud earned international acclaim in both hemispheres with Omar Khayyam, a 300-guinea yearling, triumphing in the Kentucky Derby, and Linacre, twice winner of the valuable Atlantic Stakes at Liverpool, becoming champion sire in Australia for the 1916-17 season. However the golden age for the stud proved to be the twenties with the winners of two English classics.

Papyrus provided Steve Donoghue with an unprecedented third consecutive victory in the Derby. The neat son of Tracery, who cost Basil Jarvis 3,500 guineas as a yearling, was also second in the St Leger and fourth in the 2000 Guineas, prior to being beaten in an historic match against Zev at Belmont Park, New York. Upon returning from the USA, Papyrus was sold for £30,000 to Peter Hornung for his West Grinstead Stud in Sussex.

A few months after Omar Khayyam's Kentucky Derby, John Robinson sold the yearling half-sister Lady Peregrine for a derisory 400 guineas, only to buy her back immediately afterwards. Mated with Papyrus's three-parts brother, Flamboyant, she produced Flamingo. Sold for 1,800 guineas as a yearling to Sir Jack Jarvis, Basil's brother, acting for Lord Milford, he won the 1928 2000 Guineas, was second in the Derby and fourth in the St Leger.

In those bygone days the Ascot Gold Cup carried comparable prestige to the classics, and two winners bred by Worksop Manor Stud were Bomba and Periosteum. Other Royal Ascot scorers included Horus (King Edward VII Stakes), Pillo (Ascot Gold Vase), and William the Fourth (Ascot Derby).

John Farr was the principal beneficiary when his uncle died in 1929 in his ninetieth year. Whereas the estate was bought in at public auction, the fifty-four horses were sold in separate dispersal sales at Newmarket and Doncaster. Heading the proceedings was Lady Peregrine. Lord Milford bought her for 9,200 guineas and she became a major influence at his Dalham Hall Stud.

With the war intervening, John Farr's tenure of Worksop Manor experienced rather a lean period, albeit Belle Travers (Queen Mary Stakes) and Maltravers were both smart juveniles. John died in 1951. Ironically the stud bred a top performer the very next year in the 2000 Guineas runner-up Tamerlane (St James's Palace Stakes). A 4,500-guinea yearling purchase by the present Lord Carnarvon, Tamerlane spent his stud innings at Woodpark Stud, Co. Meath.

One of the oldest established families at Worksop Manor stems from Raven Locks, dam of the 2000 Guineas fourth, Lindrick, and the Oaks fourth, Aggravate. Foaled when her dam was twenty-one, Aggravate won the Park Hill Stakes. Sold to Gestut Fahrhof, she is the dam of Acatenango (Deutsches Derby, Grand Prix de Saint-Cloud), one of the best German-bred horses of modern times. Worksop Manor Stud has contributed further to breeding in Germany as Tamerlane's sons, Dschingis Khan and Alpenkonig, both became champion sires.

Paul Kelleway secured an outstanding bargain at the 1979 Newmarket

October Sales with the 8,000-guinea Star Appeal filly Madam Gay. She was destined to provide Worksop Manor with another classic victory, winning the Prix de Diane de Revlon (French Oaks) in record time. Prior to being sold to Daniel Wildenstein, she was also second in the King George VI and Queen Elizabeth Diamond Stakes and the Oaks.

Numerous cast-offs from Worksop Manor have done well for other breeders, notably Jojo, dam of Queen's Hussar, Perennial, dam of 2000 Guineas winner Bolkonski, and Abyssinia, dam of the American sire Al Hattab. Sunshade, grandam of the half-brothers Absalom and Adonijah, was sold as a yearling.

Two valuable additions to the twelve-strong broodmare band in 1991 are Stara, an own-sister to Madam Gay and the last foal of their dam, and the winning Caerleon filly South Shore, who had changed hands for 50,000 guineas at the preceding Newmarket December Sales.

Since taking over the stud from his elder brother in 1955, Bryan Farr has had two principal stud grooms with Fred Hall, who was employed there for nearly sixty years, and Tom Mason, the present stud groom who will soon be celebrating twenty years' service. Their place of work is part of an estate which also incorporates mixed farming and forestry so that there are all the advantages that cattle and home-grown fodder and timber can provide. Furthermore there are the aesthetic qualities of fallow deer in the park and wild fowl on the lake, a wonderful environment for thoroughbreds.

Wyck Hall Stud

NEWMARKET · SUFFOLK

Fillies have carried the McAlpine colours to Group 1 victories in the 1978 Cheveley Park Stakes with Sir Edwin (later Lord) McAlpine's Devon Ditty; in the 1983 Champion Stakes with Robert McAlpine's homebred Cormorant Wood; and in the 1984 Gold Seal Oaks and 1987 Prix Morny with Sir Robin McAlpine's Circus Plume and First Waltz respectively.

Both Robin and Edwin (who died in 1990), are grandsons of Sir Robert McAlpine, founder of the great civil engineering company which bears his name. Bobby is a great grandson. All three are, or have been, involved with studs in Britain, Robin with Wyck Hall at Newmarket, Edwin with Dobson's (now Bracken Hill Stud), near Henley-on-Thames, and Bobby with Emral in Clwyd.

Robin was at Charterhouse when Shaun Spadah, owned by his father, Sir Malcolm McAlpine, triumphed in the 1921 Grand National. Sir Malcolm, who died in 1967, also won the 1952 1000 Guineas with Zabara (Persian Gulf – Samovar), whom veteran trainer Reg Day bought privately as a foal for 2,500 guineas from Lady Wyfold of Sarsden House Stud.

During the last decade, Zabara featured as the third dam of champion Mtoto, and the grandam of Circus Plume. Although this still remains the predominant family at Wyck Hall, neither Mtoto nor Circus Plume were bred there, their respective dams, Amazer and Golden Fez, having been culled at successive Newmarket December Sales.

In 1976 Amazer was purchased on behalf of Mtoto's breeder, John Moore of Biddestone Stud, for 5,800 guineas, and in 1977 Golden Fez was procured for the late Camilla Drake (Somborne Stud), breeder of Circus Plume, for 15,000 guineas. It must have rankled Robin McAlpine, a Scotsman, to have to pay 98,000 guineas to secure Circus Plume as a foal in 1981, but she was worth it.

Having originally kept his mares at Newmarket's Scaltback Stud, Malcolm

McAlpine leased Wyck Hall Stud and Cemetery Stud adjacent to the Dullingham Road from the Jockey Club before the war; afterwards he and his sons operated as McAlpine Farms Ltd. Today Sir Robin is still lessee of Wyck Hall with his erstwhile trainer John Waugh as manager. The other half of the broodmare band is boarded at Alec Head's Haras du Quesnay, near Deauville, the progeny qualifying for the generous French breeders' premiums.

Two of Malcolm McAlpine's best mares were Mesa and Allure. Bought for £13,000 after she had won the 1935 1000 Guineas, French-bred Mesa had only three foals. One of them, Solesa, an own-sister to Historic, bred Ratification (Greenham Stakes, Coventry Stakes, Richmond Stakes), and Clutha (Imperial Produce Stakes). Allure, who cost 1,000 guineas as a yearling in 1938, won the Molecomb Stakes and finished third in the New 1000 Guineas. She is dam of Infatuation (Greenham Stakes, Dewhurst Stakes, Royal Lodge Stakes), whose outstanding son, Showdown, was twice champion sire in Australia.

There were marked similarities between Ratification and Infatuation, quite apart from their names. Both were top two-year-olds trained by Victor Smyth at Epsom, both won the Greenham Stakes, but were otherwise disappointing three-year-olds, both stood at Hamilton Stud under Reg Day's management, and both were exported to Japan in 1965.

Robin McAlpine, one of whose first involvements with the family business was the building of Wembley stadium in the early 1920s had to wait a long time for Circus Plume to provide him with a first classic success. However he might well have won the 1938 St Leger had James V. Rank not outbid him for Scottish Union as a yearling. Robin's father, Malcolm, and James Rank, the flour miller, were joint founders of the Racehorse Owners' Association. In 1960 Robin succeeded his father as president; he also served two terms on the TBA council.

Long before Golden Fez, Sir Robin McAlpine sold the dam of not one but two classic winners. For Commander Peter Fitzgerald of Mondellihy Stud, Co. Limerick, Review bred Pourparler and Fleet, both winners of the 1000 Guineas during the sixties, as well as Display who was runner-up in the same classic. Another Wyck Hall cull was Saracen, who was destined to breed Wilwyn, inaugural winner of the Washington DC International at Laurel Park.

During the sixties John Waugh was private trainer to Robin McAlpine, first at Cemetery Stud stables and then at Fitzroy House. Previously he had been assistant to Reg Day, one of whose last winners for McAlpine Farms was Marsolve (July Cup). As well as supervising Wyck Hall, John is also manager to Lord Derby at Woodlands Stud; he also has charge of the animals in Newmarket owned by the Phillips family, although most of the land belonging to Someries Stud has now been taken over by Sheikh Mohammed.

Over the last two decades, Robin McAlpine has become increasingly involved in France. It was at Haras de la Vastine, near Bernay, that he stood his dual Group scorer Jefferson (Prix Gontaut-Biron, Prix Caracalla). Sire of 1979 St Leger hero, Son of Love, Jefferson was one of the first horses Robin had trained by Peter Head at Chantilly. At present the majority are based there with Edouard Bartholomew, with the remainder divided between John Dunlop, trainer of Circus Plume, and Geoffrey Wragg.

Occasionally Sir Robin McAlpine's colours of McAlpine tartan, gold hoop on sleeves, gold cap, are carried here by a French invader. Two homebreds to have made autumnal visits to Newmarket in recent times are Ranimer, winner of the 1976 Sun Chariot Stakes, and First Waltz. Having won the Prix Morny, First Waltz finished second to the brilliant Ravinella in the Tattersalls' Cheveley Park Stakes. Just like Ratification and Infatuation, First Waltz proved a disappointing three-year-old; in fact she did not win again.

A member of the Jockey Club, Sir Robin McAlpine has been an owner for nearly sixty years - his first winner was in a seller at Alexandra Park in 1932. Although he does not go racing nowadays, he still plans all the matings for his mares. He says it is one of the most enjoyable aspects of breeding, so why let someone else have all the fun?

APPENDIX I: STUD UPDATES

Group and Listed Winners (May/June 1991)

Adstock Manor Stud (J.S.Delahooke)
  Reared HATEEL (Anheuser Busch Curragh Cup) for W. and R.Barnett Ltd.
Aston Park Stud (A.J. and Mrs Cuthbert)
  Breeder of LARA'S IDEA (Gr 3 Premio Legnano-Memorial Mario Incisa della Rocchetta)
Biddestone Stud (J.L.Moore)
  Breeder of JOIE DE SOIR (Crawley Warren Heron Stakes, Kempton Park)
Cheveley Park Stud (D.B. and Mrs Thompson)
  Reared MR. BROOKS (Gr 3 Gladness Stakes, Gr 3 Compaq Ballyogan Stakes, Gr 3 Kilfrush Concorde Stakes) for Mrs J.R.Rossdale
Copgrove Hall Stud (G.Reed)
  Reared EPERVIER BLEU (Gr 1 Grand Prix de Saint-Cloud), PISTOLET BLEU (Gr 2 Prix Hocquart) for Daniel Wildenstein
Dalham Hall Stud (Sheikh Mohammed)
  Owner-breeder of KAZOO (Gr 2 ARAG Preis)
Dunchurch Lodge Stud (Major M.G.Wyatt)
  Breeder of THORNBERRY (Amethyst Stakes, Leopardstown)
Gainsborough Stud (Sheikh Maktoum Al Maktoum)
  Owner-breeder of ROCK HOPPER (Gr 2 General Accident Jockey Club Stakes, Gr 2 Hardwicke Stakes)
Hesmonds Stud (P.G.Goulandris)
  Owner-breeder of THIRD WATCH (Gr 2 Ribblesdale Stakes)
Juddmonte Farms (Prince Khalid Abdullah)
  Owner-breeder of ECOLOGIST (Gr 3 Prix Berteux), TOULON (Gr 3 Dalham Chester Vase)
Kingwood Stud (T.C. and Mrs N.A.C.Vigors)
  Reared ELBIO (Gr 2 King's Stand Stakes, Gr 2 U.B. Group Temple Stakes, Gr 3 Palace House Stakes) for Pat Samuel
Lavington Stud (Captain J. and A.R.Macdonald-Buchanan)
  Breeder of IN THE GROOVE (Gr 1 Hanson Coronation Cup)
Meon Valley Stud (E. and Mrs Weinfeld and Partners)
  Breeder of STAGECRAFT (Gr 2 Prince of Wales's Stakes, Gr 3 Brigadier Gerard Stakes)
Northmore Stud Farm (P.Trivass)
  Reared OCEAN AIR (Ballymacoll Stud Stakes, Newbury) for Charles Wacker III
Sandley Stud (S.Wingfield Digby)
  Reared MAGIC RING (Gr 3 Norfolk Stakes) for Prince Fahd Salman

Snailwell Stud (Mrs C.Brudenell-Bruce)
    Owner-breeder of PFALZ (United Breweries Stakes, Sandown Park)
Someries Stud (late N.H.Phillips, Mrs H.P.Phillips, Mrs D.Butter)
    Breeder of SYLVA HONDA (Gr 3 Diomed Stakes)
Stetchworth Park Stud ((W.J.Gredley)
    Owner-breeder of ENVIRONMENT FRIEND (Gr 2 William Hill Dante Stakes)
Woodminton Farm (Major R.B. and Mrs Kennard)
    Breeder of CLEAN CUT (Topaz Sprint Stakes, Tipperary)

APPENDIX II

Principal (Flat) Studs in Great Britain

Adstock Manor Stud (J.S.Delahooke)
  Adstock, Buckinghamshire
Angmering Park Stud (Lavinia, Duchess of Norfolk)
  Littlehampton, Sussex
Arches Hall Stud (R.D.Hollingsworth)
  Standon, Hertfordshire
Arrow Farm and Stud (Colonel Sir Piers Bengough)
  Canon Pyon, Herefordshire
Ashley Heath Stud (G.J.H.Carroll)
  Newmarket, Suffolk
Aston House Stud (A.L. and Mrs Chapman)
  Aston Rowant, Oxfordshire
Aston Park Stud (A.J. and Mrs Cuthbert)
  Aston Rowant, Oxfordshire
Aston Upthorpe Stud (Sheikh Ahmed Al Maktoum)
  Aston Tirrold, Oxfordshire
Attington Stud (C.J.R.Trotter)
  Tetsworth, Oxfordshire

Bacton Stud (B.Manley)
  Bacton, Herefordshire
Banstead Manor Stud (Prince Khalid Abdullah)
  Newmarket, Suffolk
Barleythorpe Stud (D.G.J.Gibson)
  Oakham, Leicestershire
Barton Stud (Lord Fairhaven)
  Bury St Edmunds, Suffolk
Batsford Stud (Hon R.I.H.Wills)
  Moreton-in-Marsh, Gloucestershire
Bearstone Stud (T.G. and Mrs Holdcroft)
  Market Drayton, Shropshire
Beechgrove Stud (J.R.Mitchell)
  Scamblesby, Lincolnshire
Beech House Stud (Sheikh Hamdam Al Maktoum)
  Newmarket, Suffolk
Benham Stud (R.C.Denton)
  Marsh Benham, Berkshire

Benson Stud (B.A.Wallis)
  Colchester, Essex
Bergh Apton Stud (K.Freeman)
  Norwich, Norfolk
Biddestone Stud (J.L.Moore)
  Biddestone, Wiltshire
Bishop's Down Farm (A.B. and Mrs Deane)
  Bishop's Waltham, Hampshire
Blackmore Vale Stud (C.R.C.Watkins)
  Gillingham, Dorset
Bloomsbury Stud (Lord and Lady Tavistock, Lord Howland)
  Woburn, Bedfordshire
Bottisham Heath Stud (R.H. and Mrs Cowell)
  Newmarket, Suffolk
Bracken Hill Stud (Hon.W.H.McAlpine)
  Henley-on-Thames, Oxfordshire
Brickfield Stud (S.T.A.Investments Ltd)
  Newmarket, Suffolk
Britton House Stud (R.A.Fowlston)
  Crewkerne, Somerset
Brook Stud (D.K.Harris)
  Newmarket, Suffolk
Buckhurst Stud (D.A. and Mrs Hicks)
  Westerham Hill, Kent
Burningfold Manor Stud (M.Simmonds)
  Dunsfold, Surrey
Burton Agnes Stud (S.Cunliffe-Lister)
  Driffield, North Humberside
Buttermilk Stud (A.Irvine)
  Barford St.Michael, Oxfordshire

Campbell Stud (C.C.Campbell Golding)
  Bury St Edmunds, Suffolk
Catridge Farm Stud (Catridge Farm Stud Ltd)
  Chippenham, Wiltshire
Cedar Tree Stud (A.M.Foustok)
  Newmarket, Suffolk
Charlton Down Stud (Kais Al Said)
  Tetbury, Gloucestershire
Cheveley Park Stud (D.B. and Mrs Thompson)
  Nemarket, Suffolk
Chieveley Manor Stud (C.J.Spence)
  Newbury, Berkshire
Childwick Bury Stud (H.J.Joel)
  St.Albans, Hertfordshire
Chippenham Lodge Stud (Mrs P.McAllister)
  Chippenham, Cambridgeshire

Church Hall Farm (Sheikh Mohammed)
  Newmarket, Suffolk
Clanville Lodge Stud (D.F. and Mrs.Bradstock)
  Andover, Hampshire
Cliff Stud (Cliff Stud Ltd)
  Helmsley, North Yorkshire
Cliffords Farm (A.C.M.Spalding)
  Darlington, Co.Durham
Cliveden Stud (L.Freedman and Partners)
  Taplow, Berkshire
Collin Stud (N.M.Adam)
  Newmarket, Suffolk
Copgrove Hall Stud (G.Reed)
  Copgrove, North Yorkshire
Cornbury Park Stud (Lord Rotherwick)
  Charlbury, Oxfordshire
Costock Grange Stud (C.N. and Mrs Frank)
  Loughborough, Leicestershire
Cotswold Stud (Mrs J.James)
  Lower Slaughter, Gloucestershire
Coxland Stud (Mrs J.Clabby)
  Ewhurst, Surrey
Crichel Stud (Lieutenant-Commander G.G.Marten)
  Wimborne, Dorset
Crimbourne Stud (Sir Eric Parker)
  Wisborough Green, West Sussex
Crockfords Stud (R.C.Crowhurst and Partners)
  Newmarket, Suffolk

Dalham Hall Stud (Sheikh Mohammed)
  Newmarket, Suffolk
Danemore Farm Stud (K.V. and Mrs Stenborg)
  Speldhurst, Kent
Danton and Glebe House Stud (A.D.Shead)
  Newmarket, Suffolk
Derisley Wood Stud (Sheikh Mohammed)
  Newmarket, Suffolk
Doverlodge Stud (C.T. and Mrs Spencer-Phillips)
  Rolvenden, Kent
Downclose Stud (Miss S.N.Ralphs)
  Crewkerne, Somerset
Duke's Stud (Major M.G.Wyatt)
  Newmarket, Suffolk
Dullingham Ley Stud (W.J.Gredley)
  Newmarket, Suffolk
Dunchurch Lodge Stud (Major M.G.Wyatt)
  Newmarket, Suffolk

Eagle Lane Farm (Prince Khalid Adbullah)
  Newmarket, Suffolk
Easthorpe Hall Stud (M.H.Easterby)
  Malton, North Yorkshire
Eastwood Hall Stud (Colonel K.C.Thompson)
  Barningham, North Yorkshire
Egerton Stud (M.Parrish)
  Newmarket, Suffolk
The Elms Stud (R. and Mrs Bowers)
  Denton, Northamptonshire
Elsenham Stud (D.Sullivan)
  Bishop's Stortford, Hertfordshire
Emral Stud (R.J.McAlpine)
  Worthenbury, Clwyd
Ewar Stud Farm (A.J.Richards)
  Wokingham, Berkshire
Eydon Hall Farm (G.W.Leigh)
  Eydon, Northamptonshire

Fawley Stud (D.J. and Mrs Deer)
  Wantage, Oxfordshire
Felley Priory Stud (Hon Mrs M.V.Chaworth Musters)
  Jacksdale, Nottinghamshire
Fittocks Stud (Variabetag A.G.)
  Newmarket, Suffolk
Floors Stud (Duke of Roxburghe)
  Kelso, Roxburghshire
Fonthill Stud (Hon J.I.Morrison)
  Hindon, Wiltshire
Foundation Stud (J.D.Hurd)
  Marden, Kent
Friars Farm Stud (Lieutenant-Colonel and Mrs D.E.Coker)
  Aldham, Essex
Furnace Mill Stud (D.J.and Mrs Brown)
  Kidderminster, Worcestershire

Gainsborough Stud (Sheikh Maktoum Al Maktoum)
  Woolton Hill, Berkshire
Garrowby Stud (Lord Halifax)
  Garrowby, York
Gazeley Stud (P.J.McCalmont)
  Newmarket, Suffolk
Genesis Green Stud (W.R.Swinburn Snr)
  Newmarket, Suffolk
Glazeley Stud (W.P.Jenks and Mrs A.V.Attwood)
  Bridgnorth, Shropshire
Glen Andred Stud (R.G. and Mrs Percival)
  Old, Northamptonshire

Goosemoor Stud (P. and Mrs Cockcroft)
  Cowthorpe, Yorkshire
Greenland Park Stud (R.S. and Mrs Kennedy)
  Berkhamsted, Hertfordshire
Grove Farm Stud (E.A.Badger)
  Minster Lovell, Oxford
Guiting Grange Stud (H.R.Mould)
  Guiting Power, Gloucestershire
Guyler's Stud (J.M.Greetham)
  Wymondham, Norfolk

Hackwood Stud (Mrs.J.Berry)
  Basingstoke, Hampshire
Hadrian Stud (Sheikh Mohammed)
  Newmarket, Suffolk
Hall Stud (R.Peers)
  Newmarket, Suffolk
Hardwicke Stud (E.Crow)
  Hadnall, Shropshire
Harness Grove Stud (T.Barratt)
  Worksop, Nottinghamshire
Hart Hill Stud (N.J.Dent)
  Semley, Dorset
Hascombe Stud (Sir Philip Oppenheimer)
  Newmarket, Suffolk
Heatherwold Stud (Mrs P.Longton)
  Burghclere, Berkshire
Helescane Stud (J.L. and Mrs Skinner)
  Okehampton, Devon
Heritage Coast Stud (Mrs Skepper and Associates)
  Woodbridge, Suffolk
Hesmonds Stud (P.G.Goulandris)
  East Hoathly, East Sussex
Hever Castle Stud Farm (R.A. and Mrs Popely)
  Hever, Kent
High Canfold Stud (R.E. and Mrs Crutchley)
  Cranleigh, Surrey
Highclere Stud (Lord Carnarvon)
  Burghclere, Berkshire
Higher Tregawne Stud (M.H.D.Madden)
  Bodmin, Cornwall
Hilborough Stud (H.B.E. van Cutsem)
  Thetford, Norfolk
Hillwood Stud (Dr J.A.E. and Mrs Hobby)
  Aldbourne, Wiltshire
Home Stud (J.P.Coggan)
  West Tytherley, Wiltshire

Howard House Stud (Lord Suffolk)
    Malmesbury, Wiltshire
Hunsley House Stud (R.S.A.Urquhart)
    Cottingham, North Humberside
Hyde Stud (B.H.Simpson)
    Ecchinswell, Berkshire

Juddmonte Farms (Prince Khalid Adbullah)
    Wargrave-on-Thames, Berkshire

Kennaa Farm (Mrs B.S.Facchino)
    St Johns, Isle of Man
Kilvington Stud (J.Rose)
    Kilvington, Nottinghamshire
Kingsclere Stud (Mrs.I.A.Balding)
    Kingsclere, Berkshire
Kingscote Park Stud (Lieutenant-Colonel R. and Mrs Bromley-Gardner)
    Tetbury, Gloucestershire
Kingwood Stud (T.C. and Mrs N.A.C.Vigors)
    Lambourn, Berkshire
Kippilaw Stud (Hon.Mrs N.Napier)
    St Boswells, Roxburghshire
Kirtlington Stud (A.M. and Mrs Budgett, C.M.Budgett)
    Kirtlington, Oxfordshire
Knowles Bank Stud (B.O'Brien)
    Tonbridge, Kent
Knowlton Stud (Mrs O.Fox-Pitt)
    Canterbury, Kent

Lady's Green Stud (M.J.Hall)
    Newmarket, Suffolk
Langham Stud (Mrs W.Protheroe-Beynon)
    Gillingham, Dorset
Langham Hall Stud (C. and Mrs Blackwell)
    Bury St Edmunds, Suffolk
Langton Stud (M.E.Wates)
    Blandford Forum, Dorset
Lanwades Stud (Miss K.Rausing)
    Newmarket, Suffolk
Launceston Stud (J.and Mrs Strange)
    Blandford Forum, Dorset
Lavington Stud (Captain J. and A.R.Macdonald-Buchanan)
    Graffham, West Sussex
Limestone Stud (J.W.Rowles)
    Gainsborough, Lincolnshire

Littleton Stud (J.C.Smith)
  Littleton, Hampshire
Llety Stud (W.D. and Mrs C.Hodge)
  Nantgaredig, Dyfed
Lockinge Stud (C.L.Loyd)
  Wantage, Oxfordshire
Lofts Hall Stud (Major C.R. and Mrs Philipson)
  Elmdon, Essex
Longholes Stud (late Lady Durham)
  Newmarket, Suffolk
Longstones Stud (J.B.Fenwick and Son)
  Newmarket, Suffolk
Lordship Stud (M.Parrish)
  Newmarket, Suffolk
Lowe Stud Farm (Mrs S.Owen-George)
  Wellesbourne, Warwickshire
Lower Hare Park Stud (Mrs K.M.Mack)
  Newmarket, Suffolk

Manor Farm Stud (R.T.and Mrs Watson)
  Oakham, Leicestershire
Manor House Stud (Mrs R.D.Peacock)
  Middleham, North Yorkshire
Meddler Stud (W.B.Leach)
  Newmarket, Suffolk
Melton Paddocks (Sheikh Hamdan Al Maktoum)
  Thetford, Norfolk
Meon Valley Stud (E. and Mrs Weinfeld and Partners)
  Bishop's Waltham, Hampshire
Millbrook Stud (Miss E.Drax)
  Fordingbridge, Hampshire
Milton Park Stud (Sir Stephen Hastings)
  Peterborough, Northamptonshire
Minster Stud (W.H.Carson)
  Barnsley, Gloucestershire
Molecomb Stud (D.S.W.Blacker)
  Goodwood, Sussex
Moyns Park Stud (Lord Milford Haven)
  Birdbrook, Essex

The National Stud (chairman: N.M.H.Jones)
  Newmarket, Suffolk
New England Stud (P.Stanley)
  Newmarket, Suffolk
Nidd Park Stud (Hon I.V.Matthews)
  Ripley, Yorkshire

Northgate Lodge Stud (M.A.Brittain)
    Warthill, York
Northmore Stud Farm (P.Trivass)
    Newmarket, Suffolk
North Munstead Stud (Sir Gordon Brunton)
    Godalming, Surrey
Norton Grove Stud (Major J.H.Hudson)
    Malton, North Yorkshire
Nunnery Stud (Sheikh Hamdan Al Maktoum)
    Thetford, Norfolk

Old Buckenham Stud (Thailon Establishment)
    Attleborough, Norfolk
Old Mill Stud (D.A.Shekells)
    Chippenham, Cambridgeshire
Ormsby Hall Stud (A.J.Massingberd-Mundy)
    Louth, Lincolnshire
Overbury Stud (T.D.Holland-Martin)
    Overbury, Gloucestershire

Palehouse Farm Stud (P.V. and Mrs J.P.Jackson)
    Uckfield, Sussex
Partridge Close Stud (H.Alexander)
    Lanchester, Co.Durham
Pendley Farm Stud (P.W.Harris)
    Tring, Hertfordshire
Pinfold Stud (A.C.Hall)
    Market Drayton, Shropshire
Plantation Stud (Lord Howard de Walden)
    Newmarket, Suffolk
Polhampton Lodge Stud (H.M.The Queen)
    Kingsclere, Berkshire

Qualitair Stud (P.Bottomley)
    Newmarket, Suffolk

Raffin Stud (S.M.Kelly)
    Marlborough, Wiltshire
Red House Stud (T.G.Warner)
    Newmarket, Suffolk
Roehoe Stud (B.W.Hills)
    Kinoulton, Nottinghamshire
The Royal Studs (H.M.The Queen)
    Sandringham, Norfolk

Rutland Stud (Sheikh Mohammed)
  Newmarket, Suffolk

St.Quentin Stud (Mrs R.Newton)
  Hartfield, East Sussex
St.Simon Stud (Miss K.Rausing)
  Newmarket, Suffolk
Saddlehome Stud (J.A.Haverhals)
  Slinfold, West Sussex
Sandley Stud (S.Wingfield Digby)
  Gillingham, Dorset
Sandringham Stud (H.M.The Queen)
  Sandringham, Norfolk
Sandwich Stud (D.B. and Mrs Thompson)
  Newmarket, Suffolk
Sarsden Stud (Mrs J.Taylor)
  North Aston, Oxfordshire
Saxham Stud (I.Thoday)
  Bury St.Edmunds, Suffolk
Scorrier House Stud (R.P.Williams)
  Redruth, Cornwall
Sentinels Stud (A.B. and Mrs Barraclough)
  Launceston, Cornwall
Shadwell Stud (Sheikh Hamdan Al Maktoum)
  Thetford, Norfolk
Shelton Stud (Mrs J.R.Hine and Miss J.Bunting)
  Hassocks, East Sussex
Shutford Stud (T.D.Rootes)
  Banbury, Oxfordshire
Side Hill Stud (Lord Hartington)
  Newmarket, Suffolk
Sledmere Stud (Sir Tatton Sykes Bt)
  Driffield, North Humberside
Snailwell Stud (Mrs C.Brudenell-Bruce)
  Newmarket, Suffolk
Snarehill Stud (Sheikh Hamdan Al Maktoum)
  Thetford, Norfolk
Someries Stud (late N.H.Phillips, Mrs H.P.Phillips, Mrs D.Butter)
  Newmarket, Suffolk
Southcourt Stud (E.de Rothschild and Mrs.P.Robeson)
  Leighton Buzzard, Bedfordshire
Southdown Stud (late E.H.Covell)
  Shipley, West Sussex
Spa Stud (Mrs J.Everitt)
  Droitwich, Worcestershire
Stanley House Stud (Lord Derby)
  Newmarket, Suffolk

Stetchworth Park Stud (W.J.Gredley)
    Newmarket, Suffolk
Stock Hill Stud (D.R.and Mrs Fairbairn)
    Gillingham, Dorset
Stockwell Stud (H.Easterby)
    Tadcaster, North Yorkshire
Stowell Hill (R.J.McCreery)
    Templecombe, Somerset
Strawberry Hill Stud (D.B. and Mrs Thompson)
    Newmarket, Suffolk
Stud-on-the-Chart (A.J.Lavell)
    Warninglid, West Sussex
Sturt Farm Stud (R.B.Stokes)
    Burford, Oxfordshire
Sullington Old Rectory (G.R.Rickman)
    Storrington, West Sussex
Summertree Stud (J. and Mrs Williamson)
    Robertsbridge, East Sussex
Sussex Stud (Mohammed A.A.Mutawa)
    West Grinstead, Sussex

Tally Ho Stud (A.Boyd-Rochfort)
    Chevington, Suffolk
Tancred Stud (W.G.Barker)
    Scorton, North Yorkshire
Templeton Stud (Lord Howard de Walden)
    Hungerford, Berkshire
Theakston Stud (J.McIntyre)
    Bedale, North Yorkshire
Thornton Stud (Lord Howard de Walden)
    Thornton-le-Street, North Yorkshire
Thornton Manor Stud (Lord Leverhulme)
    Thornton Hough, Cheshire
Three Gates Stud (E.Young)
    Moreton Morrell, Warwickshire
Tibthorpe Stud (L.Caley)
    Driffield, North Humberside
Ticklerton Stud (J.Young)
    Church Stretton, Shropshire
Toat Farm and Stud (J.W.Parker)
    Pulborough, West Sussex
Tregavethan Manor Stud (Mrs W.G.Clark)
    Kenwyn, Cornwall
Trentham Stud (Mrs D. and Miss L.Thompson)
    Ilkeston, Derbyshire
Tyrley Castle Stud (P.T. and Mrs Tellwright)
    Market Drayton, Shropshire

Tyrnest Stud (D.Hefin Jones)
  Tyrnest, Dyfed

Ulceby Vale Stud (E.H.Halmshaw)
  Ulceby, South Humberside
Uplands Park Stud (R.N. and Mrs Khan)
  Godalming, Surrey
Upperwood Farm Stud (N.G.Halsey)
  Hemel Hempstead, Hertfordshire

Waddesdon Stud (Lord Rothschild)
  Waddesdon, Buckinghamshire
Wakefield Lodge Stud (R.N.Richmond-Watson)
  Potterspury, Northamptonshire
Waresley Park Stud (W.Bechmann)
  Sandy, Bedfordshire
Warren Stud (Sheikh Mohammed)
  Newmarket, Suffolk
Warren Hill Stud (G.J.H.Carroll)
  Newmarket, Suffolk
Waverton Stud (J.O.Hambro)
  Moreton-in-Marsh, Gloucestershire
West Blagdon (D. and Mrs Wigan)
  Cranborne, Dorset
West Stow Stud (Mrs P.Nurse)
  Bury St.Edmunds, Suffolk
Whatton Manor Stud (P.D. and Mrs Player)
  Whatton in the Vale, Nottinghamshire
Wheelersland Stud (Mrs J.E.L.Wright)
  Ashford Hill, Berkshire
White House Stud (G.M.W.Starkey)
  Newmarket, Suffolk
White Lodge Stud (Sheikh Mohammed)
  Newmarket, Suffolk
Whitsbury Manor Stud (C.J.Harper)
  Fordingbridge, Hampshire
Wickfield Stud (N. and Mrs Brookes)
  Cheltenham, Gloucestershire
Wold Newton Stud (R.H.Mason)
  Driffield, North Humberside
Wolferton Stud (H.M.The Queen)
  Sandringham, Norfolk
Woodcote Stud (A.R.Perry)
  Epsom, Surrey
Woodditton Stud (N.S. and Mrs Yong)
  Newmarket, Suffolk
Wood Farm Stud (C.C. and W.Bromley)
  Wellington, Shropshire

Woodhaven Stud (J.N.G.Moreton and Miss J.E.Reed)
   East Woodhay, Berkshire
Woodlands Stud (Lord Derby)
   Newmarket, Suffolk
Woodminton Farm (Major R.B. and Mrs Kennard)
   Bowerchalke, Wiltshire
Woolton House Stud (Mrs R.Hue-Williams)
   Woolton Hill, Berkshire
Worksop Manor Stud (B.H.Farr)
   Worksop, Nottinghamshire
Wretham Stud (D. and Mrs Haynes)
   West Wretham, Norfolk
Wrotham Park Stud (J.M.E.Byng)
   Barnet, Hertfordshire
Wyck Hall Stud (Sir Robin McAlpine)
   Newmarket, Suffolk

Zetland Stud (Lords Zetland, Ronaldshay and Dundas)
   Richmond, North Yorkshire

INDEX OF HORSES

INDEX OF PEOPLE